THINKING HISTO~~R~~
Educating Students

Two simple but profound questions have preoccupied scholars since the establishment of history education over a century ago: What is historical thinking, and how do educators go about teaching it? In *Thinking Historically*, Stéphane Lévesque examines these questions, focusing on what it means to think critically about the past. As students engage with a new century already characterized by global instability, uncertainty, and rivalry over claims about the past, present, and future, this study revisits enduring questions and aims to offer new and relevant answers.

Drawing on a rich collection of personal, national, and international studies in history education, Lévesque offers a coherent and innovative way of looking at how historical expertise in the domain intersects with the pedagogy of history education. *Thinking Historically* provides teacher educators, and all those working in the field of history education, ways of rethinking their practice by presenting some of the benchmarks, in terms of procedural concepts, of what students ought to learn and do to become more critical historical actors and citizens.

As questions regarding history education impinge upon educators with greater force than ever, this timely study explores different ways of approaching and engaging with the discipline in the twenty-first century.

STÉPHANE LÉVESQUE is an associate professor of History Education in the Faculty of Education at the University of Ottawa.

STÉPHANE LÉVESQUE

Thinking Historically

Educating Students for the
Twenty-First Century

UNIVERSITY OF TORONTO PRESS
Toronto Buffalo London

Reprinted in paperback 2009

ISBN 978-0-8020-9259-5 (cloth)
ISBN 978-1-4426-1099-6 (paper)

Printed on acid-free paper

Library and Archives Canada Cataloguing in Publication

Lévesque, Stéphane, 1971–
   Thinking historically : educating students for the twenty-first century /
Stéphane Lévesque.

   Includes bibliographical references (p.[197]–216) and index.
   ISBN 978-0-8020-9259-5 (bound). – ISBN 978-1-4426-1099-6 (pbk.)

   1. Historiography.   2. History – Methodology.   3. History – Study and
teaching.   I. Title.

D16.2.L48 2008   907.2   C2007-906272-5

University of Toronto Press acknowledges the financial assistance to its
publishing program of the Canada Council for the Arts and the Ontario
Arts Council.

University of Toronto Press acknowledges the financial support for its publishing activities of the Government of Canada through the Book Publishing Industry Development Program (BPIDP).

Cover image courtesy Jamie Carroll/iStockphoto

Contents

Foreword

Canada, the quip goes, has a lot of geography but little history, a big country with a brief past. At one point, Stéphane Lévesque light-heartedly expressed this idea of Canada by encouraging his colleagues to embrace their 'inner northicity,' meaning, I believe, to fully claim a national identity defined by the country's geography. What is short about Canadian history, of course, is its existence in the mould of a European state; the land and people have been here for thousands of years.

Over the past several decades, historians in Canada and elsewhere have made great strides in broadening the purview of history, moving the discipline out of the shadow of Hegel, so that entities other than the state, and people other than state leaders, could take their places as agents of historical change. The main story no longer needs to centre so exclusively on the coalescing of the nation as the vehicle for the progress of human freedom, though that story certainly has its ardent defenders and still has considerable life left in it. Brought in from the sidelines are workers, women, First Nations peoples, immigrants, and the poor. The story is more confusing now, and the search is ongoing for coherent and meaningful plotlines to provide historical context for our lives today.

Historiographic ferment has immediate implications for the schools. Accompanying historians' new discontent, there is trouble in the classroom. Students are aware that women have a *new* place in school textbooks, that the history they are being taught is not the one that was always taught. They know that there are conflicting views of the forced relocation of Japanese Canadians during World War II. They are aware that the term 'discovery,' applied to Europeans' arrival in the

New World, is contentious, but only recently so. They may have been exposed – like many school children in Australia – to the notion that this was not a 'discovery' at all but an 'invasion,' interpretive stances expressed in the choice of a word.

Once the problem of historical interpretation makes itself felt in the public culture, it becomes crucial to teach students not just the one best story but the means for assessing interpretations, for weighing the evidence supporting one against another, for comparing different narratives and explanations. If young people are to get a useful history education in this cultural moment, they must not only be exposed to a good historical drama but also be allowed to see the ropes and pulleys behind the curtains.

Here is where the contribution of Stéphane Lévesque's volume is crucial. British history educators have, at least since the early 1980s, focused on 'procedural concepts' of history. That is, they have developed a vocabulary to express explicitly what is going on 'behind the curtains' of historical construction. Among the most important procedural concepts are those explored in the following chapters: significance, continuity and change, progress and decline, evidence, and historical empathy. Without working with these concepts, students cannot understand history and how it works. They can only memorize scraps of information about history in the same way they might memorize scraps of scientific information or numbers in a phone book. Without understanding terms like 'significance' or 'evidence,' they are at sea without a rudder in the interpretive storms of contemporary culture.

These procedural concepts of history may initially deceive us with their common-sense simplicity. But, as Stéphane Lévesque unpacks them, their power, their complexity, and their utility in sorting through interpretations of the past become exceedingly apparent. In skilful teachers' pedagogical repertoires, simple versions of history are potentially useful from the earliest years of schooling, whereas their higher levels of complexity can be explored through post-secondary education and beyond.

Levesque's volume is the first in North America to take these concepts on in an extended, scholarly, and systematic way. Hopefully, it will not be the last word on them but an introduction that paves the way for discussion, refinement, and empirical research by history educators. The timing could not be better. As the first printing of this volume goes to press, the Historica Foundation and the Centre for the Study of Historical Consciousness are, in a major collaboration, assembling teams of teachers across Canada to develop lessons to help them and their colleagues teach and assess historical thinking. Not coincidentally, this initiative – entitled Benchmarks of Historical Thinking – uses the same concepts, in a slightly different configuration.*

After a symposium held at the University of British Columbia in April 2006, to rough out the shape of Benchmarks project, Patrick Watson noted, 'Niels Bohr famously said about physics and mathematics that the achievement of a new formula was not, in fact, a movement towards *truth*, but rather the development of language that the research community could agree upon, as representing the objectives of the search.' Stéphane Lévesque has not given us any formula, and it would be odd to characterize his work as a 'movement towards truth.' But he has helped us in the much-needed development of a language for history education. When he first told me about his idea for this book, I was taken aback. This, I told him, was the book I had been planning to write. But 'planning to write' is not writing. Stéphane has managed to do it, while I have been caught up in other things. And so I want to join with all the readers that I hope this volume will have, in celebrating – and building on – his contribution to the literature on teaching, learning, and thinking about history.

Peter Seixas
Centre for the Study of Historical Consciousness
University of British Columbia, Vancouver
3 October 2006

---

*Recently printed is a teachers' guide entitled *Teaching about Historical Thinking*, by Michael Denos and Roland Case, from the Critical Thinking Cooperative (Vancouver: Pacific Educational Press, 2006), using some of the same concepts.

Acknowledgments

This book on history education is the result of many years of personal and collective research and thinking in the field. Its origins go back to the late 1990s when I was at the University of British Columbia. There I was first exposed to the powerful ideas of Peter Seixas, Sam Wineburg, Bruce VanSledright, Pierre Nora, Denis Shemilt, and other prominent scholars working on historical thinking. I soon realized, however, that these ideas developed in North America and Europe – divided by nationality, language, and cultural traditions – rarely encounter one another. In its own modest way, this book is an attempt to bridge this divide, a humble effort to provide history educators an additional way of thinking about history in their national and local settings.

Inevitably, several individuals and institutions along the way have influenced the shape and content of this book. Peter Seixas, at the University of British Columbia, and Geoffrey Milburn, at the University of Western Ontario, offered timely encouragement and constructive criticism on various drafts of this manuscript. The University of Western Ontario Faculty of Education, under the leadership of Dean Allen Pearson, provided a convivial and supportive environment in which to write the book. This institution has also extended financial support in the form of research and publication grants. I am very grateful to Jennifer Hedges for her keen editorial review and to Diane Nemcek and Pauline Goldie for their secretarial support and assistance in formatting the bibliography and footnotes. The Education library and Research Collection staff at Western have been remarkably prompt and efficient in responding to all my requests and book renewals. I also appreciate the feedback that I received from various colleagues when I presented chapters of this book at the conferences of the Canadian Society for the Study of Education, the Canadian Historical Association, the American Educational Research Association, the History Teacher Education Network, and the History Education International Research Network. I am also deeply indebted to my research assistant, Clare Leaper, a graduate in history education and a dedicated history teacher in Ontario. His research expertise and thoughtful professional advice proved to be extremely useful. The anonymous external reviewers offered significant revisions that have helped improved the overall quality and substance of this book. This book would never have seen the light without the support and strong commitment of Stephen Kotowych, my editor at the University of Toronto Press, and Richard Ratzlaff, assistant managing editor of the press. Finally, I want to convey my deep appreciation and respect to all the students and teachers whom I have met over the years and who have contributed, in one way or another, to my own research and thinking about history education. This book is dedicated to them.

THINKING HISTORICALLY

1 Introduction

We are witnessing a world-wide upsurge in memory. Over the last twenty or twenty-five years, every country, every social, ethnic or family group, has undergone a profound change in the relationship it traditionally enjoyed with the past.

– Pierre Nora[1]

1.1 Old and New Challenges

In times of crisis and uncertainty, historians are expected to provide instructive historical parallels and defensible responses. Because the past inexorably shapes the present, any time we try to understand present-day circumstances – particularly complex ones – we must look for preceding factors to give reasons for, or at least evidence of, what happened and what it means. Currently, it seems that this 'equilibrium between the present and the past' is severely disrupted.[2] In reflecting on the terrorist attacks of September 11, distinguished historian Sir John Keegan openly admitted in the *Spectator* (London) his incapacity to explain these aggressive 'acts of war.'

Military historians always know when there is real trouble. For years they potter away in archives, explaining to each other why Wellington won and Napoleon lost, to no one else's interest. Then some Islamic fundamentalists turn airlines into cruise missiles, and newspapers and television stations demand instant comment. During the Falklands and Gulf wars I could help. History supplied all sorts of clues as to what was happening and what the outcome would be. The nasties made familiar mistakes. One could state with confidence how they would go wrong and why our side would win. This time, stop me. Not even the Mongols – about the nastiest enemies civilisation has ever had to face – took war to the extreme of killing themselves so as to kill others.[3]

Here was an accomplished historian who had written numerous history books on warfare admitting defeat in the face of what seemed to be a new threat. All those years studying and lecturing on military history at the Royal Military Academy and Princeton University seemed futile in coming to terms with an event that, in the eyes of many, '[was] of apparently cataclysmic significance [and] spoke powerfully from the depths of modern history.'[4] As Keegan illustrates, in the aftermath of the attacks, intellectuals, governments, and teachers from around the world were soon bombarded with masses of burning questions: Who was responsible for these terrorist attacks? Why was the United States targeted? How was it possible to plan and coordinate such devastating strikes? Which country would be next? How can we make sense of this violence? Despite the value of all these – and many other – questions, few satisfactory answers could be provided. Whereas some did not hesitate to compare the attacks on the World Trade Center to Pearl Harbor, others were more careful and tentative in their historical parallels and explanations.[5] 'September 11 should have taught us,' international-politics scholars Ken Booth and Tim Dunne cautiously argue, 'that we cannot assume, for the foreseeable future, that tomorrow will be like today. The global order is being recast, and the twists and turns will surprise us.'[6] More than six years after the attacks, and an extensive report from the U.S. Congress 9/11 Commission, many are still puzzled and surprised, begging for clearer and more definitive answers from authorities, whether they are experts, teachers, or government representatives.

As shocking and powerful as September 11 was – and continues to be – these terrorist attacks are increasingly regarded as exemplifications of a deeply rooted malaise in modern civilization, characterized by collisions between ideologies and systems, struggle over resources and access to power, and transnational network's employment of unconventional, violent means to achieve moral, political, or religious purposes. It is not, as French historian Pierre Nora claims in his discussion of the 'acceleration of history,' that civilization is facing an unprecedented number of events of significance but that masses of citizens are now living in a period of remarkable and profound change in many aspects of their lives, largely because of globalization and mass culture.[7] More than a decade ago, Francis Fukuyama proclaimed that civilization had reached the 'end of history,' when market capitalism and liberal democracy became the dominant forces in world politics.[8] Yet, citizens and states now confront worldwide phenomena and threats built into this new global, liberal civilization. The dialectical tensions between cultures, ideologies, religions, states, and transnational networks are affecting people and nations with greater force than ever. Many of today's global changes have radically altered or intensified people's relationship with the past, sometimes in unpredicted and explosive ways. The recent collapse of the Soviet Union and the ensuing re-emergence of independent republics all over Eastern Europe, for example, have resulted in heated debates over what national language, history, holidays, curricula, and memories should be recognized and promoted. Clearly, the pre-Soviet order cannot be re-established and justified today on the same premises, memories, and beliefs as in twentieth-century Europe. For millions of Estonians, Ukrainians, Latvians, and the like, the approved Soviet versions of the past, once strictly inculcated at school and promoted publicly, now stand in sharp contrast to the diverse vernacular stories culturally developed, transmitted, and internalized.[9]

But one does not have to be Eastern European to find such contradictions and struggles with the collective past. In Canada, the United States, and most Western states, the recent mass migration and globalization of cultures, religions, and identities have resulted in enormous challenges for school teachers, administrators, policymakers, and even immigrants themselves trying to integrate into their new society. 'In Vancouver, Toronto, and around the world,' Canada Research Chair Peter Seixas observes, 'people whose pasts, cultures, and traditions are radically different from each other, are living in close proximity to each other.'[10] In such circumstances, it is understandable that students, and ultimately the public, wonder whose history should be taught in school. In the days of the Soviet Union, answers to such hotly debated questions were supplied by intransigent ideologies, national mythologies, and conservative educational philosophies. Even Western states were not spared from such arbitrary certitudes. The widespread assimilation of First Nations peoples in Canada, notably in residential schools, the systematic segregation of Blacks in U.S. society, and the hegemonic colonial policies and practices of European imperial powers are dreadful evidence of white Westerners' traditional relationship with the past.[11]

It is true that each historical period produces its own significant changes, struggles, progress, decline, and winners and losers and that our contemporary age is no different. In a sense, Nora's metaphorical acceleration of history can also be traced in other significant periods and civilizations. Yet, it is equally fair to claim that long-established traditions, heritage practices, deep-rooted mythologies, and even traditional inventions such as the nation state no longer appear to be adequate. The current globalization of cultures and histories thus brings people face to face with a perceived distance separating the strangeness and familiarity of past realities from contemporary actions, behaviours, and thinking.

This *fin de siècle* rift between the present and the past has provoked furious reactions within the history community and, by extension, within school-history circles. Criticism of official versions of the past and, perhaps more importantly, of the *use* of these versions has taken a variety of forms. Whereas David Lowenthal has explored the issue, by making a persuasive distinction between 'heritage' (naive use of the past) versus 'history' (inquiry into the past), Nora has recently presented a related dichotomy between 'memory-history' and 'disciplinary-history' that is particularly relevant to my discussion:

> Memory and history, far from being synonymous, are thus in many respects opposed. Memory is life, always embodied in living societies and as such in permanent evolution, subject to the dialectic of remembering and forgetting, unconscious of the distortions to which it is subject, vulnerable in various ways to appropriation and manipulation, and capable of lying dormant for long periods only to be suddenly reawakened. History, on the other hand, is the reconstruction, always problematic and incomplete, of what is no longer. Memory is always a phenomenon of the present, a bond tying us to the eternal present; history is a representation of the past ... Memory is absolute, while history is always relative.[12]

Significant events of the late-twentieth- and early-twenty-first century force citizens to rethink their traditional relationships with the past. It is not that memory-history and traditions have suddenly disappeared from human affairs. In fact, one could legitimately argue, as Benedict Anderson puts it so well, that no society could ever exist and survive without such 'imagined' references to the past.[13] But the key question is now whether memory-history can or should continue to be a legitimate ground for human actions in this rapidly shrinking world of competing views and claims about the past, the present, and, by extension, the envisioned future. Indeed, memory-history, as an unscientific study of history, subject to the dialectic of remembering and forgetting, supplies no formal evaluating principle or adequate answer to the challenges of the new global (dis)order and the conflicting memories and collective claims about the past it has engendered.

It is no surprise that the institutions that not so long ago served to shape and transmit memory-history – churches, schools, local communities, and even states – are seen by memory 'fashioners' as the cause of today's predicament.[14] As established traditions and heritage settings come under scrutiny, some wish to restore these *lieux de mémoire* so as to reinvent a collective past to seemingly solve contemporary problems.[15] And all around the world, there are noticeable signs of memory fashioners' reactionary activities: demands for nationalist curricula and content standards, commissioned history surveys showing students' blatant ignorance, promotion of patriotic days, rehabilitation of national heroes, requests for memorials and commemorative events, and last, but not least, production of mythical, historically oriented movies à la Mel Gibson and Steven Spielberg.[16]

This book outlines another approach to these recent developments in history, one that focuses on disciplinary historical thinking. Disciplinary thinking, as Howard Gardner and Veronica Boix-Mansilla contend, constitutes the most advanced way of approaching and investigating issues within the various domains of knowledge.[17] Although disciplines sometimes prove to be incomplete, as in the case of September 11 terrorism, they nonetheless represent the best scientific means available for answering 'generative essential questions' in human affairs.[18] Disciplines such as history have their own modes of inquiry, networks of concepts and principles, theoretical frameworks, symbolic systems, vocabularies, and modes of self-regulation. Because of the ways they have been devised and challenged by scholars over time, disciplines are inherently dynamic. Their objects of study, findings, methods, and theories 'stimulate controversy and evolve in time.'[19] As a result, the objects of study and boundaries of disciplines are complex and sometimes diffuse. Their methods or findings can even overlap. Despite these difficulties, disciplines offer people formidable 'ways of knowing' about past or current issues of significance. 'Shorn of disciplinary knowledge,' as Gardner and Boix-Mansilla put it, 'human beings are quickly reduced to the level of ignorant children, indeed to the ranks of barbarians.'[20]

Yet, the challenge for educators is to initiate and ultimately engage youngsters in disciplinary thinking. Although children seem to easily acquire an intuitive grasp of common-sense theories and explanatory frameworks, such as those supplied by memory-history, disciplinary thinking proves to be more intellectually demanding. Not only do people need to acquire established knowledge within their respective disciplines (e.g., facts and accounts), they must also (and perhaps above all) learn to employ their methods, procedures, and ways of thinking and inquiring. The development of this expertise is long, complex, and never complete. Achieving more mature historical thinking, as cognitive psychologist Sam Wineburg expresses it, is far from a *natural* act: '[it] depends precisely on our ability to navigate the uneven landscape of history, to traverse the rugged terrain that lies between the poles of familiarity and distance from the past.'[21]

Extensive experience with what Nora calls disciplinary-history can provide students, and ultimately the public, not only with powerful interpretative accounts of the collective past but also, more importantly, with the necessary tools, concepts, and rules to engage in the critical reconstruction and evaluation of such accounts. Rather than intuitively accepting (or rejecting) self-evident stories 'embodied in living societies,' to use Nora's terms, students could take an approach to history allowing for critical investigation, engagement, debate, and ultimately sophisticated reasoning about complex realities.

The aim of this book is to step back and reconsider the teaching and learning of history, drawing on an increasing wealth of literature in history education, largely informed in Canada by Peter Seixas's seminal work. As students enter a new century, already characterized by global change and insecurity, it is my intent to devise a conceptualization of history and identify procedural concepts of the discipline relevant to twenty-first-century students, to give students the means to a more critical and disciplinary study of the past, both inside and outside the classroom. Memory, as Nora observes, is rooted in concrete and practical application, whereas history, with its apparatus, dwells on temporal continuities and changes and their relationships, calling for 'analysis and critical discourse.'[22]

1.2 The Challenges of Historical Thinking

To date, historians – whether as researchers or as teachers – have remained surprisingly silent on recent developments in the study of history and their impact on history education and democratic citizenship. Even those few, such as Nora and Lowenthal, who have ventured into the public space of education are more eloquent in professing the wrongs of school history than in presenting and explaining the purpose of history for contemporary students.[23] In fact, the most vociferous arguments for school history have been made by advocates of memory-history, who nostalgically demand a return to the memory tradition. This is no surprise, considering that public schooling has traditionally been justified for nation-building purposes. As people do not instinctively grow into fellow patriots, the task of creating citizens was too important to be left to private or religious organizations. So nationwide educational systems gradually became the norm, and soon governments regarded history as an important builder of national consciousness. As George Ross, Ontario minister of education, declared at the annual teachers convention of 1884, 'The history of the community and nation to which we belong ... shows the young the springs of public dishonour; sets before them the national feelings, weaknesses and sins; warns them against future dangers by exhibiting the losses and sufferings of the past; enshrines in their hearts the national heroes; and strengthens in them the precious love of country.'[24] The promotion of memory-history in school did not always go uncontested. Throughout the first half of the twentieth century, a few dedicated historians and educators expressed doubts about the dominant nation-building approach to history. They outlined the flaws of teaching a consensual and mythical past that not only downplayed internal conflicts, racism, class, and gender but also failed to convey to students the contentious and relative nature of historical research and accounts. To supply an alternative, they proposed a radical shift in the purpose of the subject: introducing students to a disciplinary understanding of history through an approach such as the 'source method.'[25] Instead of simply inculcating master narratives from prescribed textbooks, teachers were to teach their pupils the nature of historical evidence and interpretation; in other words, they were to teach their students to think historically. As history educator Fred Morrow Fling once told his fellow historians in 1905, 'Let our pupils be taught that proof must be insisted on in historical work, and that when proof ends history ends. Teach them that no matter how long a story has been believed nor by how many people it has been accepted as true, if it does not rest on trustworthy evidence it is not a historical fact, and cannot be classed as history.'[26] Yet, despite successive progressive educational reforms, advocates of disciplinary history, such as Fling, largely failed to win their contemporaries over to their avant-garde views on history education. Nation-building and memory-history prevailed in schools.[27] By the 1970s, however, a combination of at least three key elements – some of which have received serious attention from Peter Seixas, Sam Wineburg, and Peter Stearns – produced an unexpectedly fertile ground for school-history reform: (1) the diversification of history; (2) the cognitive revolution; and (3) the professionalization of teaching.[28]

First, the diversification of history, which was no longer focused exclusively on the political history of the nation state, significantly increased knowledge in social, cultural, and gender history, which until then had remained marginal. This diversification led to profound reconsiderations of the nature of historiographical studies (Who gets to decide what is historically significant? What counts as acceptable evidence?) and of the use of long-established concepts such as 'nation' and 'progress.' The focus was no longer on what was perceived as the centre of political action and debate but on the peripheries of ordinary people and marginalized groups within society.[29] Increased attention to events, relics, and accounts deemed by political historians as insignificant implicitly led social historians to call into question the long-standing paradigm of nation-building so prominent in school history.[30]

Second, developments in psychology after World War II changed educators' understanding of cognitive development and teaching and learning. Following the lead of Jean Piaget, many European and North American researchers in psychology, neurology, anthropology, and philosophy have questioned the old behaviourist paradigm, focused on the repetitive model of teaching – the so-called teaching by telling.[31] Leading a movement that became known as the 'cognitive revolution,'[32] experts from these disciplines concluded that learning was not a mechanical process of assimilating agreed-on knowledge through reinforcement. Rather, it was a complex act of meaning- and sense-making requiring careful examination of the learner's mental processes. The cognitive revolution brought about a shift in educational goals and teaching methods. 'Teachers,' Boix-Mansilla observes, 'were no longer expected to train students' behaviour through positive and negative reinforcements. Instead, they faced the challenge of venturing into the "black box" of the students' minds [and reflecting on their preconceived notions and ideas] to help them construct appropriate mental representations of the world.'[33] The cognitive revolution thus emphasized the importance of each student's individuality and unique mode of learning and the need for adequate teaching methods to elicit the student's own ideas and experiences insofar as they are relevant to the discipline.

Finally, the expansion and professionalization of teaching in the 1960s was accompanied by changes in the qualifications and training of history teachers. The democratization of public schooling and the rapid growth of the student population in Western countries following World War II had major impacts on teacher education. The 'Sputnik shock' of 1957 and a general acceptance of a need to invest in human capital were important factors in the increasing interest in education. According to an Organization for Economic Co-operation and Development report, the 1960s represented a period of unprecedented worldwide growth in university enrolments. In many countries, including Canada, France, Japan, and the United States, enrolments in post-secondary education more than doubled during the period of 1960–5.[34] Not only were children staying in school longer, they were also demanding better instruction and preparation from the school system. Teacher education came under scrutiny. Many countries, including Canada, continued to have only minimal requirements for the training and competence of their teachers. Elementary teachers, for example, still had to have only a normal university degree, accompanied by a one-year teaching certificate.[35] The creation or expansion of faculties of education, coupled with the enrolments of students with professional degrees, affected the training of teachers.

In addition, the widely influential book of psychologist Jerome Bruner, *The Process of Education*, led to unexpected transformations in the teaching of subjects. The central claim of Bruner is that the structure of 'any subject [or discipline] can be taught effectively in some intellectually honest form to any child at any stage of development.'[36] According to Bruner, new findings in educational psychology clearly indicate that students are capable of learning the fundamentals of any discipline. 'Intellectual activity anywhere is the same', he claims, 'whether at the frontier of knowledge or in a third-grade classroom ... The difference is in degree, not in kind.'[37] The goal of education, Bruner adds, is to give students 'an understanding of the fundamental structure of whatever subjects we choose to teach.'[38] For him, this means that students ought to be exposed not only to natural, immediate apprehension and cognition (what he calls 'intuitive thinking') but also to the 'mediated apprehension' dependent on the intervention of formal methods of research and analysis in the disciplines.[39] But an approach to education such as this requires that teachers acquire a deeper foundation in pedagogy and a more thorough background in their own respective disciplines – fundamentals largely ignored by most faculties of education and teachers colleges at that time.

Many 'neoprogressive history' educators hoped that these three factors would 'generate a powerful dynamic' and help resolve the school-history problems engendered by the changes in methods of research in history.[40] Instead of promoting the memory-history of the nation, professionally qualified teachers would introduce students to the critical investigation of conflicting accounts of the past and invite them to create their own defensible interpretations – just like historians. Yet, it became increasingly apparent that the diversification of history, the cognitive revolution, and the professionalization of teaching only led to unrealistic expectations, and limited authentic achievements.

The new history unquestionably provided new approaches to and findings about the past and revisited established assumptions and conclusions seen as unproblematic in political history. The idea of multiple perspectives, as opposed to master narratives, including 'history from below,' gradually reached the school system. But this diversification among historians also led to a specialization of the profession. Historians gradually ceased to view themselves as public intellectuals and began to see themselves more as disciplinary experts in their own area of specialization. 'Professional historians have been so successfully socialized by demands to publish,' historians Joyce Appleby, Lynn Hunt, and Margaret Jacob contend, 'that we have little time or inclination to participate in general debates about the meaning of our work.'[41] As a consequence, historians have limited connections with history educators and lack interest in issues of public schooling, thus leading professional historians to a sense of powerlessness. As one of the few remaining historians involved in school-history reform put it in the late 1960s, 'Most disturbing to us was the difficulty we historians had in coming up with a rationale for history in the schools that was clear and convincing even to ourselves ... We became aware that our heartfelt declamations about "historical wisdom" and "a sense of the past" didn't convey very much.'[42] In the same way, the cognitive revolution alerted curriculum experts and educators to the complex cognitive processes involved in learning a particular subject. Teachers have employed more personalized approaches and child-centred pedagogy, with greater attention in the classroom to students' own ideas, preconceived notions, and structures of understanding. Equally important, new findings in psychology pointed to the inefficacy of focusing on a standard theory of instruction and learning and the benefits of 'generating theories of the middle range, narrower and more provisional theories that applied to the teaching of a particular subject.'[43] Yet, all these fascinating investigations conducted over the last decades have focused on a variety of school subjects, from physics to literacy, with inadequate reference to history. The recent interest of history educators and psychologists is refreshing and has fulfilled an urgent need for educational reform. But their findings and conclusions are still limited in scope and perhaps too tentative to generate any clear theory of school-history learning, even more so in their effects on students' progress in learning to think historically.[44]

The professionalization of teaching, finally, has undeniably helped produce better-qualified teachers, with disciplinary degrees and improved training in the methods and approaches to the delivery of subjects to a more diversified school population. As history educator M.V.C. Jeffreys once put it, 'Quite apart from keeping his knowledge up to date, the teacher (especially if he is an Honours graduate in history) has the grave disadvantage of having intensively studied a great deal of history which is of very little use to children, while he remains ignorant of much that would appeal to his pupils. The temptation to unload on to a junior form the history which the teacher has learnt at the university ... is sometimes too strong to be resisted.'[45] Jeffreys' point is well taken, but the development of more professional teachers did not necessarily help the cause of history education. On the contrary, strong advocates of disciplinary thinking in education, such as Bruner, were often unfamiliar with the history discipline, even hesitant about its overall place in the curriculum. As Bruner put it, 'History, sociology, anthropology, economics and political science may for convenience be separated as academic disciplines but they all deal with a single thing: the behavior of man in society. Accordingly we propose to teach them jointly, not separately.'[46] Facing growing and competing demands, particularly from the marketplace, many state and provincial jurisdictions reduced the number of history courses in the 1990s or simply amalgamated school history with the social studies or related interdisciplinary subjects, without any clear understanding or evidence of the consequences of such drastic decisions.[47] Perhaps more puzzling are the recent research findings revealing that even the best-qualified history teachers – with graduate degrees in history – do not necessarily engage their students in disciplinary historical thinking, so busy are they covering content for board and state examinations and controlling students' behaviours.[48]

Clearly, there is a lot at stake in history education, and, as history educator Bruce VanSledright observes, it is increasingly of concern to 'shed some light on how it could more successfully be taught.'[49] This book offers some clarifications on the nature of disciplinary-history and presents a set of five interrelated procedural concepts to help foster 'historical thinking,' that is, the domain-specific process through which students master – and ultimately appropriate (or make their own) – the concepts and knowledge of history and critically apply such concepts and knowledge to resolve contemporary and historical issues.[50]

The disciplinary notion of historical thinking is far from new or revolutionary. It has been part of the conversation in history education for over a century, as evidenced below in the 1899 report of the American Historical Association on history in the schools:

> The chief object of every experienced teacher is to get pupils to think properly after the method adopted in his particular line of work; *not an accumulation of information, but the habit of correct thinking*, is the supreme result of good teaching in every branch of instruction. All this simply means that the student who is taught to consider political subjects in school, who is led to look at matters historically, has some mental equipment for a comprehension of the political and social problems that will confront him in everyday life, and has received practical preparation for social adaptation and for forceful participation in civic activities.[51]

Yet, it is equally fair to claim that historical thinking has, until recently, remained marginal and undocumented (particularly as introduced into classroom practices), compared with the memory-history tradition based on the acquisition of factual historical knowledge. These days, this domain-specific way of knowing the past is *en vogue* in educational discourse. But it has often been reclaimed in various jurisdictions for a multiplicity of purposes, many having more to do with 'commemoration,' 'memory,' and 'heritage' than with the practice of disciplinary-history suggested by Nora.[52] Part of the problem is the divergence of views on the meaning of historical thinking. Clearly, educators cannot, as Bruner observed fifty years ago, hold students to the standards and thinking of disciplinary experts. In fact, there is no evidence suggesting that educators should do so. Yet, it is equally fair to claim that the practice of the discipline can serve as a benchmark for what might be considered sophisticated historical thinking.

1.3 Outline of the Book

'It would be nice,' VanSledright contends, 'if we could turn to the discipline of history itself in order to seek guidance in addressing the learning challenges.'[53] Indeed, if school history is to teach students to think historically, it is logical to assume that historians should provide the answers to the aims of their discipline and ways of practising and thinking about it. As distinguished French historian Fernand Braudel once pronounced, history as a discipline 'cannot be understood [or explained] without practising it.'[54] It is becoming altogether apparent, however, that the recent diversification of historical knowledge and, more generally, the critique of knowledge, notably from postmodernists, have had a considerable effect on the discipline, and on historians themselves. Historian Richard Evans argues, 'The notion of scientific history, based on the rigorous investigation of primary sources, has been vehemently attacked. Increasing numbers of writers on the subject deny that there is any such thing as historical truth or objectivity – both concepts defended, in different ways, by Carr as well as Elton. The question is now not so much "What is History?" as "Is It Possible to Do History at All?"'[55] As might be expected, epistemological disagreements between historians and philosophers of history on the nature of the discipline have raised important questions about the purpose of school history, perhaps even more so in jurisdictions where history is embedded in interdisciplinary curricular subjects.[56] Is school history a practice of memory-history, meant to introduce children to their cultural and national heritage? Or, is it about a critical inquiry about the collective past? If it is the latter, what are the concepts and knowledge of the past that students should learn and master in order to think historically? What abilities do they need to *practise history*?

To date, educators have provided few clear or definitive answers, especially in North America. Perhaps much of the pedagogical problem, a Canadian educator recently acknowledged, 'comes from not understanding history as a discipline.'[57] If theorizing history, as Evans contends, is 'too important a matter to be left to the theoreticians,' then, it follows that theorizing school history and historical thinking is too important to be left to professional historians or, *faute de mieux*, to current memory fashioners, alone.

Starting from the premise that the past (what happened in human affairs) and history (constructed accounts or narratives of the past) are inseparable but quite different, the first part of chapter 2 discusses the nature of history. Traditionally, the focus of school history has been on students' mastery of the 'substance' of history (the official narratives), without understanding the process through which historians come to acquire and develop knowledge of the past, with the result that students have tended to accept the epistemologically naive view of history as the true (and indisputable) description of 'what actually happened.' Yet, students cannot think historically if they have no understanding of the structuring concepts of the discipline.

The next section of chapter 2 examines the nature of historical knowledge by developing a useful distinction, initially proposed by history educator Peter Lee, between the 'substantive' (first-order) and 'procedural' (second-order) knowledge of history. Disagreements in history education often arise from a misunderstanding or failure to define these different ideas in history. I hope to show that considering history in both its substantive and its procedural knowledge can help clarify the notion of historical thinking and the (too-often-differing) learning expectations of ministry officials, teachers, students, historians, and other agents in history education.

The difference between substantive and procedural knowledge can be seen as one between the substance, or 'content,' of the past (what history is about: wars, revolutions, women, workers, etc.) and procedural concepts for structuring or giving sense and coherence to events in history (concepts giving shape to historical practice and thinking about the past). These concepts (e.g., 'evidence' and 'historical empathy') are not what history is about (substance), but they implicitly arise in the act of doing history.[58]

Perhaps Canadian historian Chad Gaffield's useful analogy from sports can help clarify the distinction I am making. 'In the history courses I took in school,' Gaffield observes, 'we read about history, talked about history and wrote about history; we never actually did history.' He goes on, 'If I had learned basketball in this way, I would have spent years reading the interpretations and viewpoints of great players, watching them play games, and analysing the results of various techniques and strategies. Instead, though, I was soon dribbling a basketball and trying to shoot into the hoop after just a few instructions.'[59]

Today, students are still very much taught in class what the sport (history) is about: the great players' stories of political leaders, military generals, social activists, etc., statistics on their successes and failures, viewpoints and remarks from historians or narrators, and so forth. This information and these accounts delivered to students typically represent the substantive knowledge of the 'sport.' They surely help novices know more about what happened in the past from the interpretative viewpoints of others. However, they do not (and cannot) make intelligent 'players' – no matter how self-motivated and engaged they are. What they need as well is to master and appropriate the procedural concepts, to ultimately play the game themselves. Put differently, watching amateur or professional basketball or hockey players on television can stir up the crowd and motivate novices, but there is clearly no guarantee of novices' understanding or ability to play the game.

This sports analogy shows all the challenges involved in considering a complex and intellectually sophisticated discipline such as history. Without procedural thinking, students are left passively absorbing the narratives and viewpoints of authorities, too puzzled or indifferent to use the tools and mechanisms for making sense of the past. Thus, students *cannot* practise history or even think critically about its content if they have no understanding of how one constructs and shares historical knowledge. More specifically, the second part of chapter 2 introduces the following procedural concepts:

- Historical significance
- Continuity and change
- Progress and decline
- Evidence
- Historical empathy

In chapters 3 to 7, I present these concepts and explore ways of employing them in history education through sets of essential questions. It should be noted that the distinction I am drawing between substantive and procedural knowledge is highly theoretical. Historians would certainly agree that there are many fuzzy boundaries between them in practice. However, separating them serves the analytical and pedagogical purposes of this book.

2 The Nature of History and Historical Thinking

Contact with the past extends the experience of each individual, enriches his mind and gives him points of comparison which can guide his present judgment and his future actions. The lessons of history are of use not only to the politician but also to the ordinary citizen; they give him some idea of collective behaviour, help him to see contemporary problems in perspective and sharpen his social perception and political outlook. They also provide a firmer basis for freedom, developing his social conscience and political judgment.

– Royal Commission of Inquiry on
Education in the Province of Québec, 1965[1]

Writing in the pivotal period of Québec radical changes of the 1960s, commonly referred to as the Quiet Revolution, members of the Royal Commission of Inquiry on Education in the Province of Québec expressed, in their three-volume report, their views on the kind of history education that students ought to receive. What may appear to be self-evident to a twenty-first-century educator was, in many ways, revolutionary at the time. Instead of reinforcing the long-established religious and patriotic memory-history that was in place in the province – as well as in many other jurisdictions – the members of the Commission took another side on the struggle over the nature of history and how it should be used and taught in the classroom. Rejecting the traditional nation-building approach to history, the members of the Commission did not want students to be inspired simply by the heroic exploits of French Canadian martyrs who struggled for the survival of the *Canadiens* in British North America. Instead, they proposed to redefine the very nature of history as a discipline that 'aims to develop the human mind by the objective and honest study of the past.'[2] They wanted students to experience the craft of the historian by using historical methods and evidence, even if this new inquiry-based model would reveal less-inspired heroes. The goal was no longer to perpetuate *la survivance* of a mythical past but to prepare students for the demand, in a changing world, for critical and educated citizens. Teachers were no longer expected to deliver a recital of historical facts and figures of the collective past but to prepare students for a more sophisticated critical investigation and analysis of the evidence of the past. Conceivably, the most drastic change was to make history useful, engaging, and relevant to the lives of young Quebecers. The goal was to cultivate an interest in the study of the past and a sense of historical agency and to instil in students an understanding of the connectedness of the past, the present, and the future by making them 'feel a certain presence of the past.'[3]

Yet, as I suggested in the introduction, the disciplinary approach to history education did not go unchallenged. Vocal and influential critics opposed the implementation of disciplinary-history on various (notably, educational and nationalist) grounds. Students, it was argued, were immature, not-yet-competent persons, unable to fully grasp the complexity of the world in which they lived and, thus, incapable of learning the methods of history. On another, more emotionally powerful ground, there was growing fear, particularly among the new Québec nationalists, that such an approach to the collective past would undermine the survival of the *Canadiens* – now referred to as Québécois – and challenge their historical struggle for national recognition and sovereignty.[4]

Overgeneralizations and misunderstandings about the nature and purpose of history and school history have had a detrimental effect on history education in Québec – and elsewhere. Even today, much of the debate over school history suffers from the same flaws. Memory fashioners criticize the emphasis on disciplinary-history for its *soi-disant* damage to the civic and socializing mission of public schooling, whereas historians – at least those still involved in the discussion – claim that the discipline has its own intrinsic purpose, that is, the study of the past for its own sake, without regard for any other aim. To paraphrase Keith Barton and Linda Levstik's most recent book, 'What a mess!'[5]

In this chapter, I propose to bring some conceptual order to the present debate by looking at the nature of disciplinary-history. Using a variety of historians and philosophers of history, notably Leopold von Ranke, I show that although there are disagreements about the nature and role of the discipline, the same scientific methods developed over the last two centuries continue to inform historical practice and shape the landscape of historical scholarship. Building on this conception of history, I then present, in the second part, my own conception of historical thinking. To do so, I begin by discussing a model of historical-knowledge development, based on two interrelated forms of historical knowledge: substantive and procedural knowledge. Then I present a colligatory set of history benchmarks and competences, defined by five procedural concepts found in the scholarly practice of history.

The discussion of this chapter – and by extension, subsequent ones – deals primarily with procedural ideas, ideas about *how to think historically*. It focuses on what historical thinking entails for our understanding of the discipline and its impact on history education, not so much on the cognitive processes involved in thinking historically. Despite this qualification, I hope to show that my conception of history and these concepts can stimulate the development of historical thinking in schools and better equip students with 'the rules of the game' so they can make sense of the conflicting views of history they encounter in and outside their classrooms. Too often, the current discussion among educators has taken the simplified form of supposing an unbridgeable gap of 'content' versus 'skills' or of the realms of historical fact versus the processes of mastering these indisputable facts.

2.1 On the (Evolving) Nature of History

Professional historians have debated for centuries the very nature of their discipline. The result is that, to this day, there is no clear consensus on its exact definition and justification, particularly not in the schools. The problem, as historian E.H. Carr cautiously observes, comes from the fact that the answers to the question 'What is history?' consciously or not, reflect our own frame of reference (or 'positionality') in time. For example, Herodotus, often called the Father of History, produced the first official accounts of life in the Near East (Greece, Persia) in his legendary *Histories*, written in the fifth century BCE. His successor, Thucydides, also offered passionate stories of major events of his own time, notably the Peloponnesian War. Although Thucydides found Herodotus's explanations insufficient and biased, both historians have been under serious attack for representing the past in imaginary ways, by often using fictional sources to supplement actual documentary and oral evidence.[6] In the *History of the Peloponnesian War*, for example, Thucydides claimed, 'As for the speeches made on the eve of the war or during the course, it was hard for me, when I heard them myself, and for any others who reported them to me to recollect exactly what had been said. I have therefore put into the mouth of each speaker the views that, in my opinion, they would have been most likely to express, as the particular occasions demanded, while keeping as nearly as I could to the general purport of what was actually said.'[7]

This tendency of confusing historical evidence and fiction largely went by unnoticed for centuries, until about the early nineteenth century, when a new generation of historians reassessed the previous study of history. Building on the rationalist belief of the Enlightenment that human rational thinking (as opposed to God's sacred purposes in the human world) could explain human societies, a branch of pioneer historians, initially located in Germany, reassessed the notion of 'historicism,' that is, 'the belief that truth is found in the single, particular object or event, something with its own spatio-temporal location ... rather than in universal but abstract and unobservable theories.'[8] The premise of historicism was that each historical period or change in history was unique, with its own 'manifestation of the human spirit,' so that historical actors and their actions could only be understood historically, with reference to their own time and positionality (frame of reference).[9]

Possibly the most influential thinker of the time was German historian Leopold von Ranke, who, in the words of Evans, 'was the lead in this change of direction,'[10] a conclusion shared by many other modern historians.[11] Originally a philologist and school teacher, Ranke was first attracted to history by reading historical novels and finding they contained inaccuracies.[12] Adapting philological techniques to history, he proposed to approach the study of the past with complete detachment.[13] He determined that history ought to be a discipline with its own methods of research and writing. The core of this new scientific approach was to access the primary sources, the relics and records of the past, and verify scrupulously their authenticity. Ranke believed that scientific history could only be achieved if the historian, through archival research, could get and rely on the 'purest, most immediate sources' originating at the time.[14]

In addition, Ranke maintained that the historian has to study and critically analyse *all* the sources on the period or event to determine (1) the internal consistency of the sources (and thus avoid using forged documents); and (2) their consistency with other sources of the time (corroboration). Secondary sources, which do not necessarily originate from the period, were to be avoided as much as possible. After gather-

ing and scrupulously verifying the sources, historians could reconstruct the past accurately – give what Ranke referred to as the 'strict
presentation of the facts' – only if they understood the past as the people who lived in it, that is, with 'historical empathy.'[15] The past, in his
view, could only be judged on its own terms, not by the ever-changing
standards of the present. As Ranke explained, in the much-quoted preface of his Histories of the Latin and Germanic Nations from 1494 to
1514 (*Geschichten der romanischen und germanischen Völker von 1494 bis
1514*), 'To history has been assigned the office of judging the past, of
instructing the present for the benefit of future ages. To such high
offices this work does not aspire: It wants only to show what actually
happened [wie es eigentlich gewesen]. But whence the sources for such
a new investigation? The basis of the present work, the sources of its
material, are memoirs, diaries, letters, diplomatic reports, and original
narratives of eyewitnesses; other writings were used only if they were
immediately derived from the above mentioned or seemed to equal
them because of some original information.'[16]

The scientific methods of history proclaimed by Ranke at the University of Berlin immediately received serious attention in European and
U.S. scholarly communities.[17] 'The German mode of "doing history,"'
Ernst Breisach observes, 'influenced the idiosyncratic development
through the so-called Oxford and Cambridge schools of historiography
and American historiography through the numerous Americans who
studied at German universities.'[18] Even France, with divergent political
and historiographic traditions, was not spared by the German scientific
upsurge. French historian Fustel de Coulanges did not hesitate to
declare during a public lecture in 1862 that 'history is something more
than a pastime, that it is not pursued merely in order to entertain our
curiosity or to fill the pigeonholes of our memory. History is and should
be a science.'[19] Talking about the influence of the German scientific tradition, Cambridge professor John Bagnell Bury declared a few years
later, 'The proposition that before the beginning of the last century the
study of history was not scientific may be sustained in spite of a few
exceptions ... A few stand on a higher level in so far as they were really
alive to the need of bringing reason and critical doubt to bear on the
material, but the systematised method which distinguishes a science
was beyond the vision of all, except a few like Mabillon. Erudition has
now been supplemented by scientific method, and the change is owed
to Germany. Among those who brought it about, the names of Niebuhr
and Ranke are pre-eminent.'[20] During the same period, Professor

Edward Gaylord Bourne proclaimed in his address before the meeting of the American Historical Association of 1895 that 'It is hardly possible so soon to decide what has been the dominant intellectual characteristic of our century, but certainly, in the increase of positive historical knowledge, the elaboration of sound historical method, the enlargement of the range of historical evidence, and especially in the development of the historical way of looking at things, the nineteenth century stands out conspicuous above any century since the Renaissance. To these immense changes no one contributed so much as Leopold von Ranke, the centenary of whose birth was celebrated last week.'[21] Whether Ranke was the greatest nineteenth-century historian is still open to debate. Several historians, notably after World War I, did not hesitate to criticize him for his positivistic history.

One of the most vocal critics was British historian George Macaulay Trevelyan, grand-nephew of Whig historian Lord Macaulay, who strongly objected to the influence of the German scientific tradition: 'Who is the Mother Country to Anglo-Saxon historians? Some reply "Germany," but others of us prefer to answer "England." The methods and limitations of German learning presumably suit the Germans, but are certain to prove a strait waistcoat to English limbs and faculties. We ought to look to the free, popular, literary traditions of history in our own land.'[22] Trevelyan likely had his Whig great-uncle in mind here. Indeed, if Macaulay is no longer seen as the authority in history, even in his native England, he surely epitomizes an important development in the study and writing of national history, the notion of progress. As a result of the eighteenth-century Enlightenment, and as part of the nineteenth-century Industrial Revolution, the view of history as progress became a dominant trend in historical scholarship – especially so in England. Not only is history seen as the product of historical changes created by human actors (and no longer by divine providence), but these changes are advancing in a unique direction in human evolution, that of liberty, modernity, and Western civilization. This view is very perceptible in Macaulay's *History of England from the Accession of James II*, where he announced that his focus would not be exclusively on politics, because 'it will be my endeavour to relate the history of the people as well as the history of the government, to trace the progress of useful and ornamental arts.'[23]

But just as Macaulay, Trevelyan, and their Whig contemporaries looked to more national traditions as the source of historical study and interpretation, historians from other countries soon rejected, or at least publicly objected to, the positivist views of Ranke. Italian philosopher Benedetto Croce and his English counterpart R.G. Collingwood made it clear that historians are guided in their selection of topic and interpretative judgment not only by the sources they select and use but also by their own positionalities, interests, and perspectives. 'All history,' Croce argued, 'is contemporary history.'[24] Collingwood took Croce's argument further by noting that 'All history is the history of thought; and when an historian says that a man is in a certain situation this is the same as saying that he thinks he is in this situation.'[25] He went on, 'the hard facts of the situation are the hard facts of the way in which he conceives the situation.'[26] History was thus, and perhaps first and foremost, about interpretation and judgment. No document, as close as it was in its origin to the event in question, could tell exactly what the original author thought or believed. Selecting and reading historical sources implies re-enacting in the mind of the historian the thought of the author (to empathize), a notion largely overlooked by Ranke.

Pushing these ideas further, others such as Carl Becker, William Gallie, E.H. Carr, and more recently Paul Ricoeur and David Carr have focused more explicitly on narrativism as a method in history and the complexity of the relation between historical facts and the historian's narrative explanation. Indeed, one of the conventional tools for communicating historical interpretations is the 'narrative,' that is, a coherent representation of past human actions as the story of these events.[27] Unlike a chronicle, which presents a chronological list of historical happenings, the narrative, by virtue of its retrospective view, 'picks out the most important events, traces the causal and motivational connections among them, and gives us an organized, coherent account.'[28] Because the narrative must hang together, it is typically shaped with a beginning, subject, actors, events, setting, plot, and conclusion. Narratives, as novelists know well, can be either real or imaginary (some would say both) without losing their internal structure and power. Yet, the narrative used in history, as Trevelyan once argued, would form a distinct literary genre: 'The appeal of history to us all is in the last analysis poetic. But the poetry of history does not consist of imagination roaming at large, but of imagination pursuing the fact and fastening upon it ... The poetry of history lies in the quasi-miraculous fact that once, on this earth, once, on this familiar spot of ground, walked other men and women, as actual as we are today, thinking their own thoughts, swayed by their own passions, but now all gone, one generation vanishing into another, gone as utterly as we ourselves shall shortly be gone, like ghosts at cockcrow.'[29] With the recent postmodernist critique of knowledge, the connection between history and narrative – as defined above – has been the subject of lively debate among historians, linguists, psychologists, philosophers, and other *bien-pensants*. Can we get rid of narrative in history? Is narrative a fictional imposition on a disorganized past? What is the relation between a narrative and the actions and events it depicts? Are historical actors and events shaped by the form of narrative?

Answers to these questions have been offered by different domains and theories of knowledge, including cultural anthropology, linguistics, and postmodernist thought. It is not necessary here to follow all the debates, except perhaps to note that scholars by and large agree with the general principle that history and narrative are not identical. History can take the form of narrative, but a narrative does not always speak in the name of history, because it is constructed – as opposed to rescued – by an outside narrator, who can only attempt to recreate 'what actually happened' in the past. Put simply, not only can the selected facts be distorted, but their arrangement (notably the causal relation between events) could be misconstrued by historians, as a result of their own misjudgments or predilections. As David Thomson observes, '[An] interesting and meaningful narrative, as distinct from a mere chronological annal, rests (if only implicitly) on a whole series of judgments about the relative importance of some events or people in "causing" other subsequent developments. So the historian cannot escape the obligation to consider relationships of cause and effect, even though he may often have to confess himself baffled by the problems which they raise.'[30]

Clearly, the Rankean revolution in historiography has led to much writing and debate in the history community, as evidenced above. Yet, the application of scientific methods to historical sources was – and still is – a major advance in the discipline. As Tosh observes, '[Ranke] certainly founded the modern discipline of academic history – largely because he developed the techniques of research necessary for the fulfilment of the historicists' programme, especially the use and interpretation of primary documentary sources.'[31] Perhaps more appealing to educators, the revolutionary ideas advanced by Ranke, and subsequently challenged and revised by his followers, were accepted not only by a few obscure academics but by visionary scholars of history education who believed in a *rapprochement* between the educational and academic worlds. As early as the 1890s, for instance, some historians from

Europe and North America advocated the so-called New History in schools. 'Progressive' historians, such as Mary Sheldon Barnes, Edward Freeman, Charles Beard, James Harvey Robinson, Fred Morrow Fling, Charles Seignobos, and M.W. Keatinge, all believed in a theory of school history anchored in the practice of teaching history with primary sources, sometimes referred to as the source method.[32] Yet, this method, though proclaimed in academic circles, never led to a revolution in history education. Not only were history teachers unprepared to accomplish this *tour de force*, but detractors within the history community simply believed it was a *folie de grandeur* to teach masses of youngsters the complexity of this science. As prominent British historian G.R. Elton once argued,

> School courses of history dominated by the ultimate academic principles involved in the most highly developed forms of historical studies must be thought ill-advised, however honourable. This is not, however, to throw the schools back on producing some inferior kind of history, so that the universities may have a free run ... On the contrary, what is urgently required is the discovery of an alternative principle by which the study of history at school can be justified and therefore animated, and one, moreover, which is more appropriate to a group of students many of whom are not specialising in history. One must ask once again just why children and adolescents should be asked to concern themselves with history.[33]

Despite the fact these avant-garde historians largely failed to win their contemporaries over to the necessity and usefulness of teaching disciplinary-history, the key principles they advanced over a century ago still remain relevant today. As I argue in the next section, the process of studying and communicating knowledge about the past is also applicable to historical thinking in school. Teachers and their students simply cannot make sense of, or even critically employ, historical accounts without some understanding of how one creates these accounts.

2.2 On Historical Thinking

Knowing how the discipline of history has developed over the past few centuries is certainly useful and illuminating for history educators. It shows the importance of the study of historical knowledge, as well as the dynamic nature of the profession. New ideas, concepts, and theories of history have challenged and gradually changed earlier orthodoxies. Yet, as useful as they might be, these disciplinary developments do not address the ways students, educators, and historians *think histor-ically*. The intellectual process through which an individual masters – and ultimately appropriates – the concepts and knowledge of history and critically applies such concepts and knowledge in the resolution of contemporary and historical issues is extremely demanding and com-plex. In fact, one could argue that school history has typically failed to promote historical thinking because of its persisting (and often dog-matic) focus on the transmission of memory-history, largely in the form of master narratives. Limited but growing research indicates, with increasing academic acceptance, that historical thinking is not limited to (and is probably not, above all) the mastering of factual knowledge of the past, such as dates, names, characters, and events established by authorities in historical accounts. It is also about the *self-appropriation* of the procedures and concepts that arise in the act of doing history.[34] Of course, it is essential for students to master the claims (substantive his-torical knowledge) made by historians, teachers, or related authorities. This type knowledge – commonly referred to in the schools as 'content' – constitutes the foundation of historical thinking. As Lee observes, 'it is misleading to juxtapose "developing concepts" against "transmitting content." Presumably the concepts in question, as well as being devel-oped through content, are developed in order to allow pupils to ask and answer historical questions more successfully [that is, practise history].'[35]

Historical thinking is, indeed, far more sophisticated and demanding than mastering substantive (content) knowledge, in that it requires the acquisition of such knowledge to understand the procedures employed to investigate its aspects and conflicting meanings. 'While all thinking results in knowledge,' as John Dewey once summed it up, 'the value of knowledge is subordinate to its use in thinking.'[36] To think historically is thus to understand how knowledge has been constructed and what it means. Without such sophisticated insight into ideas, peoples, and actions, it becomes impossible to adjudicate between competing ver-sions (and visions) of the past. One can clearly see the power but also the limit of memory-history when the past, to paraphrase Nora, becomes no more than a useful resource of everyday experience, subjected to the dialectic of remembering and forgetting.

But this type of disciplinary understanding is only possible and effec-tive if another element in the construction of knowledge is considered: the ability to apply what is learned in other contexts. Thus, Gardner

argues that sophisticated thinking (he refers to it as 'disciplinary expertise') occurs when a person can take information and concepts learned
in one setting 'and apply them flexibly and appropriately in a new and
at least somewhat unanticipated situation.'[37] This type of thinking is
complex and never complete because it requires from the learner a
capacity not only to master knowledge or concepts as taught in one
context but also to apply such knowledge or concepts to different or
new phenomena. In other words, to understand a concept or piece of
knowledge is to be able to represent it in more than one way or context.
For Gardner, such disciplinary performances occur 'When history students who have studied the French and Russian revolutions are able to
discuss the factors that have precipitated a contemporary revolutionary
movement and to offer grounded predictions of what is likely to occur
during the coming months.'[38] Gardner's disciplinary ideas are hardly
new. Bruner had already argued some thirty years earlier that the structure of a discipline could best be understood by students through the
adequate transfer of training across contexts. 'To understand something as a specific instance of a more general case – which is what
understanding a more fundamental principle or structure means,' he
observes, 'is to have learned not only a specific thing but also a model
for understanding other things like it that one may encounter.'[39]

Bruner carefully sets limits to such transferability. He notes that generalizations, notably in history, are highly problematic because of the
specificity of historical contexts, something Ranke had already established. The recognition of this limit is not as much a problem for him,
because he believes that understanding the fundamentals of a discipline is to be familiar precisely with those instances that cannot be
explained by a given mode of knowing – as clearly evidenced in Keegan's introductory remarks on September 11.

From this definition, then, it is fair to claim that historical thinking, as
presented above, can make an important contribution to democratic citizenship. Historical knowledge of political, social, cultural, and economical systems overlaps with the democratic knowledge necessary
for active citizenship, and hence mastering the knowledge of history,
and ultimately the practice of history itself, can allow students to more
effectively engage in democratic society, well beyond acquiring a deep
sense of patriotism (i.e., sense of attachment to the polity). According to
historian Peter Stearns, history can contribute to democratic citizenship
in at least four ways: (1) the study of political institutions; (2) comparative historical analysis; (3) comparisons of past and current events; and
(4) development of democratic habits of mind.[40]

Given this relationship between history and democratic citizenship, it is no surprise that several jurisdictions have identified history as the subject *par excellence* to teach citizenship education. Many history teachers already recognize that their mission is highly political. What they choose to teach (or not to teach), how they teach it, and what students are expected to do in their classes are all implicitly about politics and power. Yet, if the attainment of citizenship education goals can be transferred to history education, one nevertheless needs to be careful and put limits on what they can be expected to accomplish. 'If we expect the history teacher to be the sole guarantor of such ambitions,' as James Arthur and his colleagues rightly contend, 'we will only raise hope unrealistically and condemn teachers to take the blame for problems that are actually beyond their capabilities.'[41] Indeed, history and citizenship education are subjects closely related, but they are not interchangeable. Whereas school history can contribute to citizenship education, education for citizenship does not necessarily support or rely on the standards, procedures, and rationale of history. Part of the current debate in school history emerges from the failure to make these limits clear. A better understanding of how historical expertise intersects with, but also diverges from, history education may facilitate the discussion.

Substantive and Procedural Knowledge of History

'Historians,' VanSledright observes, 'reconstruct (some might say create) the past based on questions they attempt to answer. Criteria are involved in selecting and reconstructing the past, and these criteria relate to what is considered generally acceptable practice within the field.'[42] In an attempt to conceptualize historians' ways of practising historical scholarship, Lee, drawing on the influential works of Kitson Clark, William Burston, William Walsh, and others, has laid out an interesting and extremely helpful model of historical-knowledge development, based on two types of interdependent historical knowledge: substantive and procedural knowledge.[43]

The first type of historical knowledge focuses on the substance of the past. It is what historical knowledge is *about* – the 'content' of history.[44] Typically, this type of knowledge focuses on certain historical themes or actors. Substantive knowledge, as discussed in the previous section, has traditionally been framed in narrative form, with all the consequences of such historiographical 'emplotment.' Examples of the forms of substantive knowledge are history books and textbooks (often entitled 'The story of ...'), movies, and oral histories. In curricular language, this form of historical knowledge is typically found in expectations of students' learning, such as the students' understanding of certain terms, events, phenomena, or personages (e.g., names of the prime ministers of Canada). It is the substantive knowledge that has been the subject of lively debate in various jurisdictions because it is highly political and contentious and frequently misused and justified by competing groups for a variety of collective purposes (identity, memory, patriotism, public policy, etc.).

The second type of historical knowledge, referred to as procedural, concentrates on the concepts and vocabulary that provide 'the structural basis for the discipline.'[45] These concepts (evidence, empathy, progress, decline, etc.) are not what history is *about* – the substance. They are, rather, conceptual tools needed for the study of the past as a discipline and the construction of the content of historical knowledge. Without these concepts, it would be impossible to make sense of the substance of the past, as 'they shape the way we go about doing history.'[46] Because these concepts are rarely apparent in use, they are often left hidden in historians' investigations and even more so in school textbooks, thus leading to the naive assumption that they do not influence historical inquiry and are unworthy of study.

It is important not to misconstrue the distinction and transition from substantive to structural knowledge as the simplistic dichotomy of content versus skills, as too often happens in school history. It is impossible for students to understand or make use of procedural knowledge if they have no knowledge of the substance of the past. To claim, for example, that there has been remarkable *progress* in human rights over the last century makes no sense unless one knows some *content* (key dates, events, declarations, charters, etc.) relating to the history of human rights. To understand the various claims made about the past, therefore, students need to be introduced to the disciplinary concepts and procedures that led to the crafting of these historical claims. 'The acquisition of more powerful procedural or second-order ideas,' Lee and Ashby contend, 'is one way – perhaps the best – of giving sense to the notion of progression in history.'[47]

Equally important is the 'progression' in historical thinking that Lee and Ashby talk about. There has been a misleading tendency, even in academic circles, to place substantive and procedural knowledge on a linear scale of historical reasoning, leading to the belief that progress in historical thinking should be from the former to the latter, that is, from lower- to higher-order thinking. This understanding is highly misleading and likely stands behind the rhetorical and unproductive debate over teaching content versus skills in the classroom. Progression in historical thinking ought to be developed simultaneously *within each* of these domains of knowledge and not from one to the other. In other words, sophisticated historical thinkers are not those who have successfully moved away from content acquisition to the mastery of procedural knowledge but those who have made significant progress in understanding both the substance of the past and the ideas (procedures and concepts) necessary to make sense of it. School history can help with this type of progression.

In recent years in North America, Europe, and the Asia-Pacific (especially, Australia), an interest has grown in teaching students about the procedures and ideas needed to engage in the study of history. Given the early developments in historiography discussed in section 2.1 above, the current return to the practice of history may leave the reader with a sense of *déjà vu*. Yet, the terms 'doing history' and 'historical thinking' are now so widespread and *en vogue* in educational jargon that educators may wonder about their meaning and significance. Clearly, the historical thinking of elementary- and secondary-school students does not (and cannot) match that of disciplinary experts. VanSledright is thus correct to argue that scholars must not unfairly hold novices to standards of disciplinary expertise. There is simply no evidence showing that students naturally grow into historians. Historical thinking is, indeed, an *unnatural* act, to borrow Wineburg's cliché.

Nevertheless, it is fair to claim, as Bruner observes, that 'there is a continuity between what a scholar does on the forefront of his discipline and what a child does in approaching it for the first time.'[48] Therefore, the development of historical scholarship, as outlined so far, can serve as a benchmark for students' own historical development, a benchmark that may help educators narrow the gap between the two worlds and assist students in developing more a sophisticated understanding of past and contemporary issues – as opposed to a strict accumulation of content knowledge. To this day, the problem in history education has been the failure to understand how educators can improve students' historical thinking by introducing them to disciplinary concepts and procedures allowing for such progression in historical thinking. More focus has been on how students could more successfully acquire knowledge of specific claims about the past (i.e., retention of facts, dates, and stories), without it being realized that success in this depends on a second feature of historical knowledge. A student simply cannot, for example, make sense of the Holocaust without being exposed to the concepts of historical significance (why is the Holocaust important to study?) and empathy (what was it like? How did people feel?). 'It it now generally accepted,' as Terry Haydn, James Arthur, and Martin Hunt contend, 'that the more sophisticated [students'] understandings of these concepts, when relating to historical content, the greater will be the depth of their historical understanding.'[49] But what exactly are these concepts? How do educators go about using them?

As I discuss in the following chapters, historians and philosophers of history have employed procedural concepts for a long time in their works. Yet, the problem has been the absence in the literature of a coherent and explicit articulation of them, particularly for history education purposes. Even the revolutionary arguments of the 'new history' presented a century ago by Fling and his contemporaries have remained largely silent on procedural knowledge. Because of a drastic change in British history education from memory-history to disciplinary-history in the early 1990s, some scholars in the United Kingdom engaged in the study and dissemination of ideas about historical thinking in general, and procedural concepts in particular. This movement was also fuelled by the interests and findings of a highly influential history project established in the 1970s, the Schools' Council History Project (SHP). Based on studies of students' understanding of causation, change, evidence, and empathy, the SHP not only offered a more accurate picture than the largely deficient one of British students' thinking current until then but also examined the important role of these concepts in students' progression in learning and practising the discipline of history. Following the lead of the SHP, several history educators, such as Peter Lee, Rosalyn Ashby, Martin Hunt, and Chris Husbands, have enriched the field of history education by presenting complementary arguments and findings revealing a more comprehensive and perhaps more accurate representation of historical learning, at least for England.

However, the ideas developed across the Atlantic during the late-twentieth century were not always disseminated and were far less adapted to the North American context. Notably because of the 'progressive education' movement of the late 1910s, which stressed teaching interdisciplinary subjects as part of the new 'social studies,' the focus in the field of history education has been on issues of citizenship education, republican democracy, and the 'common good.'[50] The recent debates over the teaching of U.S. history in schools and the subsequent

National Standards for history offer perhaps some indications of a *rapprochement* between the two school-history traditions. But, as VanSledright recently claimed in light of his history teaching experience, 'the British example may help us understand that, in order to learn to think historically, an obsession with asking children to commit a nationalist narrative to memory is a misguided approach.'[51]

In Canada, where the provinces have followed various, sometimes divergent traditions, it is difficult to point to the systematic and influential role of the British history education movement. Even if some revolutionary ideas and authors (e.g., W.M. Keatinge) made their way into some Canadian schools during the twentieth century, history education reforms have traditionally focused on 'fears for the future of the country,' rather than on concerns for the purpose and nature of school history. As Osborne observes, 'the not-so-hidden assumption in every case was that if only the schools were to do a better job of teaching history, Canada would be safer and stronger.'[52] Perhaps the most significant contribution to the field of history education in the last decades has been made by Peter Seixas, director of the Centre for the Study of Historical Consciousness at the University of British Columbia, the first scholar to conceptualize the notion of historical thinking in Canadian history education. Seixas is, for instance, the one who offered North American educators a creative conceptualization of growth in historical understanding centred on a set of related elements initially developed in historiography. These elements are, for him, 'closely related core issues that must be confronted in order to foster growth in historical thinking.' Seixas goes on, 'Without addressing these core issues, we could not begin to think historically, nor could we become more expert.'[53] For Seixas, the ability to move from a naive historical understanding to sophisticated thinking is rooted in the understanding of key elements in the structure of historical inquiry: significance, epistemology and evidence, continuity and change, progress and decline, empathy and moral judgments, and historical agency.

Seixas is careful to note that these disciplinary elements should not be viewed as fixed or given but as developing, always problematic and incomplete, contingent on and limited by people's own historiographical culture. Like any other discipline, history has meaning and justification within 'the context of the questions, procedures, and debates in which it develops.'[54] Perhaps more importantly, because history is a dynamic discipline, new discoveries or methods in the discipline gradually challenge and ultimately undermine current tenets. This cautionary point is crucial, as other communities of scholars and educators have also come up with similar concepts, more in tune with their research culture or national curriculum. In England, for example, the 'key' concepts of the National Curriculum for history are time and chronology, evidence, importance, causation, change and continuity, empathy, interpretation, and enquiry.[55] Although the United States does not have the exact notion of procedural concepts for its history curriculum, the National Standards for history do provide a list of five related historical-thinking skills as arising in the actual practice of the discipline: (1) chronological thinking; (2) historical comprehension; (3) historical analysis and interpretation; (4) historical-research capabilities; and (5) historical-issues analysis and decision-making.[56] Related to the U.S. National Standards, a Deweyan approach has recently been taken by Barton and Levstik, who offer their own set of 'stances' they claim students should be 'expected to perform when they learn history.'[57] These stances include identification, analysis, moral response, and exhibition (display). Other jurisdictions and scholars, notably in Australia, France, and Germany, have also developed history programs with related structures, concepts, and procedural ideas.[58] Perhaps Finnish scholar Sirkka Ahonen best sums it up when she claims that the recent changes in history have been confronted by 'different traditions of research into history education' that, unfortunately, rarely encounter each other.[59]

In relying on the influential works of British, U.S., Canadian, German, and Australian scholars, this book offers a more inclusive and coherent study of historical thinking and procedural concepts than offered so far in any of their traditions of scholarship on history education. If applying such an approach to history education in specific jurisdictions or school curricula is problematic, it is also its advantage. In a world where the validity of knowledge is more and more widely contested, the dynamics of divergent and, in themselves, contentious historical practices may help reduce the tendency of historians to make absolute claims to knowledge and give way to other equally important types of claims. Instead of promoting creative discussion and exchange, sharp and unworkable distinctions between British and U.S. historical traditions or between the viewpoints of history scholars and educators are likely to favour resentment and mutual ignorance.

In many ways, the approach taken in this book reflects the process of inquiry through which historians create knowledge of the past. The Rankean revolution has produced useful intellectual tools that the history community largely accepts and still employs, notably in its peer reviews. 'The fact that historians disagree,' Rogers contends, 'is exactly what makes historical knowledge reputable by providing the most rigorous check upon its provenance and content.'[60]

Five Procedural Concepts

In their influential book *Understanding by Design*, educators Grant Wiggins and Jay McTighe claim that 'essential questions' are doorways to sophisticated thinking because they help educators focus on *what is worth knowing* by employing a problem-solving approach to the subject.[61] Not only do essential questions go to the heart of the discipline but they also raise other, equally important questions whose answers do not seem self-evidently true or false. They should be deliberately thought-provoking and '[help] students effectively inquire and make sense of important but complicated ideas, knowledge, and know-how – a bridge to findings that experts may believe are settled but learners do not yet grasp or see as valuable.'[62] In an attempt to uncover the various and complex disciplinary practices and concepts of history outlined earlier, essential questions can be useful in orienting the selection of concepts, as they have been in structuring my own argument. Perhaps more importantly, Wiggins and McTighe's inquisitive-teaching design (they call it 'backward design') offers history educators a deliberate and active-learning approach to historical knowledge that shifts the focus from 'coverage' to 'uncoverage.'[63] Instead of presenting an overview of the past by marching through a vast body of information and topics within a limited time (i.e., textbook coverage), educators who uncover the past make students inquire, interrogate, and go into depth, so as to find defensible answers to meaningful questions – just like scholars when they study and uncover a given problem.

I mentioned in the first section that historians have developed a time-honoured process of investigating – *uncovering* – aspects of the past that goes back to Ranke's principles of scientific history. This process of turning the past into history more or less resembles something like this the following. Historians approach the past with some personal interests, areas of significance, and questions in mind. These interests and questions are typically informed by historians' positionalities and knowledge (or lack of knowledge) of certain historical subjects – often in terms of stories. Implicit in the questions historians initially consider of significance are their own historical narratives, hypotheses, and evaluative judgments about these events as signifying continuity and change or progress and decline. Then begins, for historians, a complex research process of gathering, selecting, and making sense of the evidence that they think is worth collecting and analysing. When they believe they have gone as far as possible into the subject and possess a good understanding of it, they offer some interpretative answers to their initial questions, which, in turn, may prompt them to investigate some other related aspects of the past.

Of course, this simplified model of inquiry does not do justice to the complex practice of historical research and writing. It implies, for example, that historians arrive at their interpretations of the past only *after* they have collected all the available and necessary evidence. In practice, however, the construction of answers to initial questions can be ongoing. 'For any historian worth his name,' Carr contends, 'the two processes of what economists call "input" and "output" go on simultaneously and are, in practice, parts of a single process.' He goes on, 'The more I write, the more I know what I am looking for, the better I understand the significance and relevance of what I find.'[64] That being said, separating this process of historical inquiry into a number of temporally and conceptually distinct elements provides a didactically useful and convenient sequence of interrelated steps. Perhaps more importantly, by doing so, we uncover the careful, analytic process involved in investigating the past. Unlike memory-history, disciplinary-history is not primarily an act of 'intuitive thinking,' intended to arrive at a given answer, with little or no awareness of the process of reaching that answer, although the answer may well be right or wrong.[65] Historical investigation involves a deep understanding of both the power and limits of history (why histories and historians might be right or wrong) and the rigorous disciplinary steps or procedures necessary for crafting a defensible response to a given problem. Intuitive thinking, in contrast, is more instinctive and unconscious, based on prior perceptions and a sense of familiarity with the domain of inquiry.

So if one considers the analytic model above, a number of different steps can be identified. First, historians investigate aspects of the past because they think they are worth studying and uncovering. Why would historians question, research, or think about certain historical events or personages unless they strongly believe these are historically significant? Second, historians approach the significant past with some judgments and understanding of events in the past as part of a larger narrative or sequence of events that provides meaning and direction to the event. This understanding implicitly rests on a process of perceiving past events as signifying the complementary concepts of continuity and change and those of progress and decline. Because historians' interpretations must rely, as Ranke made it clear, on supporting evidence, the third step of an inquiry is the research. It is at this point that the evidence must be selected and analysed, carefully and with a deep sense of historical empathy to avoid naive or intuitive 'presentist' judgments of past actors. This whole process finally brings historians back to their initial significant questions, which they then attempt to answer, usually in writing.

Building on Wiggins and McTighe's teaching design, I have developed a set of five essential questions at the heart of the practice of history. Each question logically leads to the inquiry and analysis of a certain concept that in turn provides a doorway for uncovering the answer to this type of question in history education practice. Thus, each question is framed to uncover a certain procedural concept in ways that will lead to a better understanding of, and potentially a better use of, that concept in history education. These are epistemic concepts employed by historians in studying and interpreting the past, although not necessarily in the sequence I am suggesting in this book. They are often considered 'background' concepts because 'they are seldom discussed in history texts' and are traditionally overlooked in school-history teaching.[66] Yet, they are fundamental to the discipline because one simply cannot progress in historical thinking without adopting some procedural understanding of significance, evidence, empathy, and so forth. These essential questions and associated procedural concepts are

1 What is important in the past? – Historical significance
2 What changed and what remained the same? – Continuity and change
3 Did things change for better or worse? – Progress and decline
4 How do we make sense of the raw materials of the past? – Evidence
5 How can we understand predecessors who had different moral frameworks? – Historical empathy

Consistent with my earlier discussion, I recognize that these practice-informed questions could be construed as subjective, as they emerge from a given cultural and historical standpoint. The choice of these questions in particular is also personal, in that other, equally important questions at the heart of the discipline could be asked in the study of historical thinking. However, partial as they might be, I believe that they are still pertinent (some might say *sine qua non*) for making sense of historical thinking and offering targets for what history educators might accomplish with their students in the twenty-first century.

2.3 Conclusion

In this chapter, I have argued that the discipline of history rests on several assumptions about the nature of historical knowledge. Using the works of various historians and philosophers of history, notably Leopold von Ranke, I have shown that the nineteenth- and twentieth-century scientific revolution, emerging from the idea of modernity, has provided historians with a set of distinctive procedural ideas still largely employed in the history community. Yet, evidence suggests that history educators often fail to engage students in the practice of uncovering the past, notably because of an overemphasis on the coverage of narratives and the substantive knowledge they contain.

In trying to foster historical thinking, I have stated that history educators can narrow the gap between disciplinary experts and novice students by examining more explicitly a set of procedural concepts of the discipline. These concepts, actually employed by historians in their investigations, are rarely discussed in class and are typically left implicit in historiographical research, thus leading to the belief that historical thinking does not advance by a careful, analytical process. The following chapters each start with one of these essential questions and more thoroughly examine one of these five concepts and ways they could be employed in history education.

3 What Is Important in the Past? – Historical Significance

> The reciprocal process of interaction between the historian and his facts, what I have called the dialogue between present and past, is a dialogue not between abstract and isolated individuals, but between the society of today and the society of yesterday. History, in Burckhardt's words, is 'the record of what one age finds worthy of note in another.'
>
> – E.H. Carr[1]

In the fall of 1993, Canadian General Roméo Dallaire was officially appointed Force Commander for the United Nations Observer Mission Uganda–Rwanda. Leading what was supposed to be a modest and straightforward peacekeeping mission of confidence-building between Rwandese Governmental Forces and Rwandese Patriotic Front belligerents, General Dallaire turned out to be a key witness to one of the most dreadfully rapid and neglected genocides in modern history. During a one-hundred day reign of terror, over three-quarters of a million Rwandans, among whom were 300,000 children, were savagely slaughtered with machetes and clubs by *génocitaire* militias and extremist Hutus. Restrained by a strict UN mandate, international community indifference, and a poorly trained and equipped military contingent of fewer than 500 troops, General Dallaire found himself powerless, unable to intervene and stop the ongoing slaughter taking place in this small country already devastated by famine and poverty. In the introduction to his award-winning book, *Shake Hands with the Devil*, General Dallaire recounts,

> The following is my story of what happened in Rwanda in 1994. It's a story of betrayal, failure, naïveté, indifference, hatred, genocide, war,

inhumanity and evil. Although strong relationships were built and moral, ethical and courageous behaviour was often displayed, they were over-shadowed by one of the fastest, most efficient, most evident genocides in recent history. In just one hundred days over 800,000 innocent Rwandan men, women and children were brutally murdered while the developed world, impassive and apparently unperturbed, sat back and watched the unfolding apocalypse or simply changed channels.[2]

General Dallaire never recovered completely from his experience in Rwanda, a mission that he does not hesitate to qualify as a personal, but also collective, failure. In 2000, he was released from the Canadian Forces for post-traumatic stress disorder. After contemplating suicide several times, he embarked on a personal and immensely emotional journey of writing a first-hand account of what happened during his mandate in Rwanda. Ten years after the mission, General Dallaire finally returned to Kigali, and the (too many) sites of massacres, to com-memorate the genocide. As if the international community had not learned any lesson from its mistakes, no Western leader even deigned to attend the official remembrance ceremony, not even Secretary Gen-eral Kofi Annan, who was then Under Secretary General for Peacekeep-ing. The only exception was Belgium, Rwanda's former colonial power, which had initially deployed a contingent to the region but had brought all its troops home hastily when ten of its soldiers were killed in action during the early stage of the mission. A decade after the geno-cide, General Dallaire is more than ever convinced that the interna-tional community deliberately closed its eyes to an escalating conflict that, despite daily updates from his headquarters, UN members sys-tematically refused to call a 'genocide' because of the political and mil-itary implications it would have had for them. As he told an Amnesty International journalist, '[the] world is racist, Africans don't count; Yugoslavians do. More people were killed, injured, internally dis-placed, and refugeed in 100 days in Rwanda than in the whole eight to nine years of the Yugoslavia campaign. And there are still peacekeep-ing troops in the former Yugoslavia while Rwanda is again off the radar.'[3] To this day, General Dallaire could not explain why interests in Yugoslavia, Afghanistan, and Iraq have proved to be more significant than those of Rwanda. Why was military intervention necessary in the Balkans during the same period and inevitable in the Middle East fol-lowing 11 September but pointless in Africa in 1994? E.H. Carr once argued that in history 'numbers count.'[4] One would think the 800,000 victims of the Rwandan genocide were more significant than the 3,000 in New York City and Washington, DC, on 11 September. But numbers cannot offer the only defensible answer, particularly in the realm of politics. General Dallaire has supplied his own response: 'Because there was no self-interest ... No oil. They didn't come because some humans are [considered] less human than others.'[5]

General Dallaire's comments, if warranted, have serious implications for the future of international affairs. If human rights have spread to the global community, the very idea of global intervention to protect these rights is still unclear and inconsistent, at least in the Western world. Military intervention, Michael Ignatieff contends, is undermining the international community's legitimacy, 'both because our interventions are unsuccessful and because they are inconsistent.'[6] He goes on, 'Failing to intervene in Rwanda has proven even more damaging to the credibility of human rights principles than late and partial interventions in Iraq, Bosnia, and Kosovo.'[7] Put differently, if human rights are universal, human rights abuses everywhere should be condemned, and sanctions should everywhere be imposed. Yet, the international community does not (and perhaps cannot) intervene everywhere. In a world of limited resources, collective interests, and national sovereignty, choices must be made about what to do and where to intervene. But why should the UN intervene in Bosnia and not Rwanda? According to what principle? What criteria?

'Significance' is determined by the valuing criteria through which politicians, diplomats, scholars, and even the defenders of human rights covenants assess which event, conflict, or war is worth considering and ultimately worth intervening in to restore human rights. Ignatieff argues that at least four criteria of significance have emerged in the 1990s for validating military interventions: (1) human rights abuses must be systematic and pervasive; (2) abuses have to be a threat to international peace and security; (3) interventions have to have a real chance of succeeding; and (4) the region must be of vital interest to intervening states.

The notion of significance is not an issue exclusively for military interventions and political aspirations in a world of conflicting rights and self-interest. It is a key concept for historians as well. Because they cannot study everything that happened in the past, historians are necessarily selective in their own investigations. Certain historical events, personages, dates, or phenomena are more important to their studies than others. In an anecdotal passage, Carr notes that the past often comes to us through the interpretive choices of historians, so that Caesar's crossing of the Rubicon is, whereas the crossing of the same insignificant stream by millions of others before or after him is not, seen as significant.[8] Pushing this understanding further, Tim Lomas argues that in trying to make sense of history, 'one cannot escape from the idea of significance. History, to be meaningful, depends on selection and this, in turn, depends on establishing criteria of significance to select the more relevant and to dismiss the less relevant.'[9] For Lomas, historians necessarily use certain criteria to decide between significant and trivial events. But what criteria?

This chapter looks at the concept of historical significance and the necessity of defining criteria to make selection and use of the past. Using the works of Geoffrey Partington and others, it presents a set of five factors of significance largely employed by professional historians: importance, profundity, quantity, durability, and relevance. It then examines the notion of significance in school history in light of educational research on the topic, presents an additional set of three related criteria of significance – intimate interests, symbolic significance, and contemporary lessons – and concludes by discussing the implications of the use of criteria of significance in history education.

3.1 Criteria of Historical Significance

Ranke's original principle of scientific history was grounded in the belief that historians had 'to show what actually happened.' Yet, this task would only be conceivable if historians first make a decision on what it is that they want to show and provide justifications for wanting to do so. In other words, before showing what happened, they must decide what historical events, characters, or period they want to study. Ranke never clarified his selection of events in his research or even offered the reasons for it. In fact, Ranke and his contemporaries completely neglected the notion of significance, thus overlooking the fundamental claim that certain aspects of the human past deserve more interest than others from historians. Each epoch, he once argued, 'was immediate to God.'[10] The goal of historians was therefore to keep their eyes 'on the universal aspect of things.'[11] More recently, Elton also expressed the belief that 'no argument exists which successfully establishes a hierarchy of worth among historical periods or regions as such.'[12]

The argument of Ranke, and of his followers, suggests that all human actions are of equal value and interest to historians. The choices they make are either scientifically irrelevant (as no choice is necessary in the universal aspect of things) or purely arbitrary and subjective. If Ranke was correct, as Partington observes, 'there can be no point in even considering criteria of significance, since all experiences would be in principle of equal value (or futility).'[13] Yet, historians simply cannot study everything from the past, even if they are engaged in what Braudel and his colleagues at the Annales school called the *longue durée* of history – the long-time span and flow of structural realities.[14] Their initial interests, research questions, and selection of relics are inevitably influenced by how they ascribe significance to past events and actions. To claim, for instance, that an historical event, a character, or a piece of evidence is significant is to say that it is for the historian worthy of historical investigation, a claim that implies an evaluative judgment on particular aspects of the past. Perhaps more importantly, the historian's ability to make sense of the past actions and events and ultimately create coherent interpretations is necessarily tied to what he or she sees as significant. As Rogers contends, in constructing an account one must inevitably differentiate 'between the various members of a mass of crude facts and of showing their significance in relation to some theme or development.'[15]

The question, then, would not be whether or not historians employ the concept of historical significance but whether there could be any disciplinary framework for ascribing significance to the past. Until the mid-twentieth century, questions of significance appeared to be unproblematic in Western historiography because historical studies were largely framed in reference to political power and impact. According to this view, wars, revolutions, political changes, and leaders were all considered to be highly significant. 'History,' as British historian Thomas Carlyle openly claimed, 'is the biography of great men.'[16]

Yet, with the late-twentieth-century redefinition and enlargement of the field of history, notably with social and women's history, a growing number of historians are now engaged in investigating subjects previously ignored or marginalized – not because of the lack of sources but because they were initially deemed *in*significant. The recent historical studies and reproductions of Métis artist E. Pauline Johnson's works are a good Canadian example of this redefinition of significance. This daughter of a Mohawk chief and an English woman became in the late nineteenth- and early twentieth-century Canada the first Native poet to have her work published. She was also one of the few female writers at the time who could make an independent living from what she wrote and performed. Johnson (also known in Mohawk as *Tekahionwake*) was particularly proud of her Native heritage and once declared that 'my aim, my joy, my pride is to sing the glories of my own people.'[17] Her most famous poem, 'The Song My Paddle Sings,' has been read by thousands of school children in Canada and elsewhere.

Yet, despite her popularity and the significance of her work, Johnson, who was also a strong activist woman fighting against rampant racism in post-Confederation Canada, virtually faded into obscurity after her death in 1913. It is only recently that scholars and historians have reconsidered E. Pauline Johnson.[18] As Canadian historian Veronica Strong-Boag puts it, 'Canadian history has many significant, yet largely untold stories to tell.'[19] She goes on, 'A recognition of Johnson's role as counter-hegemonic figure, one among many who have been lost to the historical memory, helps us to reconsider long-standing assumptions about the Canadian story as it has often survived in school texts.'[20]

The growing number of historical studies of once 'insignificant' actors, such as Johnson, exposes the problems that historians, and ultimately the whole public, face in thinking about the concept of historical significance. Because of these historians' innovative inquiries, they have brought to the foreground of historiography the stories of actors, events, transformations, and patterns previously relegated to the margins. In doing so, these historians have in many ways challenged the older, established norms of historical significance as found in memory-history narratives now seen as ideologically *dépassé*.

Given this state of affairs, Seixas contends that an historical event or character does not become significant only because of its place or importance in the past itself, nor because of someone's special interest in it. 'Standards of significance,' he argues, 'apparently inhere not only in the past itself, but in the interpretative frames and values of those who study it – ourselves.'[21] Historical significance is thus a quality determined by historians (or other investigators) in response to the past. An event, to paraphrase Seixas, becomes significant when contemporary people see its relevance to other events and ultimately to themselves in the present. Its historical significance might better be understood in relation to contemporary circumstances, that is, its relevance to people living in the present. Indeed, historians are both the 'products' and conscious or unconscious 'spokespersons' of the society and era to which they belong.[22] The historian, Carr suggests, is not a distant spectator or a 'V.I.P. at the saluting base' watching a procession;

he is part of 'the moving procession ... [and] the point in the procession at which he finds himself determines his angle of vision over the past.'[23] Faced with almost limitless human evidence and past events and actions, historians look at the past with a contemporary eye and with questions, concerns, and values emanating from the society and culture of their own time.[24] People's relationship with the past is thus influenced by their inherent positionalities. But what really makes an event significant to historians is still not clear, even within the history community. It is commonly assumed in historiography that professional historians will come up with their own defensible selection of events and collection of sources and evidence if their work is to be scientifically accepted, even if this implicit understanding is likely to change from one generation of historians to another.[25]

As a result, there has been only limited research on this procedural concept of history, even in England, where it is formally part of the school curriculum. To this day, studies that have looked at the notion of historical significance have largely ignored the criteria of historical significance. Rather, the focus has been on the substance (or selected topics) of historical significance (e.g., freedom, justice, nation-building), without an analysis of the procedures that illuminate how and why people's explanations have focused on certain topics of the collective past. In other words, attention has been paid to the content of teachers' and students' selection of what they consider significant, as opposed to their procedural knowledge.

British scholar Robert Phillips, drawing on the influential works of Geoffrey Partington and Martin Hunt, contends, however, that the criteria of significance depend on a variety of related history factors often informing the initial questions, interests, and selection of events by historians.[26] These factors do not, in themselves, tell whether one character or event is (or ought to be) significant; nor are these factors universally shared and employed by historians. Because inquiries and research questions are essentially 'a matter of [historians'] judgement,'[27] there is no scientific rule or procedure for investigating the past, thus coming up with a mechanical set of criteria – so much depends on the historian, the past in question, and the sources available. That being said, the factors presented below are nonetheless useful constructs from Western historiography that provide disciplinary guidance in understanding historical investigations. They can be seen as 'disciplinary' not only (or so much) because they are employed in the field but more precisely because they offer historians formal and defensible concepts to apprehend the past. They are, in other words, clearly defined and useful 'analytic' concepts, to go back to Bruner's distinction between intuitive and disciplinary thinking, for advancing sophisticated forms of knowledge in history. Equally important, because historians are aware of their use and importance for investigating the past, their use renders historical explanation, justification, and even re-evaluation possible. These factors of historical significance are importance, profundity, quantity, durability, and relevance. Below I briefly outline each of these factors with some practical applications.

Importance

One way to appreciate the significance of an historical event is to contextualize the past and consider what was perceived as important to those who lived then, irrespective of whether their judgments about the importance of the event were subsequently shown to be justified. Was the past in question important to predecessors? Why? In what ways? 'We may not,' as Partington argues, 'restrict ourselves to what interested them, but we can hardly begin to learn from the dead unless we know what was important to them and why.'[28] From this view, importance might be understood as what affected predecessors, that is, the actions that had an influence on their thinking or behaviours of the time. For example, World War II might be considered important for historians because it was perceived to be so by Holocaust survivors. A history of the concentration camps can thus be presented as significant from the perspective of those who lived or died in, or were directly affected by, these camps.

Yet the problem, as historians know well, is that people at all times have thought their own interests or concerns important, even more important than those of past times. It becomes, therefore, difficult to assess the importance of events for past actors if historians refer only to sources of self-centred judgments that could have been highly inappropriate for the time and if they lack corroborating evidence or direct access to the opinions, judgments, or beliefs of other past actors. But at the same time, attempting to consider other historical periods not only as different from contemporary ones but also as having their own importance for those who lived then may offer historians a means to counter 'presentism,' the imposing of present-day values on the past, and to realize that every present can have its own meaning, salience, and prominence. As I discuss in chapter 7, such an assessment necessarily demands a deep sense of contextualized history and empathy.

Profundity

The notion of profundity offers an evaluative component to the factor of importance. In trying to appreciate and contextualize the importance of the past for those who lived then, it might be valuable to consider how deeply people were affected by an event. Was the event superficial or deeply affecting? How were people's lives affected? Partington argues that in selecting a topic or event for study, historians and educators must 'ensure that the hopes, fears, and other concerns of all the interested individuals or groups must be adequately investigated.'[29] Asking questions relating to historical profundity may, at the outset, reveal crucial information regarding people's different reactions to the same event. If people at the time all considered a particular event to be important, their perceptions might have been totally different. Profundity can thus provide an instructive factor for understanding various people's reactions to a significant event (e.g., natural disaster, pandemic, elections, or military conflict). A study of the treatment of German and Japanese Canadians during World War II, for example, may reveal interesting elements of analysis and comparison about how racism affected members of these communities. It may even lead to a compelling study of Canadian policies during the period toward immigrants and ethnic minorities.

In a broader perspective, looking at the notion of profundity may help people understand the nature of change in society. In fact, there is a compelling reason to believe that history educators should seek to help students understand events that profoundly changed people's lives. As I argue in the following chapter, because history is about perceived changes, profundity can help students understand more about the nature of particular changes in past human affairs and ultimately appreciate that changes have not occurred evenly at all times and have not been lived and experienced in the same way by our predecessors. For example, by analysing a range of diverse accounts of Japanese Canadians during their internment in camps in the British Columbia interior, historians may come to understand more about the profundity of the changes, during and following their internment, that this terrible, 'enemy aliens' policy decision brought to these citizens of Japanese ancestry.

Quantity

One of the most common ways of ascribing significance to the past is to look at the number of people affected by an event: How many victims? How many survivors? How many more were affected by this event than by another one? As long as history was primarily focused on the 'great men,' numbers were hardly necessary. But once historians became interested in issues of economic growth, social change and development, or histories of communities and workers, questions of numbers had to assume greater importance. The so-called history by numbers has thus redirected historians to elements, relics, and phenomena once perceived as insignificant from the point of view of the study of great men.[30] Demographic history is arguably evidence of this growth of interest in historical numbers, as attested by the creation of academic journals such as *The Economic History Review, Journal of Economic History, The Australian Economic History Review,* and *The European Review of Economic History.*

Yet, the focus on numbers must be taken up extremely carefully in history, as it may lead historians to ascribe significance only to events affecting masses of people or events lending themselves to quantification. I have already pointed out the pitfall of using numbers (e.g., of victims) exclusively to determine the magnitude of a massacre and the need for international intervention. The same is true in historical research. If numbers, for example, may help historians to examine more accurately the impact of certain changes for various people (according to age, gender, household size, etc.), historical numbers do not in themselves reveal the significance of a change. 'Cause and significance,' Tosh concludes, 'remain matters for the interpretative skill of the historian.'[31]

Durability

Related to the factor of number is that of the durability of an event. How long does an event have to endure to be considered significant? Should it be lasting or may it be ephemeral? The Hundred Years War, for example, spanned from 1337 to 1453, whereas the war in Iraq of 2003 officially lasted forty-two days. 'Campaigns so brief,' Keegan maintains, 'are rare ... For comparisons one has to reach back to the "cabinet wars" of the nineteenth century, Prussia's victory over Austria in six weeks in 1866 or over the French field army in less than a month in 1870.'[32] So which of the two, the Hundred Years War or the war in Iraq, is more significant? According to the length of these military conflicts, it is necessarily the first one. But historians, including Keegan, would be more careful in their assessment and likely find problematic the notion that they should ignore the ephemeral and especially consider the long-lasting.

At first glance, it is not always easy to draw a line between the beginning and the end of an event. Some, for example, would argue (and with good reason) that despite President Bush's declaration, on board USS *Abraham Lincoln*, of the end of the major military operations on 1 May 2003, the war in Iraq was far from over. More coalition troops have, in fact, fallen to attacks after that famous declaration than during the war itself. Although historical events are, by definition, circumscribed in time, their existence largely depends on the historical context and the criteria used by historians to make those delimitations. Put differently, different lengths can be attributed by historians to the same events because these people may not necessarily agree on what they perceive as a change in a given state of affairs.

But even when historians agree on the exact length of an event, the notion of durability can lead people to believe that the longer the event lasts, the more significant it becomes. For example, even if it is not entirely clear when the war in Iraq officially ended, its duration is unlikely going to match that of the Hundred Years War of fourteenth–fifteenth-century Europe. Does this shortage of time, so to speak, on the continuum of durability automatically make an event less significant? Obviously not. Both the historical context and historians' relationship with the past are necessary to making that evaluative judgment.

Relevance

Should relevance inform historians' selection and study of past events? The idea that what is significant in history must be relevant to current interests has been the subject of lively debate in disciplinary-history. In 1931, for instance, British historian Herbert Butterfield furiously attacked the so-called Whig history, advanced by historians such as Macaulay, for its liberal, progressive, and glorifying misinterpretation of the British past. In his once influential book, *The Whig Interpretation of History*, Butterfield launched his attack by arguing that the study of the past with one eye on the present 'is the source of all sins and sophistries in history.'[33] Using the analogy of the trekker on a mountain top observing a valley, he went on to criticize twentieth-century historians as follows:

> The whig historian stands on the summit of the 20th century, and organises his scheme of history from the point of view of his own day; and he is a subtle man to overturn from his mountain-top where he can fortify himself with plausible argument. He can say that events take on their due proportions when observed through the lapse of time. He can say that events must be judged by their ultimate issues, which, since we can trace them no farther, we must at least follow down to the present ... The fallacy lies in the fact that if the historian working on the 16th century keeps the 20th century in his mind, he makes direct reference across all the intervening period between Luther or the Popes and the world of our own day. And this immediate juxtaposition of past and present, though it makes everything easy and makes some inferences perilously obvious, is bound to lead to an over-simplification of the relations between events and a complete misapprehension of the relations between past and present.[34]

Butterfield was not alone in his attack on the Whig view of the relevance of history. Philosopher Michael Oakeshott presented a similar charge by drawing a sharp distinction between the 'practical' and 'historical' past. Only the latter was, for him, the proper subject for historians, that is, the study of history with complete detachment. 'Whenever the significance of the past lies in the fact that it has been influential in deciding the present and future fortunes of man,' he claimed, 'the past involved is a practical, and not an historical past.'[35] To him, historical importance, as lived and experienced by predecessors, was the only valuing criteria of significance in historical scholarship.

Yet, other historians, notably Becker and Carr, have insisted that those who study history cannot divorce themselves from the present in which they work and live. Historians are social actors influenced by the forces and concerns of their own time. 'The historian,' Carr observes, 'is also a product of history and of society; and it is in this twofold light that the student of history must learn to regard him.'[36]

Indeed, historians make decisions of significance with an eye in the present, even if their investigation is driven by scientific principles. The recent focus in the United States on African American history is evidence of the contemporary relevance and influence of history. 'Historians,' as Appleby, Hunt, and Jacob observe, 'are frequently exposed to the charge that they write the present back into history ... The reverse holds true for African American history.' They go on, 'When scholars began researching the details of slave life in the Chesapeake and free black communities in the urban south, they were recovering stories that had always been there.'[37] When, therefore, historians respond positively to the notion of relevance, they do not necessarily (or unconsciously) falsify the past, as Butterfield and Oakeshott argue. On the contrary, they may bring to the surface of historical knowledge aspects of the past previously deemed irrelevant and thus insignificant to study.

But the factor of relevance holds another implication for history. Society (and possibly historians themselves) also expects studies and interpretations of the past to be relevant and useful to their understanding of both past and current affairs and potentially illuminating for the future. Historians may argue that their work, expertise, and duty are not with the public but with the discipline itself. Yet, historians are, in many ways, extremely well qualified to provide society with sophisticated perspectives on the past and the present and, thus, counter the naive, presentist representations of the past found in memory-history. Faced with the social menace of being ignored, Becker proposed therefore a *sortie de secours* to his fellow historians: 'Our proper function is not to repeat the past but to make use of it, to correct and rationalize for common use Mr. Everyman's mythological adaptation of what actually happened. We are surely under bond to be as honest and as intelligent as human frailty permits; but the secret of our success in the long run is in conforming to the temper of Mr. Everyman, which we seem to guide only because we are so sure, eventually, to follow it.'[38] Using the factor of relevance in history does not, therefore, inevitably impose presentist cataracts on historians with regard to periods, events, or relics to study. Rather, it can offer the possibility of appreciating aspects of the past not only as filtered through contemporary eyes but also as signifying what these particular pasts *now mean* to contemporary actors. The significance of the past thus becomes tied to its contribution to present-day meaning-making and understanding of aspects of history. Put differently, the significance of an event is influenced not only by the past itself but also by subsequent use of this event according to contemporary priorities and present-day developments. The famous Treaty of Versailles of 1919, for example, is typically presented in Canadian history textbooks as having historical importance for making sense of World War I and World War II. Yet, the contemporary significance of this peace treaty has suddenly re-emerged in the literature because of its relevance for understanding current conflicts over nationalism in states born out of this treaty (Iraq, Israel, and Yugoslavia). As a *New York Times* book review states, in its appraisal of Margaret MacMillan's best-seller *Paris 1919*, 'the history of the 1919 Paris peace talks following World War I is a blueprint of the political and social upheavals bedeviling the planet now.'[39]

One can see, in light of this example, how important it is to keep in mind the ever-changing orientations and priorities of the present, as well as the inherent positionalities of historians, when ascribing significance to past actions and events. 'The narrator's perspective and predilections,' Lowenthal concludes, 'shape his choice and use of historical materials; our own determine what we make of them.'[40]

3.2 Students and Historical Significance

Schools are official sites where some forms of common history are explicitly introduced to students. 'Schooling,' Barton and Levstik contend, 'is one important forum for [the] transmission [of cultural constructs] – a site where contending forces in the culture try to influence what history will be publicly commemorated.'[41] In Canada, as in any other country, the selection of historical events and characters to study, as evidenced in the design of curricula and textbooks, implicitly relies on the notion of historical significance – or perhaps on some political views of significance. In one way or another, educational authorities do (voluntarily or not) make distinctions between what they perceive as historically significant and what they perceive as historically trivial, between what they 'approve' and what they 'ignore.'

The recent debate over the establishment of national history standards for K-12 students in the United States provides an illuminating example of how conflicting cultural ideas of significance can affect school history. In 1992, following the 1983 report of the National Commission on Excellence in Education, entitled *A Nation at Risk*, Congress passed Bush's *America 2000 Act*, which calls for national standards in K-12 education. That year, the National Endowment for the Humanities and the Department of Education joined to fund the National Center for History in the Schools (NCHS), a $1.6 million project aimed at developing comprehensive standards for U.S. and world history. By October 1994, the NCHS – made up of a coalition of professional historians, teachers, history organizations, and parents – released the first version of the standards. Almost immediately, a major political controversy broke out in the country. With the involvement of conservative Republicans, notably Lynne Cheney, chair of the National Endowment for the Humanities, the standards became the subject of a fierce war over *which* national history and cultural identity should be promoted in school. After intense public debate, little of it informed by hard evidence, the Senate resolutely put an end to the case by voting 99 to 1 to condemn what was perceived to be a 'hijack' of U.S. history by progressive, multicultural, and politically correct social leftists. 'What is a more important part of our Nation's history for our children to study – George Washington or Bart Simpson?' asked Senator Slade Gorton in his speech before the Senate. Although the choice between the two figures seems absurd, the lack of explicit identification of President Washington in the standards – despite a full unit on the 'Revolution and the New Nation' – simply represented, for Senator Gorton, a frontal attack on U.S. civilization, ideas, and institutions. In her recent analysis of the struggle for history standards, NCHS project assistant Linda Symcox writes, 'The Standards controversy serves as a case study that illuminates the broader issue of how educational policy is made and contested in the United States. It reveals how policymakers and opinionmakers, including academics, pundits, politicians, and the press, used their positions to advance particular intellectual and ideological agendas, and how their contending efforts drove curricular policy throughout the 1980s and 1990s.'[42] Parallel 'history crises' have also affected Canadian history education.[43] Perhaps the most recent debate has been precipitated by historian Jack Granatstein, who argues, in his book *Who Killed Canadian History?* '[there] has never been an attempt to establish national standards here and, should there be, there would probably be just as little agreement as in the United States. Canadians appear to have concluded that history is unimportant at best or divisive at worst; in either case, it is not something worth fighting about or worth teaching. Yet, Canada can never be a strong nation (or even two nations) if it does not teach its past to its people. The country needs a nationally based history curriculum with its content defined for each grade, and with publishers given specific targets for their texts to meet.'[44]

Clearly, the result of this general confusion over the significance of key aspects of the collective past has serious implications for teachers and students, whether they live in Canada, the United States, or elsewhere. Because of the potential differences between the official versions of school history presented by teachers, views of history defended by professional historians, and the vernacular stories commemorated at home or in the community, students can face contradictory and puzzling accounts of their past. And, if not well addressed in class, these collisions and contradictions can lead youngsters to be highly suspicious of historical study. In the face of unsupportive or inconclusive evidence and accounts, uncritical students can turn to simple answers or, more bluntly, refute *tout court* all the conflicting histories they encounter.[45] With this state of affairs, one may wonder how students, notably those of different linguistic and cultural backgrounds, respond to such contradictions.

Although limited, research findings suggest that 'students construct their own historical understandings according to the schemata of their historical knowledge.'[46] Perhaps more importantly, the means by which they judge what is important to remember, know, and use 'constitutes the foundation for all further encounters with history.'[47] Thus, even at an early age, students do not passively absorb or take for granted the (competing) historically significant information presented to them publicly. 'Even in their most naïve structuring of historical information,' Seixas contends, 'young people can establish ... connections and define themselves through new knowledge of their relation to the past.'[48]

According to this constructivist view, students, no less than educational authorities, teachers, and historians, confront the study of the past with their own mental framework of historical significance shaped by their own cultural and linguistic heritage, family practices, popular culture influences, and last, but not least, school-history experience. It thus becomes extremely important to understand more accurately students' conceptions of historical significance if educators want to further their historical thinking.

A closer look at their conceptions can help clarify the extent to which students' development of historical knowledge is shaped by school communities. In other words, what students see as historically significant in the past and the reasons they offer for their selection do not occur in a vacuum or by accident. Rather, they are to varying degrees shaped by classroom teaching and the school community. By paying more attention to students' understanding and reasoning, educators can more precisely identify what school authorities see as historically significant in what students develop, acquire, and internalize in their respective history classes. 'Just because someone is exposed to a cultural tool,' Wertsch observes, 'does not mean that the individual has made it his or her own.'[49] Indeed, Seixas found in his study that BC students typically articulate the notion of historical significance either as part of a larger narrative of historical events useful in explaining past and present circumstances or as a concept necessary to connect past events to the understanding of, and more frequently as guidance for, their own lives (i.e., history as 'lessons'). In either case, the processes by which students ascribe significance to the past involve their particular ways of conceiving of the past as useful. Perhaps more interesting is that even when students are not explicitly introduced to the study of *their* collective past but to the past of other civilizations, the usefulness and practical relevance of history continue to be central to them. This is notably the case in Northern Ireland, where elementary-school students do not look at their contemporary history and identity, because the subject is deemed too explosive in the political and religious context of the region. Yet, the result, as Barton observes, is that 'the potential for the subject to lapse into irrelevance is perhaps the greatest obstacle to sustaining students' interest.'[50] Clearly, removing national history and identity from school to avoid sectarianism or political manipulation does not seem to detract students from acquiring at home or in larger society what they see as meaningful stories of their nation or, more dangerously, detract them from misusing such stories for social, political, or eventually even terrorist acts.

Furthermore, studying students' own concepts of significance can help us look at, and compare, the unclear environmental influence of family, language, culture, and gender on students' understanding of their national past. More and more, the evidence suggests, as in the study of Northern Ireland, that class, ethnicity, culture and language, and popular culture are important factors in defining students' positionalities and their decisions regarding what they perceive as important or trivial in history.[51] For example, in a study of African American and European American adolescents, Terrie Epstein recently found that 'African American students' historical experiences ... were shaped by their own [African American culture] and their family members' race-related experiences, many of which were marked by racial discrimination and oppression.'[52] Dominant versions of the national past, as presented in official curricula and approved textbooks, often conflict with the vernacular forms developed by ethnic and linguistic minorities, who may have a divergent understanding of their nation, as well as of their country's accomplishments.

Faced with this challenge, we may find it necessary to reassess the whole notion of historical significance in history education by recognizing the diverse communities that largely define its domain, and thus define *their* historical significance. As a general rule, professional historians have addressed questions of significance by employing the set of analytic criteria defined earlier (importance, profundity, quantity, durability, and relevance).

Yet, these criteria, familiar as they are in historiography and the philosophy of history, have not necessarily been fully articulated outside the history community. As a result, the public and school teachers have developed and used additional criteria, a bric-a-brac of standards, many driven by present-day use of memory-history. These 'memory significance' criteria emerge out of their practical use in decisions about historical relevance. They have a more collective and intimate function, designed to tailor the collective past for personal and collective purposes.[53] More specifically, they can be seen as identifiable contemporary and personal reasons for ascribing significance to events of the past. Unlike the previous criteria, they are more intuitive, subject to the dialectic of collective and intimate remembering and forgetting. They also tend to be unconsciously employed and thus more likely to generate naive, distorted views of the past that are not open to revision. These criteria are nonetheless conceptually useful, as they help explain how and why people (including perhaps historians) may establish different connections of significance with the collective past. These types of memory significance, which I briefly review below, are at least threefold: intimate interests, symbolic significance, and contemporary lessons.

Intimate Interests

One way people ascribe memory significance to the past is through their intimate interests and questions about particular events: Is the event important to me personally? My family? My ancestors? Family history, ancestral obligation and belonging, and personal experience of events in history are some of the factors (or even motives) for people to connect with the past. In his survey of *How Americans Use and Think about the Past*, Roy Rozenzweig found, for example, that respondents felt most connected to the past when they encounter it with the people who they knew or who mattered most to them. 'Although respondents described the past as being with them in many settings,' Rozenzweig argues, 'they share the sense that the familiar and intimate past, along with intimate uses of other pasts, mattered most.'[54] Family reminiscences and reunions, as well as the collection of, and reference to, photographs or videos (to preserve memories), were the most cited examples.

My own study of historical significance with French Canadian and English Canadian students in the province of Ontario also leads in this direction.[55] In explaining the rationale for their selection of key events in Canadian history, many students were inclined to refer to the interests of their intimates. This criterion was by far the dominant reason the French Canadians gave for relating to Canada's past. One possible explanation for this finding is that minorities are traditionally more suspicious of dominant historical interpretations of the collective past, because they are traditionally tailored by the majority (in this case, the English Canadians). As such, they are more likely to endorse personal or intimate connections to the same past. These connections, and the interpretations they ultimately generate not only appear to be more authentic to them but also, and more problematically, appear to be more reliable and legitimate, regardless of the internal or external validity of such connections and interpretations.

Wertsch also came to this conclusion when looking at Estonians' understanding of the official and vernacular stories of the Soviet invasion of 1940.[56] People who had memories of this period reacted negatively to the official narrative inculcated in school, preferring the more reassuring 'truth' of the local vernacular stories developed and shared in the community. These stories, Wertsch found, tend to be very partial, fragmented, and inaccurate and to be shaped by incoherent historical reasoning. He concluded the study by suggesting that '[the] interviewees demonstrated what might be called a pattern of "knowing but not believing" in the case of the official history and perhaps even "believing without knowing" in the case of the unofficial history.'[57]

Symbolic Significance

The use of particular historical events for collective or patriotic justification is of an entirely different order of memory significance. In this case, it is not the intimate connectedness to the past but the symbolic nature of the event that matters most. Is the event emblematically important? Does it represent something significant in the collective consciousness? Here, the line between the 'personal' (or intimate) and 'national' (or collective) past often becomes blurred. Events are selected because they reflect the importance of certain aspects of the past in defining a community of identity. In their study of national identity and significance, Barton and Levstik found that such use of the past often leads students to employ 'our' and 'we' in talking about the events in question, as if the collective connection had defined their own personal sense of identification and relation to these events. 'Their explanations,' they contend, 'suggested that they considered events related to America's creation and settlement important because those events defined the community with which they identified.'[58] In my own study, a large majority of students (particularly among English Canadians) also chose historical events because they carried a symbolic significance. Canada's participation in World War I is a typical example. Students' responses gave pride of place to the celebration of Canada's war participation and recognition on the international stage as an independent Dominion and no longer as a British colony. The following explanation of the role of Canadian soldiers at the famous Battle of Vimy Ridge in 1917 is telling: 'This marked the first time Canada fought together on a global scale. People drew closer together. A Canadian identity was starting to form and with the success at Vimy Ridge Canadians could be proud together.'[59]

Yet the notion of symbolic significance has serious national and patriotic implications, particularly in terms of how individuals within the collectivity conceive of the first person plural (i.e., 'we' and 'our'). Who is included or excluded from the community? On what grounds? What are the consequences for what is perceived as significant in history? Identity is always an interactive process by which reference to 'others' is important, possibly necessary, to one's own sense of belonging and place in the collectivity – and ultimately in history. In taking for granted the experience of the collective 'we,' students may naively invoke the past to legitimate social order, bind past and contemporary peoples in a collective venture, and, more dangerously, exclude disparate or ethnically different peoples from the nation's past and envisioned future. World history is replete with such ideological attempts to censor history and historians. As a result, school reference to symbolic significance, as Levstik observes, leads students to face 'a history long on myth, short on intellectual rigor, and extraordinarily slow to incorporate the wide range of behavior that has characterized ... history.'[60] Following this reasoning, it is thus no surprise that few French Canadian students in my own study saw World War I as a symbolic event for Canada, given the limited role and influence of French Canadian troops (notably senior officers) in the Canadian army.[61]

Contemporary Lessons

A different approach is taken by people who conceptualize the present by using events for simple historical analogies: What lessons should we learn from the past? The use of past events for contemporary lessons is often regarded by historians as the sin of history. 'I'm allergic,' British historian Simon Schama remarks, in reference to President Bush's use of the 1930s policy of appeasement to muster support for his war in Iraq, 'to lazy historical analogies. History never repeats itself, ever. That's its murderous charm.'[62] Novices in all spheres of society frequently misuse the past by drawing simplistic lessons from it to guide them in the present, without acknowledging the historicity of the actors and the contextualization of events.

This direct relationship between the past and present presupposes a basis for the discipline of history in scientific principles, universal laws and generalizations, as traditionally defined in the natural sciences. Although some nineteenth-century positivist historians, notably Henry Thomas Buckle, believed it would be only a matter of time before historians could 'ascertain the whole of the laws which regulate the progress of civilization,' such an assumption is perceived today as exceedingly dangerous.[63] As Lee argues, 'there are clearly summative generalizations in history, which are explanatory in an everyday sense, but they make a weak basis for prediction.'[64] In chapter 2, I argued that history is based on the logical accumulation and causal relation of historical events by historians looking at the past retrospectively (i.e., backward referencing). Yet, both events and actors are unique in that they have their own historical contexts, which render application and generalization to other (including contemporary) events and actors highly problematic – a notion that goes back to Ranke's historicism. 'If we wish to explain an action (characterized in everyday terms),' Lee goes on, 'we do not need (and cannot have) a law to the effect that people who believe so-and-so and want such-and-such will always act in a certain way.'[65] There is no such thing in history as a universal law that could bear the weight of scientific prediction. It is difficult, not to say impossible, to imagine an historical lesson to which there is no counter example or evidence. Even the common-sense idea that the most experienced general with the best army always wins cannot hold the course of historical evidence. Thus, the application of laws or generalizations in history should always be in question because the discipline is based on historians' retrospective judgments of past events and of what counts as the 'same' events in different contexts. Perhaps the best historians can do is to supply what Lee calls 'vicarious experience,' that is, to offer knowledge of what might be expected, knowing that what is expected is rarely exactly what happens.[66] In this sense, history can be useful for historical analogies, provided that the historians can clarify the distinctions between past and contemporary events.

The notion of historical analogy is something often largely unknown to students. In a comparative study of British and U.S. students, Elizabeth Yeager, Stuart Forster, and Jennifer Greer come to the conclusion that those students who believe people need history 'to stop doing the same stupid things' are likely to oversimplify the past, avoid reference to evidence, and come up with simple historical interpretations of both past and contemporary issues.[67] Related to this view, a finding of Seixas's own study was that those students who use this notion of significance generally speak as if 'history were now under control.'[68] Embedded in a larger narrative of historical progress, a concept I address in chapter 5, these students view the present as the result of our progress away from the errors of the past. When talking about the Holocaust, for example, one student said, 'I'm sure we can take steps to prevent it from happening again because I'm sure people, like some will think if there's another war everyone will be thinking, oh, no, will there be another Holocaust or what type will it be and whatever.'[69] The recent mass killings in Rwanda should provide a convincing enough argument to put a stop to such progressive thinking.

3.3 Conclusion

Whether people use the past for academic research or contemporary meaning-making, whether they are professional historians or bored history students, they cannot escape from the concept of historical significance. To be meaningful, the past must be somehow coherently organized. And this implies distinguishing and selecting 'significant,' by contrast to 'trivial,' history.

Yet, the key educational problem, I have argued, is the current absence and even awareness in history education – and to a certain extent in the literature – of such historical criteria and terminology. Teachers and students are then left with their own *bricolage* of criteria of historical significance. The result can sometimes be astonishing, but it leaves students highly vulnerable to the use or influence of constructions and concepts that are far from enhancing of historical thinking. As VanSledright contends, 'decisions about historical significance [in school] have serious consequences for identity politics and sociopolitical control.'[70] So instead of authoritatively imposing on students pre-digested historical events that appear to be unproblematic in textbook content and learning objectives, educators who are conscious of their own and the provincial or state authority's selection are in a better position not only to help students reconsider their initial interpretations of the collective past but also to advance the learning of other equally significant events deemed irrelevant or alien to them. In other words, clarifying the concept of historical significance – in regard to both procedural concepts and substantive topics – can help identify and question those aspects of the past the authorities see as significant to study, as well as helping compare these with teachers' and students' approaches to significance. One step in this direction would be to ask students, 'What are the reasons and consequences of believing this event is more important than that?,' and then engage in the study of what makes such events significant.

It can also be argued, from recent research findings, that without a defensible conceptualization of historical significance, students and teachers find it becomes extremely problematic to articulate their own conception of the collective past and develop more sophisticated historical understandings of it. So far, the notion of historical significance and the disciplinary and educational criteria to define it have largely been overlooked in both history and history education. There is thus a need for more research in this area of history education, notably in multicultural and multinational societies, such as those of Canada, the United Kingdom, and the United States, in which self-evident versions of the national past conflict with the official history and too often lead to deep-rooted divisions and even conflicts between groups.

Related to this point, findings also indicate that high-school students not only need to receive direction and guidance on this complicated historical terrain but also need to be made to consider or reconsider the implicit and explicit interpretative frames and collective values they use to make sense of the past. Often, the criteria they intuitively employ to select and justify a selection of the collective past are shaped by their cultural communities, without their understanding how the conceptual tool of historical significance operates and could inform their decisions. If educators ignore this concept, as well as ignoring how students from different communities relate differently to events of the collective past, their history teaching is likely to fail to address students' misconceptions of the past. Perhaps more importantly, questions of curriculum design, textbook selection, and the whole notion of historical interpretation itself will remain entirely obscure to history students.

4 What Changed and What Remained the Same? – Continuity and Change

> The only sensible deduction to be made is that neither change nor continuity can survive without the other; they are both integral parts of history. Preoccupation with one or the other produces distortion and ignores the immanence of both.
>
> — Timothy Donovan[1]

During the federal election campaign of 1963, Liberal Party leader Lester B. Pearson promised voters to provide Canada with its own national flag before the end of the first two years of his mandate. The Centennial of Canada (1967) was approaching rapidly, and growing political turbulence, dissatisfaction, and alienation among Canadians, notably in the Province of Québec, had led to a sense of crisis. Canada, a North American country born out of a nineteenth-century compact between the French and the English, was still relying on British traditions and emblems for its definition and identity. Securing a distinctively Canadian flag was now seen as a question of national unity. Taking the offensive for the flag, the newly elected prime minister addressed the twentieth Dominion Convention of the Royal Canadian Legion in May 1964. Being a World War I veteran himself, and now recognized internationally for having won the Nobel Peace Prize (1957), Pearson put it to his comrades in these terms:

> I had as comrades in my section, men whose names were: Cameron, Kimora, English, Gleidenstein, de Chapin, O'Shaughnessy. We didn't fall in or fall out as Irish Canadians, French Canadians, Dutch Canadians, Japanese Canadians. We wore the same uniform, with the same maple leaf badge, and we were proud to be known as Canadians, to serve as Canadi-

ans and to die, if it had to be, as Canadians ... We are all and should be Canadians – and unhyphenated; with pride in our nation and its citizenship, pride in the symbols of that citizenship. The flag is one such symbol.[2]

Although Prime Minister Pearson had already supplied his own idea for a Canadian flag (the so-called Pearson Pennant), a joint committee of the Senate and the House of Commons (compromising fifteen members, representative of all political allegiances) was created in September 1964 to study the question and report back to the House of Commons within six weeks. Having reviewed thousands of flag sketches coming from all over the country, the committee finally retained three designs: the Red Ensign bearing the Union Jack and the fleur-de-lys, a flag made up of three maple leaves between two sky-blue borders (the Pearson Pennant), and a single red maple leaf on a white square between two red borders. In a unanimous decision, the committee recommended to the House of Commons the adoption of the single-maple-leaf flag. But most Conservative members of parliament rejected the selection, preferring the Red Ensign, with the conventional Union Jack. Conservative opposition leader John Diefenbaker seized every opportunity to block the adoption of the maple-leaf flag, but in vain. Resorting to a motion of closure, the Liberal government of Pearson finally approved the new flag on 15 December 1964, in a vote of 163 to 78. In his inflammatory and memorable speech to the House of Commons, Diefenbaker declared in a *cri de cœur*,

> I ask this House: In what way does the design now proposed embody our history? It denies Cardinal Newman's saying that all greatness rests upon the shoulders of past generations. In what way does it represent the sacrifices, the experiences, the achievements of the past? Are we to eradicate the past, to remove all vestiges of the things which brought my forefathers here on both sides, and the forefathers of Hon. gentlemen everywhere in this House? Edward Burke said all human society was a partnership between the living and the dead. This design denies that partnership.[3]

For Diefenbaker, the maple-leaf flag symbolized a drastic and perilous departure from the traditions, values, heritage, and institutions that had shaped *his* country. Unlike Pearson, Diefenbaker deeply believed that his contemporaries had purposely broken the memory-history 'partnership between the dead and the living,' thus creating a rupture with the collective past of the country. In his *Memoirs*, he explains,

'Pearson believed that a distinctive flag was one in which there should be no relationship with the past, nothing to indicate our heritage.'[4]

But Prime Minister Pearson took another stand on the issue. Convinced that the maple-leaf flag did not eradicate Canadians' relationship with the past, he declared, 'The past can and must be honoured, but surely the past must not be permitted to prevent the changes that are necessary to adapt to the future ... The British Empire has changed. We do not talk about the British Empire now in the sense that we talked about it 25 or 50 years ago, and quite rightly so.'[5] A brief survey of Canada's flag question may lead to the conclusion that the two political leaders, and their respective constituencies, were engaged in very different relationships with the past. Diefenbaker seems to have taken the ideology of memory, considering the dominant commemorative consciousness that had survived in English Canada until then to be indicative of what the collective future should retain and be. To accept the red-and-white maple-leaf flag was clearly forgetting the past of the nation. Pearson, the skilful diplomat, appears to have distanced himself from this memory-history, preferring to exploit present tumultuous circumstances to solicit drastic changes for the future of his country. A flag that embedded distinctively Canadian characteristics would symbolize its fabric – its future. As he once put it, 'No one would deny that we have a responsibility to the past. But we have also a greater responsibility to the present and to the future.'[6]

Yet, such an understanding of the flag debate would be misleading. Both politicians were (consciously or not) engaged in a complex relationship with the past, the present, and the future of the country. Diefenbaker, for instance, was adamantly opposed to the removal of the Union Jack symbol, because of the historical character and presence of the British in the shaping of the country. Yet, the Red Ensign he defended so ardently was a typically Canadian invention. Initially used for Canadian merchant ships in the nineteenth century, the familiar Red Ensign was later employed by Canadian troops in Europe to distinguish themselves from the British and was at one time adopted by an Order-in-Council, in 1945, as the Canadian flag. Diefenbaker himself officially approved a change to the coat of arms in the Red Ensign during his mandate.[7]

In the same way, Pearson's initiative in adopting a distinctively Canadian flag was far from *avant-gardiste*. As early as 1925, the federal government of William Lyon Mackenzie King had been struggling with the question of a national flag, particularly in the context of having

Canadian troops fighting overseas. The reference to the maple leaf was not unique to Pearson, either. As he recognized, this Canadian symbol had been in usage for over a century as a *de facto* emblem of Canada, notably on soldiers' badges and for navy ships.

The Canadian flag controversy provides an interesting example of all the complexities of studying people's relationships with the past. The perceived drastic change of a dominant national symbol in Canadian politics only makes sense if the adoption of the maple-leaf flag is placed in the broader historical context of Canada's struggle for independence, which may subsequently offer more historical continuity than initially expected. The concepts of continuity and change are not only 'relational' (relative to one another) but also necessary to one another. To study particular changes in human affairs, historians must implicitly accept certain elements of continuity in other aspects of life. Without the ability to see relationships between events in a larger historical context, historians cannot have a coherent understanding of the events they study or appreciate the significance of these events for subsequent ones and ultimately for contemporary purposes.

In this chapter, I consider the importance of the concepts of continuity and change for giving meaning and coherence to the past. To do so, I use the work of Louis Mink on synoptic judgments in history (section 4.1). Building on Mink's features of historical practice, I introduce two elements pertinent for understanding the connection between past events: (1) understanding the sequence of events; and (2) making connections between events by means of colligation. In section 4.2, I look at the implications of synoptic judgment and the concepts of continuity and change for school history and show that despite a dearth of educational research on these procedural concepts, continuity and change are key to students' historical thinking.

4.1 Continuity and Change and the Need for 'Synoptic Judgment'

I argued in chapter 3 that historians study past human actions in the form of significant events. These events are understood as perceived changes in a given state of affairs worth recording and studying. The adoption of the maple-leaf flag in December 1964, for example, could be construed by historians as a significant event to study because it focuses on a perceived change in Canadian affairs (from the Red Ensign to the maple leaf) delimited in time and space and considered significant because of its political importance (relevance) and societal impact (profundity). The same can be said of September 11, the Battle of Water-loo, or the U.S. Declaration of Independence. These are all events that occurred over a certain period of time in particular locations and circumstances that historians notice because of the significant changes they brought about.

Louis Mink argues that to get a holistic understanding of an event, one must use hindsight to trace what he calls the 'intrinsic relations' of the event to others, thus locating it in its historical context.[8] He refers to this bird's-eye view process of studying the past as 'synoptic judgment.'[9] The historian, he argues, 'tries to understand a complex process as a function of its component events plus their interrelationships (including causal relationships) plus their importance, all interpreted in a larger context of change.'[10] For Mink, it would be possible to understand historical events only if historians define what they want to look at, consider the intrinsic relations of *prior* and *later* events (including causal relations) and the importance of each in a series, and use hindsight to comprehensively and coherently judge what happened. Historical understanding, in other words, would be achievable only if one '[comprehends] a complex event by "seeing things together" in a total and synoptic judgment.'[11]

Mink discusses several features of historical practice to explain the pertinence of synoptic judgments in historiography, with two of these features having direct relevance to this chapter. For practical purposes, I have renamed these: (1) understanding the sequence of events; and (2) making connections between events by means of colligation.[12] These two complementary features are, I believe, extremely important to the discussion because they help historians grasp the complex relationship of changes over time and of continuity in times of change. Only with a sophisticated sense of synoptic judgment, I argue, can contemporary people compare and assess the meaning and significance of past events for other events and ultimately for the present. Below I review briefly each feature, with some practical examples.

Understanding the Sequence of Events

First, Mink contends that although historians may legitimately study and write on circumscribed (or unique) events in time and space, the events selected must be set and understood in a sequence. 'It is at least in part a claim,' he argues, 'that for the historical understanding of an event one must know its consequences as well as its antecedents.'[13] In trying to understand or explain what happened and why, one has to look for the causes of the change, as well as the consequences of the change for future actions and events. Otherwise, history becomes a mere chronological list of disconnected events, having no historical meaning – or what history educator Dennis Shemilt refers to as the naive 'logical possibilities' of history.[14]

Collingwood offered a similar viewpoint where he claimed that the processes of history could not be properly described as a mere sequence of events logically connected by time alone, but only as 'processes of actions.'[15] He believed that these processes could only be understood by our considering both the 'inside' and 'outside' of actions. Whereas the outside is the observable action, the inside comprises the thoughts expressed by an action. Yet, the problem is that historians have difficulty accessing and 'observing,' so to speak, the thoughts of past actors. These can only be inferred and imagined from the evidence through *historical empathy* (see chapter 7). Because this process of rethinking the past is far from unambiguous, the ability of historians to create a rational explanation of historical events has been a point of criticism of the theory. The sequence of events, as Lowenthal believes, is necessarily created and imposed by outsiders, since historical actors would lack, in his view, any perception of the flow of time and sequencing of events. As he puts it, 'It is so customary to think of the historical past in terms of narratives, sequences, dates, and chronologies that we are apt to suppose these things attributes of the past itself. But they are not; we ourselves put them together ... Historical facts are timeless and discontinuous until woven together in stories [by us]. We do not experience a flow of time, only a succession of situations and events. Much historical apprehension remains almost as temporally vague as memory, lacking dates or event sequences.'[16] If Lowenthal's remarks remind historians of the danger of imposing contextualized beliefs on the past, he completely overlooks the fact that predecessors (some more than others) did have some influence on the events that historians are studying. And, more importantly, these influences were largely the result of intended motives or purposes (thoughts) as part of a larger chain of events known to actors. Predecessors had, in many ways, a temporal and chronological awareness of their actions, often by placing them in the larger context of the time. 'Man,' as historian Sydney Pollard claims, 'always assumes regularity in his environment, all his actions are based on a purposive use of his rational environment.'[17] Supporting this view, William Burston claims that both historical actors and historians implicitly refer to the inside and outside of events when engaged in actions or in the study of these actions. He writes, 'Human behaviour in the past has both an inside and an outside, and the inside consists in the motives, intentions, designs, purposes and policies expressed by the action or event. In most of our language describing past events, we refer obliquely to the inside of such events. If we describe an event as a "battle" we are not merely asserting that it looked like one, we are saying that it was a battle, and that in addition to all the external signs there were the internal purposes present to make it a real battle.'[18] Given this state of affairs, it is reasonable to claim that when studying events from the past, historians cannot abstract from the sequence of these events in history – if it is kept in mind that this sequence is not given but constructed by historians. The essence of this claim is that, since historical events are normally the outcomes of certain human actions (except for the so-called acts of God, such as a hurricane or tsunami), these actions must be explained in terms of the purposes and motives that inspired them, as well as their consequences for future events. It is with this thinking that historians approach the past and construct narratives.[19]

One contentious aspect of human actions and their consequences is, of course, the perverse fact that some actions intended to bring about certain changes sometimes lead to the exactly opposite results. It is well known in economics, for example, that the fear of a possible financial collapse can drive consumers to withdraw all their savings. This impulsive action can cause financial institutions to crash. To cause the crash would not be, in this case, an intention of the actors, but the consequence would definitely be the outcome of their actions. Enlightenment thinkers clearly departed from the old tradition in the study of history when they conceived of history itself as a result of human agency, as opposed to divine providence. The actions of men and women, taken individually or collectively, are now seen as the main causes of what happens in history – even if historians and philosophers may not (and often do not) agree on the rationality of historical actors. 'Men to a great extent,' as Thompson concludes, 'do make their own history.'[20]

Yet, the critical and delicate task of understanding the motives of actors as found in the sources available does not necessarily offer historians an understanding of a larger sequence of events connected in a narrative explanation. 'Time, and the order of occurrence in time,' as Richard Tawney puts it, 'is a clue, but no more.'[21] Because of the historicist preoccupation with the study of events as unique, historians often debate the way a series of events, of which historical actors may have been totally ignorant, is connected in a sequence.[22] One key element of this debate revolves around the nature of the *causes*. 'Explanation in history,' Burston observes, 'is the process by which the historian explains why and how events happened. It is therefore another way of saying that he shows the *causes* of an event.'[23] Taking the transfer of Bosnia from the Ottoman Empire to the Austro-Hungarian Empire in 1908 as an example, he argues, 'If we "explain" the Bosnian crisis of 1908 we do so in terms of Russian and Austrian policies and ambitions, of the meeting between the two foreign ministers, of subsequent misunderstandings, and of the degree of backing either party obtained from its allies and so forth. We do precisely the same thing if we are asked to state the "causes" of the Bosnian crisis. Hence, "explanation" and "giving the causes of" are, at least for our purposes, synonymous terms.'[24] But, as historians well know, events in history often have many causes, some more important than others, that they must evaluate carefully. Historians' judgments can be (and often are) debated and challenged by their colleagues, on what might be perceived as purely subjective grounds.[25] 'The historian,' as Carr confesses, 'is simultaneously compelled, like the scientist, to simplify the multiplicity of his answers, to subordinate one answer to another, and to introduce some order and unity into the chaos of happenings and the chaos of specific causes.'[26] With this state of affairs, the sequence of events constructed by historians should be understood as one of 'causal possibilities,' as opposed to definite necessities.[27] I believe this distinction is crucial because it reveals the contingency of historians' claims, which otherwise could be construed naively as ascribing necessity to a certain sequence of events (i.e., alternative outcomes would be illogical). In this sense, probability, rather than certainty, governs the crafting of historical explanations. 'We evaluate one cause in a sequence of events as more important,' as historian Michael Stanford argues, 'because of the greater *probability* of its consequences. Now we are able to make judgments of probability only in the light of *our experience.*'[28] It is thus historical perspective and detachment that allow historians to make judgments of probability. As a matter of fact, Mink contends, historians can predict the outcomes of an historical event only by virtue of their perspective on the period. 'Historical explanation,' he argues, 'requires a certain "perspective," which the historian can achieve only after a connected sequence of events (such as a revolution or a reign) has been completed.'[29]

Hence, the advantage that historians possess over historical actors is to know with hindsight the consequences of past actors' actions, which they could not necessarily have predicted. This competence enables historians to create coherent interpretative accounts from their contemporary perspectives, accounts typically offering a sense of coherence and continuity, as embodied in past and present experiences.[30]

But, as I stated in chapter 2, the creation of historical narratives by contemporary actors is highly contentious. For postmodernists, the process is fraudulent because it leads to the present-day belief that events happened as they did because they had to (i.e., out of logical necessity), whereas past realities could have been more open, fortuitous, and incoherent than imagined. As White creatively puts it, 'narrative strains for the effect of having filled in all the gaps, of having put an image of continuity, coherence, and meaning in place of the fantasies of emptiness, need, and frustrated desire that inhabit our nightmares about the destructive power of time.'[31] Although this hyperbolic statement may appear to be extreme in historiography, it should nonetheless remind historians of the contingency of their claims vis-à-vis perceived historical change or continuity in human affairs. Historical thinking, as I have argued, starts from a present-day perspective and interest in aspects of the past. And typically the construction of interpretative accounts resulting from such inquiry is comprehensive and coherent. Yet the past may not have been organized in this way at all.

Making Connections by Means of Colligation

Consideration for, and study of, the past in light of present circumstances (hindsight) implies the need for an analysis of the second, related element of synoptic judgment: colligation. In the previous segment, I argued that historians can look at a sequence of significant events and explain the outcomes (as causal possibilities) because they possess some historical perspective largely lacking to the actors themselves. Yet this advantageous point of view, which allows historians to create coherent historical narratives retrospectively, would also require what William Walsh refers to as 'colligation,' that is, the tracing of the *intrinsic* relations of one event to others in a series.[32] Explaining, and ultimately understanding, the past by colligation is, in his view, possible (and, in fact, necessary) as a result of the fact that historians select and study events of the past not only as occurring in chronological order but also as parts of a larger phenomenon or movement. 'If an historian is asked to explain a particular historical event,' Walsh insists, 'he is often inclined to begin his explanation by saying that the event in question is to be seen as part of a general movement which was going on at the time.'[33]

These 'general movements,' also called colligatory concepts, would be sets of ideas or 'pervasive themes' manifest in a sequence of changes studied by historians.[34] Walsh lists the 'Enlightenment,' the 'Romantic movement,' and 'Monopoly capitalism' as examples of colligatory concepts employed by modern historians. Whether one agrees with his personal list is not so much the issue here, although the list is certainly questionable and incomplete. What is more *à propos* with respect to the discussion is the nature of these colligatory concepts. Walsh supposes that to study a period in history and thus develop a coherent understanding of its events, historians must create or reveal a common theme *intrinsic* to these changes. As he puts it, 'The historian and his reader initially confront what looks like a largely unconnected mass of material, and the historian then goes on to show that sense can be made of it by revealing certain pervasive themes or developments. In specifying what was going on at the time he both sums the individual events and tells us how to take them. Or again, he picks out what was significant in the events he relates, what is significant here being what points beyond itself and connects with other happenings as phases in a continuous process.'[35] But the paradox of studying a series of significant changes is that to conceptualize events occurring at particular times, historians must conceptualize colligatory concepts, or themes, as continuous or transhistorical categories extending over time. Using Hitler's access to power as an example, Walsh argues that the German policy of 'self-assertion and expansion' of the late 1930s could be used to explain the series of events leading ultimately to World War II. He writes, 'Hitler's reoccupation of the Rhineland in 1936 might be elucidated by reference to the general policy of German self-assertion and expansion which Hitler pursued from the time of his accession to power. Mention of this policy, and specification of earlier and later steps in carrying it out, such as the repudiation of unilateral disarmament, the German withdrawal from the League of Nations, the absorption of Austria and the incorporation of the Sudetenland, do in fact serve to render the isolated action from which we started more intelligible. And they do it by enabling us to locate that action in its context, to see it as a step in the realization of a more or less consistent policy.' If Walsh is correct, then, historians would need some transhistorical or continuous categories (such as a 'policy') as backdrops for their investigation and construction of narrative explanations. 'Without such a transhistorical category,' as Seixas observes, 'it becomes difficult or impossible to understand change within that category.'[36] For example, the acceptance of the maple-leaf flag, discussed in the introduction to this chapter, could be understood as a drastic change in Canada's official symbols only if one posits the colligatory term 'symbol' or 'emblem' as a transhistorical political convention traceable back in history. Without such a term, this key event in Canadian history makes no sense.

Following Walsh, one could argue that the whole notion of change in historical studies only makes sense if historians can study the past with a set of tools allowing them to see things at once and together.[37] Burston, a strong supporter of Walsh, has indicated that the notion of a cause is also essential to understanding a sequence of events. But as useful as citing causes might be, they are not pervasive themes intrinsic to events. So what are the larger phenomena or colligatory tools that Walsh is talking about?

Walsh suggests that colligatory concepts are ideas or themes that meet three key principles in the study of history: they must (1) be well-founded in the facts; (2) serve to illuminate the facts; and (3) be thought of as concrete and universal. For him, colligatory concepts are pertinent to historians only if, first, such concepts are embodied in the evidence and capable of leading to 'a series of relevant and connected lower-level statements which count in [their] favour, [and] are framed, by comparison, in untheoretical terms, and about whose acceptability historians are generally agreed.'[38] In other words, to be recognized as relevant by historians, concepts must emerge from the sources. Second, Walsh argues, colligatory concepts are relevant only if they illuminate the facts in question and thus render 'the past real and intelligible *to us*.'[39] As the whole object of colligation is to 'increase understanding,' in Walsh's terms, it is thus necessary to ground the concepts in the available sources, but in a way that makes the past more accessible and understandable.[40] But Walsh also adds a final principle to his notion of colligation: the concepts must be not only concrete enough to be intelligible but also general (or 'universal') so that 'the central subject [of historians' concern must be one] possessing something like a form of life of its own, a life expressed in phenomena which are diverse but recognizably related, and in which the same themes keep recurring though never in a simply repeated way.'[41] Walsh is convinced that the persons, communities, institutions, and movements that historians investigate must lead to an understanding of these particulars as part of something more universal in history.

Taking Walsh's argument further, philosopher Behan McCullagh contends, however, that although some colligatory concepts, as originally defined by Walsh, could be understood as 'formal,' indicating intrinsic structures of an historical process, others should be considered 'dispositional,' referring to a disposition of historical actors or a set of their ideals that the sequence of events could be set to manifest to the historian.[42] Hence McCullagh suggests that because historians have their positionalities and sets of questions and evidence, the colligation process would not exclude the possibility of other understandings of the same events if historians used or revealed different colligatory concepts or even relationships between events.

Equally pertinent is McCullagh's reconsideration of 'universal' colligatory concepts as defined by Walsh. McCullagh contends that colligatory concepts should not be understood exclusively as general instances of classification, describing whole sequences of events across periods. Revolution, for example, can serve to describe more than one historical series of events (e.g., French Revolution, U.S. Revolution, etc.). But other colligatory concepts emerging from the study of a particular series of events (e.g., Québec's Quiet Revolution) could be far more restrictive and unique in their application. At some point, these terms may even be inappropriate for describing some events, as the changes could be so drastic or sudden that new colligatory terms would be necessary. Also taking Hitler as an example, but this time to show the limits of colligatory concepts, McCullagh argues,

> There is only one set of events which is 'the implementation of Hitler's intention to control Austria.' It would include such diverse events as movements of the German army before and during the occupation of Austria in February and March 1938, Hitler's negotiations with the Austrian Chancellor Schuschnigg, the events by which Hitler got Schuschnigg replaced by the Nazi Seyss-Inquart as Chancellor of Austria, and his instructions to Prince Philip of Hesse to get Mussolini's consent for the invasion of Austria. The collection is not a neat one from a formal point of view; but it is unified by being a total manifestation of a particular disposition, namely the intention of Hitler at that time to seize control of Austria. It therefore does constitute a unique historical whole: no other set of events in history could be so described.[43]

Clearly, the interaction between continuity and change has serious implications for historians. Though historical events are, by definition, changes perceived as significant in a given state of affairs, changes are possible, and perceptible, only if historians posit a certain continuity in human affairs, often by employing transhistorical colligatory concepts to study or illuminate the phenomena they wish to describe. The recent redefinition of historical studies has led historians to consider aspects of the past previously ignored or deemed insignificant (e.g., gender, childhood, the body, ethnicity). This redefinition has resulted in not only a richer and more complex understanding of continuity and change in human affairs but also the creation of colligatory concepts formerly either absent or largely ignored in the discipline (e.g., masculinity, human rights, and multiculturalism). In many ways, these concepts now serve to illuminate significant aspects of the past that had lacked the terms or ideas needed to make them more intelligible.

4.2 Students and the Concepts of Continuity and Change

If history is, by definition, concerned with the study of historical change, it is reasonable to assume that continuity and change should be concepts of crucial consideration in school history. As Haydn, Arthur, and Hunt contend, for many decades history teachers in England have been aware of their importance, but 'only in the last two decades have the reasons for [their] importance been articulated in pedagogical terms.'[44]

In many ways, the same could be said for Canada and the United States. Curriculum guidelines and content standards now acknowledge the need to use concepts such as these in structuring courses and, to a certain degree, introducing students to perceived changes and continuities in historical affairs. The Ontario history curriculum, for example, uses 'change and continuity' as a strand to organize the content of all its high-school history courses. In the overall expectations, the curriculum guidelines state that students must demonstrate an understanding of the historical process of change and continuity in the context of the course of study.[45] The United States National Standards for History are even more specific in their consideration of these concepts. In the section on 'chronological thinking,' the standards discuss the need to engage students in the historical analysis of past events so as to 'reconstruct patterns of historical succession and duration in which historical developments have unfolded, and apply them to explain historical continuity and change.'[46] Even textbook publishers have followed the movement and included continuity and change in their content and exercises. The concepts are now so *en vogue* that one

Canadian history textbook is even entitled *Canada: Continuity and Change – A History of our Country from 1900 to the Present.*[47]

Yet, like the concept of historical significance, those of continuity and change are rarely presented to students as concepts to be employed in their historical learning but as implicit elements for structuring the content of textbooks or curriculum guidelines, notably as ways of establishing periods in history (e.g., the Roaring Twenties or the Dirty Thirties). It is no surprise, therefore, that the limited number of studies conducted on these concepts suggest that 'change is a historical concept that adolescents initially find difficult to entertain in any but everyday use.'[48] In England, for example, Shemilt found that teachers often take 'continuity and change' for granted in their course planning or lesson objectives. History is typically presented as an overcrowded list of disconnected events falling under a variety of subject titles (revolutions, reforms, battles, bills, inventions, etc.). The result is that students largely see change 'as an episodic not a continuous process, and one change (event) is not constructed in any way connected with changes (events) preceding it in time.'[49] 'The fabric of History,' as he eloquently puts it, 'is like a volcano occasionally convulsed by random explosions. Recorded history is seen as a chronicle of disruptions within the crater of the volcano.'[50] The difficulty for students may well come from a poor ability to imagine and create a mental picture – a colligatory picture – of the larger sequence in which the event is situated. Because of curriculum design or teaching approaches focused on a mere sequence of happenings, students typically lack the ability to engage in the study of the motives and causes of events, preferring to adopt a logical (and often inevitable) explanation of the past.

Equally problematic to Shemilt is the finding suggesting that continuity is a concept recognized and accepted by students but 'not necessarily the right one.'[51] As students often lack narrative understanding (as of sequence, coherence, and colligation), they operate with either an image of the *longue durée* of certain causes, and including everything as a cause of history, or with a superficial view of the past funnelled through a naive contemporary lens, often leading students to consider past actors as inferior or less advanced (i.e., as suffering a deficit from the students' point of view).

Other studies conducted in the United Kingdom and North America highlight similar difficulties for students at elementary- and secondary-school levels.[52] In a U.S. study of grade 4–5 students, for example, VanSledright and Brophy observed that they typically used contemporary human beliefs and standards to discuss causal relations between events during the Civil War, and without proper knowledge of the events or their sequence.[53] In a subsequent study of the views of other grade 5 students on the causes of the U.S. Revolution, VanSledright not only confirmed earlier findings but also discovered that students purposely select certain causes to support or even justify their prior understanding and penchant for U.S. independence. 'Virtually without exception,' he concludes, 'the essays contained arguments about significant causes that were tilted in favour of citing types of repression visited on the colonials by an intolerant British regime bent on dictating life in North America largely through unfair tax policies.'[54]

Barton's study of the views of grade 4–5 students on the origins and evolution of U.S. slavery and immigration also provides interesting evidence. Whereas students did implicitly use colligatory concepts (e.g., slavery) to structure their narrative explanations, they simplistically conflated entire historical periods and sequences of events with a few significant historical happenings – often unsupported by historical evidence. For example, one student participant explained the origins of slavery in these terms: 'During the Revolutionary War and stuff, people sailed down to Africa ... to like get away from the war, and they found these black people, and they thought they were monkeys or animals, and they thought they were really neat, and they crowded them up on boats and stuff, and sold them.'[55] As part of a post-evaluation study of the School Council History Project, Shemilt recently addressed the issue of students' conflation of larger sequences of historical events. Not only did the students in the study see necessity and faith where contingency and possibility might have worked better and more accurately, but the construction of their interpretations of the past offered lists of chronological changes (pictures of the past) 'separated by periods of quiescence in which nothing happens.'[56] The result, as Shemilt argues, is that students treat the past in a 'binary mode,' that is, by alternating selected events and temporal spaces, a simplistic model that inevitably leads students to believe that nothing happened during the 'holes in history.'[57]

Part of the current problem may well emanate from factors that lie outside the formal historical classroom. Like all historical actors, students understand continuity and change according to their own experience of history.[58] Age is possibly an important factor to consider in such experience. If one leaves aside differences in cognitive development, older people (such as senior citizens) have naturally lived through and experienced more historical change than teenagers and thus 'have more direct experience with how fundamentally things can change.'[59] A Holocaust survivor, for example, is more likely than a student born after the Cold War to comment on the development and persistence of genocide in contemporary history.

But, aside from age, people's own historical location can influence their thinking. People, whether they are infants, teenagers, or elders, who have lived through a coup d'état or a tsunami or who are immigrants to a new country will have different understandings of change than those who live in relatively traditional stability. My own study of Ontario high-school students and terrorism supports this line of reasoning. When asked what had changed or remained the same since the attacks of September 11, immigrant students and those from religious minorities (notably Muslims) had clearly different perspectives on the tragic event than their white, Canadian-born counterparts. While some students mentioned trivial changes (e.g., longer airport security checks), students from visible minorities did not hesitate to comment on the more racist attitudes of Canadians toward Arabs and Muslims.[60]

Saying that students' articulation of continuity and change is largely shaped by their own experience is not to say, however, that history educators should ignore the teaching of these concepts altogether. On the contrary, with the recent influence of global change, it becomes even more important to engage students in the study of the concepts of change and continuity so they can better understand the past and current events that have, in many ways, shaped their views of history. It could well be, as Seixas contends, 'that younger people growing up in an era of uncertainty and instability have a more profound experience of change than their elders.'[61]

Given the limited attention and focus of education scholars on these procedural concepts for the study of history, it is difficult and even speculative to provide any firm recommendations on the use of these concepts in history education. It is nonetheless possible, in light of the previous discussion, to advance the following two objectives for better integration and use of the concepts of continuity and change in class: (1) to foster chronological thinking; and (2) to promote synoptic judgment using colligation.

Fostering Chronological Thinking

'The first characteristic to be noticed [about the form and structure of history],' Stanford observes, 'is that the past had a chronological order; things happened either one after another or at the same time.'[62] But chronology is only a prerequisite for historical understanding, not an end in itself. The United States National Center for History in the Schools has thus emphasized the need to develop not only a sense of chronology but also a more comprehensive notion, namely, chronological thinking. As stated in the National Standards, 'Chronological thinking is at the heart of historical reasoning. Without a clear sense of historical time – time past, present, and future – students are bound to see events as one great tangled mess. Without a strong sense of chronology – of when events occurred and in what temporal order – it is impossible for students to examine relationships among them or to explain historical causality. Chronology provides the mental scaffolding for organizing historical thought.'[63] Too often, chronological thinking is understood in school history as the linear sequencing of historical events in the 'proper' temporal order.[64] The presentation or design of timelines of varying kinds (political, technological, etc.) is a typical example encountered in textbooks or even in class activities. The predictable result is that 'pupils often forget the sequence of events while, as a rule, remembering something or other about the events themselves.'[65] The usefulness of organizing the past in a sequence of historical events is not disputed, but this aspect of historical thinking is surely not sufficient to acquire, as the U.S. National Standards state, a sense of 'historical reasoning.' What is also needed, perhaps above all, is the complex study of the nature and significance of events, as well as of the connections between them. Studying a long series of disconnected happenings from the past often leads students to remember the chronological sequence presented to them (or, more realistically speaking, some *fragments* of this sequence), without constructing or even questioning the sequence and timeline offered. The problem they face is not so much the failure to master the events (although many do miss that aspect, too) as the failure to conceive the purposes and motives that inspired them, as well as their future consequences; a failure, in other words, to look at the processes of the 'inside' and 'outside' of these actions, to use Collingwood's *façon de parler*.

Unfortunately it is not clear in the literature how to achieve this complex goal in schools. At least three related approaches seem to emerge from recent studies in the field: narrative, thematic, and contemporary. Each approach has its own merits and limitations and can be used, sometimes concurrently, in history education, depending on teachers' perspectives, goals, courses, and familiarity with the approaches.

The first approach, largely supported by the U.S. National Standards, suggests that students learn chronological thinking by constructing their own narrative understanding of past events. This approach has the merit of putting students in the situation of apprentice historians who learn how to build coherent accounts of the past by considering the unfolding of the events (forward thinking), as well as thinking about their origins and development (backward thinking). As I argued in chapter 2, an historical narrative is a particular form of writing that forces students to create a series of significant events and look at possible causal connections between them. As the U.S. National Standards document puts it to teachers, 'Establish temporal order in constructing [students'] own historical narratives: working forward from some beginning through its development, to some end or outcome; working backward from some issue, problem, or event to explain its origins and its development over time.'[66]

The second approach recommends that teachers discuss the concepts of continuity and change by identifying what historians Frederick Drake and Lynn Nelson refer to as 'key turning points without reducing history to earthquakes of change.'[67] Instead of covering the collective past with a master narrative, Drake and Nelson suggest, teachers and students should select and analyse key events or larger phenomena thematically (e.g., the U.S. Declaration of Independence) so as to reveal patterns of historical duration (e.g., democracy, self-government) and succession (e.g., from slavery to civil rights). By doing so, it becomes possible to discuss rapid changes that a society can undergo in certain aspects of life (e.g., politics), as well as the accompanying continuities in other aspects (e.g., religious beliefs). Similarly, with this approach, students are led to study certain significant actions during periods that may initially appear stable and continuous to them but that may reveal more social changes than expected, if examined thematically.

As an addition to this approach, Seixas suggests, third, that teachers make explicit use of the relation between the present and the past to discuss elements of continuity and change. As the present in which students live is necessarily the outcome of past events, having students examine or question contemporary concepts (e.g., freedom and justice) or elements (e.g., a contemporary scene from different historical pictures) that they may take for granted or simply ignore can be a valuable way of introducing them to the concepts of continuity and change. In a particular history exercise called the Names Project, for example, Levstik and Barton reveal that even the simple study of students' own names in an historical context can be an engaging activity, with teachers asking such questions as How have the reasons for people's names changed over time? How have people's names gotten longer or shorter? Why have some people adopted nicknames?[68] But, perhaps more importantly for Seixas, the use of the present as an approach to teaching the concepts of continuity and change can encourage teachers to be more conscious and careful of the various perspectives and experiences that students have acquired during their lives and bring to class. The classrooms of Canadian schools are more and more made up of students from diverse religious, cultural, and linguistic backgrounds. These young people have diverse and possibly conflicting experiences of change that are, unfortunately, largely neglected in school history. Attending to students' perceptions of continuity and change can, therefore, allow for better representations of the students' own ideas, as well as allowing an opportunity to challenge or enhance their relationship with the past.

Promoting Synoptic Judgment Using Colligation

Having students develop a sense of chronology or consider elements of continuity and change between the past and present is definitely an important objective, as it serves to 'map the past' with certain orders, sequences, and relationships. But this does not necessarily provide teachers and students with the opportunity to develop more advanced forms of synoptic judgment, notably in the form of a structured narrative. As I argued in the previous section on colligation, interpretative accounts of the past have an internal coherence and logic largely shaped by the phenomenon or theme intrinsic to the events historians wish to describe. Taking colligation into account may have serious implications for at least two aspects of history education: (1) course planning; and (2) students' practice.

COURSE PLANNING
First, the notion of colligation can help teachers structure or restructure the planning and periodization of their courses of study. One of the key challenges in school history is to organize it in such a way as to render the past intelligible and significant to students to help them appreciate and to understand what happened, what it means, and how people lived, thought, and acted back then. As a convention, curriculum guidelines present teachers with extensive lists of various expectations and learning outcomes, but these do not prioritize learning or help anyone see things at once and together. The Ontario curriculum,

for example, structures all Canadian and world-history courses according to five learning strands, which may not be adequate for colligating historical knowledge: communities; citizenship and heritage; continuity and change; social, political, and economic structures; and methods of historical inquiry. Textbooks can be more helpful in their structuring of historical content but are often conventional, rigid, and highly progressive (or Whiggish) in their periodizing and may not be appropriate for what teachers wish to do. The modern Canadian history course, for example, is typically shaped as follows:

Unit 1: The birth/rise of a nation, 1900–13
Unit 2: Canada and World War I, 1914–18
Unit 3: The Roaring Twenties, 1919–29
Unit 4: The Dirty Thirties, 1930–8
Unit 5: Canada and World War II, 1939–45
Unit 6: Canadian identity and unity, 1946–82
Unit 7: Canada and the world, 1983–today

There are clearly merits to organizing Canadian history around the strands and periodization outlined here, which I am not going to debate. The question I want to examine here is about the grouping and arrangement of events for such a course, as it may have vital effects on history teaching and, ultimately, on students' learning. Chronology and concepts such as citizenship and communities are key aspects of history, but they are certainly not sufficient for introducing students to historical thinking. In Walsh's terms, historians have to show the meaning of the past by *picking out* what is significant in the events they relate. In chapter 3, I argued that certain criteria are used by historians, educators, and the public to ascribe significance to past events. Although indispensable, these criteria do not necessarily provide a particular grouping of events in a coherent framework. What historians and educators need for this complex task is to consider the criteria of significance in light of pervasive themes or ideas to increase the synoptic understanding of the sequence of events but to avoid extensive chronological coverage.[69] Put differently, colligation is valuable only if it renders the past more intelligible as a consequence of the grouping. As Thompson puts it,

The way in which the material for a lesson or a series of lessons is handled and grouped is vital to the effectiveness of the teaching. If it is so organized that the facts are presented as a series of more or less unconnected events then the lesson will have little interest or meaning. The pupil will not recognize any significant interplay between the various happenings, will understand little and be much bored by what he is doing. If, on the other hand, the connection between events is brought out, explanation and interpretation emphasized, and where possible the individual events seen as parts of a whole, the chance of understanding and therefore of successful history learning is greatly enhanced.[70]

Perhaps my earlier sports analogy would help to reinforce the essence of this notion of colligation. When a hockey coach works out with each of his or her players a specific series of actions during a practice (holding respective positions, making passes, skating to the net, etc.), the coach does so for an ultimate objective (e.g., to have the players work together as a team in scoring a goal). If the spectators focused exclusively on the steps during a practice, they would not necessarily comprehend the overall purpose of these individual actions. It is only when all the players' separate actions (or steps) are placed in a sequence and relationship with other stages in a game that the spectators comprehend their significance.

The challenge for educators is, therefore, to find colligatory ways of selecting and organizing the content and expectations of history courses to achieve pedagogically sound groupings consistent with historical conceptions and practices. Would the notion of colligation therefore offer any help or guidance in course or unit planning?

I believe so, if teachers carefully analyse and rework the material and periodization already presented to them in textbooks and curriculum guidelines. In some cases, teachers may realize that the proposed expectations (or strands) and structure meet their pedagogical and historical needs. In these instances it might be possible to organize specific units or lessons to reinforce or emphasize the colligatory concepts already proposed (e.g., Canada and World War I). But in other cases, teachers may want to change or prioritize a certain periodization or grouping of events. The 'Roaring Twenties,' for example, may not necessarily offer an appropriate colligation for the period. It may well be that teachers wish to study or render intelligible certain sequences of events or phenomena of the 1920s (e.g., crime and poverty or factory development) that do not suit the colligatory idea of 'Roaring.' In such cases, teachers may wish to change the periodization or develop more appropriate colligatory concepts (e.g., Prohibition or the Depression). With adequate direction, focus, and hindsight, then, it becomes possible to render the past more comprehensible and accessible to students if teachers reorganize their course planning according to colligatory concepts that are (1) intrinsic to the events or series of events in question; and (2) useful for meaning-making. In the example of a modern Canadian history course, reconsideration of course planning could lead to something like the following:

Unit 1: Canada and nation-building
Unit 2: Empire, race, and war
Unit 3: Prosperity, the Depression, and horror
Unit 4: Canadian revolution and the welfare state
Unit 5: Affirmation and globalization

Alternatively, a teacher could restructure the same course of study entirely around one or two colligatory concepts, as opposed to a specifically chronological colligation. In this case, one could use the concept of 'collective identity' to arrange the grouping of events and periods for the entire course of study. The result might look like this:

Unit 1: Nation- and state-building, now and then
Unit 2: Canadian identity and contribution in war times
Unit 3: Canadian social programs and the welfare state
Unit 4: Identity and French-English relations
Unit 5: Multiculturalism and regionalism
Unit 6: Constitution, rights, and freedoms

By organizing the same course of study (and the various units) according to these different structures, teachers can perhaps more easily meet both the demands of the curriculum and those of students for historical meaning-making. Employing the relevant concepts could help render the past more intelligible and meaningful to students.

STUDENTS' HISTORICAL PRACTICE
The second educational aspect of colligation in history has to do with students' own learning. If the past ought to make sense to students, it is reasonable to expect them to engage in exercises that are both meaningful and reflective of the discipline. As previously discussed, constructing coherent narrative explanations can be central to historical thinking. Because historical narrative works with connections, patterns, and colligatory concepts, as well as with time and space (past and present), it is thus a valuable exercise for engaging students in historical learning.

Yet, the inherent structure of the historical narrative largely determines what is included and excluded from the evidence and events of the past. Not every causal relation or action of predecessors is mentioned or even considered worth studying or recording. The significance of each of these elements is dependably established by the focus of the historians and these elements' meaning within the historical narrative itself. 'Narrative,' as Tosh argues, 'imposes a drastic simplification on the treatment of cause ... It can keep only two or three threads going at once, so that only a few causes or results will be made apparent.'[71] Colligation can be particularly well suited for creating or analysing the 'simplified' narratives of the past. The U.S. National Standards, as I noted earlier, suggest that students advance their historical thinking by constructing their own historical narratives. The standards are not clear, however, on how to achieve this goal or, more specifically, on how to employ the concept of colligation. At least two different but related approaches could be envisaged here.

First, teachers can purposely assign students the colligatory concepts that they wish the students to consider. Consistent with my inquiry-based approach (chapter 2), teachers should not only plan lessons and activities around realistic historical problems to be solved (inquiries) but also offer students the intrinsic concepts or themes framing these cases. By doing so, teachers would not necessarily impose their logic or rationality on the inquiry but would guide students in their investigation and writing up of narrative explanations. A major deficiency of students' historical explanations, as evidenced in several studies, has to do with the students' limited ability to conceive of a chronologically coherent picture of the past. Having them perform realistic historical tasks may encourage the students to experience the historians' craft. However, their mapping and sense-making of the past could be seriously hampered by their inability to 'see things together.' Offering students particular colligatory concepts can, therefore, help explain the pertinence of the case (with its respective questions and evidence), as well as offering them some guidance in the discipline of historical thinking. To go back to my earlier example of the Canadian flag, teachers could present the concepts of national identity, sovereignty, French-English relations, and political symbols as colligatory terms to be employed by students for their narrative explications of the changes that occurred during the period.

The second approach to consider is to allow students to elaborate, with the teacher's assistance, their own (general or specific) colligatory concepts for larger historical periods. Culminating activities are often praised by teachers because they draw attention to the key goals and elements of a unit of study that were introduced in a series of specific lessons. Perhaps more importantly, they allow students to demonstrate, and even celebrate, their learning in realistic and engaging ways. Historical narratives on particular themes can play that crucial role in the history classroom. Shemilt contends that it is important for students to structure and conceptualize the chronological content of the past in narrative frameworks that address the 'material, social, and organizational aspects of human history.'[72] By doing so, students can more effectively understand change (or even continuity) over a period of time and thus avoid the naive tendency to view the past as a series of abrupt disconnected events, like a chronicle of volcanic eruptions. The construction of colligatory concepts by students may thus help clarify the relations of continuity and change between the many historical events presented to them, if it is kept in mind that such relations should be understood as causal possibilities and not logical certainties.

Equally important, the teacher's use of colligatory concepts to create historical narratives may discourage students' drawing simplistic or 'universal' lessons from past events about the manifest destiny of their own contemporary society or their memory obligations to certain predecessors. In the case of the Canadian flag, for example, students could investigate the series of events that ultimately led to the adoption of the maple leaf in 1964 and look at the consequences it has had for Canadian identity and citizenship. Teachers could provide students with a question such as 'In your opinion, what has changed and what has remained the same since the adoption of the flag in 1964?'

4.3 Conclusion

Understanding continuity and change is crucial to historical thinking. Because history is about perceived changes in past human affairs, historians need some kind of synoptic judgment to make sense of these events in larger historical contexts and sequences. Yet, change is only possible if historians posit certain continuous phenomena or concepts as backdrops for their investigations. Colligation can be a useful tool for constructing logical, coherent, and intelligible interpretations of historical change, as it can reveal pervasive themes, ideas, or phenomena to historians (such as terrorism, revolution, and transportation).

Yet, I have argued that although school history is increasingly attentive to the relational concepts of continuity and change, students, and perhaps teachers as well, continue to have only a limited understanding of their use in historical studies. (Is not this a sign of the pervasive importance of 'continuity' in history?) To make sense, history cannot be presented or understood as disconnected 'bits and pieces that can validly and usefully inform the present.'[73] For this reason, teachers and students should be more conscious and critical of the various accounts or 'lessons' of the past that they read, absorb, create, or take for granted. Promoting chronological thinking and synoptic judgment can help in doing so.

5 Did Things Change for Better or Worse? – Progress and Decline

> Whenever humans are involved in histories, experiences of transformation or change are to be found, for better or worse, for those affected in a given time.
>
> – Reinhart Koselleck[1]

The eighteenth century was marked by unprecedented progress in the study of history. During the Age of Enlightenment, thinkers conceptualized and disseminated revolutionary ideas about nature, humanity, society, and history that soon affected the whole Western world and beyond. Among these thinkers was a young French ideologist, François-Marie Arouet, known as Voltaire, who believed in the advance of happiness and the progress of civilization. For Voltaire, the emancipation of rationality – which implied a rejection of the belief in divine providence in favour of faith in humanity – could lead to a more civilized and free society. True *avant-gardiste*, his ideas critical of established French authorities were apparently not welcomed by the establishment and caused him numerous imprisonments and exiles.

In his famous *Age of Lewis XIV*, he argued that human history comprised four key ages (those of Philip and Alexander of Greece, Caesar and Augustus of Rome, Mahomet II of Constantinople, and Louis XIV, the last one being the 'nearest to perfection'). 'True philosophy,' Voltaire contended, 'was discovered only in this age: and it may with truth be said, that, from the last years of cardinal Richelieu to the death of Lewis XIV there happened a general revolution, not only in our government, but in our arts, minds, and manners.'[2] This revolution was, for Voltaire, by no means 'confined to France, but extended into England, where it excited the emulation which that sensible and thinking nation then wanted.'[3]

Taking Voltaire's ideas further, the Marquis de Condorcet claimed that there would be virtually no limit to the perfectibility of human beings. In his *Esquisse d'un tableau historique des progrès de l'esprit humain*, Condorcet wrote, 'Such is the goal of the work which I have undertaken, of which the result will be to show by reason and by evidence that no limit has been set to the perfection of human faculties; that the perfectibility of man is really indefinite; that the progress of this perfectibility, henceforth independent of every power which might wish to stop it, has no limit other than the duration of the globe on which nature has cast us.'[4] Writing at the time of the French Revolution, Condorcet was convinced that the liberation of human beings from the tyranny of nature and irrational social authorities (such as the clergy) would now be inevitable. 'Having long been engaged in pondering the means of improving man's fate,' he once declared, 'I have not been able to avoid the conclusion that there is actually only one such means: the speeding of the progress of enlightenment.'[5]

The optimism of Voltaire, Condorcet, and other such Enlightenment crusaders was not purely utopian or limited to a small French philosophical élite writing to each other in a period of profound social agitation. The U.S. Revolution, and its rhetorical emphasis on the inalienable rights to life, liberty, and the pursuit of happiness, coupled with the French Revolution and its famous *Déclaration des droits de l'homme et du citoyen*, provided first-hand evidence of the powerful impact of the messages circulating on both sides of the Atlantic. The hundreds of thousands of workers, plebeians, vagabonds, illiterates, and other have-nots of the *tiers état* could now hope for a better life, or at least rhetorically consider themselves of a status equal to that of the few 'haves' who had governed and oppressed them for so long. The ideas on the advance of progress were highly contagious. They were, as eighteenth-century French economist and political leader Jacques Turgot put it, 'passed on from country to country.'[6]

But the beliefs in the human capacity for self-improvement, as well as the rejection *en masse* of the orthodoxy of the *ancien régime*, did not go unchallenged. Among the various critics of inevitability of progress was an inquisitive Anglican curate whose father knew and had corresponded with Voltaire, Thomas Robert Malthus. In his famous *Essay on the Principle of Population*, first published in 1798, Malthus presented the results of his inquiry on 'the causes that have hitherto impeded the progress of mankind toward happiness.'[7] The growing mismatch between people and the available resources, if unchecked, presented to Malthus a bleak picture for the future of the human species. The thrust of his argument was that the 'power of population' to expand was far greater than that of the earth to produce subsistence. This growing imbalance would potentially result in a period of drastic decline, famine, and misery. As he pronounced, 'The power of population being in every period so much superior [to the power in the earth], the increase of the human species can only be kept down to the level of the means of subsistence by the consistent operation of the strong law of necessity acting as a check upon greater power.'[8] Malthus was right to maintain that late eighteenth-century Europe was engaged in an unprecedented surge in population. While the overall population of Europe in 1650 was about 100 million, it was almost 170 million a century later, and well over 200 million by the time Malthus wrote his book.[9] Asia and the so-called New World were also witnessing a drastic increase of inhabitants, notably in the city slums. Taking the United Kingdom as an example of his calculations, Malthus believed that the population would increase by factors of 1, 2, 4, 8, 16, 32, 64, and so forth, whereas the means of subsistence would increase by factors of 1, 2, 3, 4, 5, 6, etc. The predictable result, for Malthus, was catastrophic. 'In two centuries,' he pessimistically estimated, 'the population would be to the means of subsistence as 256 to 9; in three centuries as 4096 to 13, and in two thousand years the difference would be almost incalculable.'[10] From his calculations, the population would thus continue to grow exponentially while millions of people everywhere would be dying of famine and disease, if drastic measures were not immediately adopted.

Malthus did not live long enough to see whether the United Kingdom would fall into a period of drastic decline – he died in 1834. Although the advocates of human progress suffered frequent disappointments in the decades that followed, Malthus's pessimistic picture for humanity faded out, at least in his native country. To be sure, the United Kingdom did witness a period of population increase and localized famine and misery in the nineteenth century, notably in Ireland. But at least three unanticipated developments permitted the United Kingdom to avoid the so-called Malthusian trap. First, a vast movement of emigration, notably to the New World, resulted in a massive exodus of nearly 20 million Britons between 1815 and 1914.[11] Second, developments in agriculture led to more efficient and productive techniques, so the 'the power in the earth' actually could match 'the power of the population.' Finally, the United Kingdom initiated and largely controlled the Industrial Revolution, which led to a major leap in productivity, employment, and prosperity for the British people.

With hindsight, it may seem evident today that progressive optimists decisively won the debate against the pessimists of decline, although not necessarily for the reasons they had initially advanced. More remarkable would be the contemporary view, as Ignatieff contends, that the Enlightenment project, developed two centuries ago, is very much on its way to accomplishment: 'The political and social history of Western society is the story of the struggle of all human groups to gain inclusion. This vast historical process, which began in the European wars of religion in the sixteenth century, has been brought to a successful conclusion only now, in the rights revolution of the past forty years.'[12] Despite this optimistic claim, one could argue that the old debate between progressive optimists and the pessimists of decline is far from over and is even now an issue pertinent to the twenty-first century. Now, more than two hundred years after the first publication of Malthus's *Essay*, the same views of humanity's decline have recently been put forward – this time concerning decline on a more global scale. Writer Ronald Wright, for example, claims in his Massey Lectures that Western societies still believe deeply in the Enlightenment project of Voltaire, Condorcet, and their followers. 'Most people in the Western cultural tradition still believe in the Victorian ideal of progress, a belief succinctly defined by the historian Sidney Pollard in 1968 as "the assumption that a pattern of change exists in the history of mankind ... that it consists of irreversible changes in one direction only, and that this direction is towards improvement."'[13] Yet, the experiment in progress, Wright believes, 'must be [brought] under rational control, and guard[ed] against present and potential dangers.'[14] Using the Mayan and Roman civilizations as examples and plausible models to predict collapse, he contends that increasingly rapid overpopulation (in the developing world), coupled with relentless exploitation of the earth's resources (predominantly in the Western world) 'is typical of failed societies at the zenith of their greed and arrogance.'[15] Reading Wright in light of Malthus's *Essay* may lead readers to a sense of *déjà vu*.

That being said, Wright is far from alone with his pessimist views.[16] Historian Paul Kennedy also believes that the same issues 'still confront us today, with greater force than ever.'[17] The recent world transformations have, for him, affected significantly the earth and human populations in extraordinarily many fields, including technology, production, consumption, and the environment. The test would be, once again, to confront the 'powers of technology and population' with 'the power in the earth.'[18]

All these past and contemporary discussions on the future of humanity provide clear illustrations that history is not only (or exclusively) about perceived changes in human affairs but perhaps more fundamentally about the direction and meaning of these changes as those of progress, decline, or even collapse of civilizations. Enlightenment progress was welcomed *à bras ouverts* by optimists because they could take advantage of the means to bring about positive change in their own lives and societies. However, the same historical changes did not have the same benefits for everyone on the globe. On the contrary, some societies (and their economies in particular) were largely devastated by the progress of the West. For example, the British and Indian peoples had roughly similar per capita levels of industrialization at the time Malthus wrote his book. By 1900, however, India's level was only one one-hundredth that of the United Kingdom.[19] It is no surprise, therefore, that progress would be, in Koselleck's terms, 'a concept specifically calibrated to cope with modern experiences'[20] and not only modern but exceedingly Eurocentric.[21]

In this chapter, I discuss the relational concepts of progress and decline. Building on the argument presented in the previous chapter on continuity and change, I claim that since their appearance over two centuries ago the concepts of progress and decline have provided historians with additional evaluative components to use in their interpretations of change in historical affairs (section 5.1). I then present a set of three principles that may be useful for judging the past in terms of improvement or decay (section 5.2). Finally, I discuss the implications of these principles for students' historical thinking (section 5.3). I show that without a sense of both progress and decline in history, students typically fall into the naive trap of Western progressive ideologies that lead them to view the past as essentially a place of inferiority and deficit.

5.1 On the Value Judgments of Progress and Decline

In the previous chapter, I claimed that historians make sense of the past by creating sequences of significant events, using colligatory concepts to structure and give coherence to their interpretations. These two complementary features, I argued, are crucial because they help historians grasp the complex relationship of changes over time and continuity in times of change. Yet, as useful as they might be, these two features do not provide historians with a clear evaluation of the direction of change. As historical actors and events have changed, have they improved? In what ways? For whom? To address these critical questions, a third element is required: an evaluative judgment to assess these changes as for better or worse.

Although historians may find common ground on the first two elements (sequence and colligation), the third one is more contentious in the discipline, as it requires the acceptance of a certain value judgment on the direction of change. It necessitates a shared belief in a particular direction of progress or decline for a series of perceived historical changes set by historians. With the decline of religion as a dominant socio-political force and the rise of a multiplicity of belief systems, Pollard claims it is increasingly problematic to share a belief in improvement: 'With the decline in the belief of supernatural sanctions, which began with the Enlightenment, it has, indeed, become much harder to find a firm resting place, a fixed point on which a moral system or a social objective greater than the individual can be built up. What is a crime from one point of view, is heroic self-sacrifice from another, and all the civic virtues of one system become persecuted vices over the border, where political power is built on a different class structure.'[22] As debatable as this statement might be, there is nonetheless merit and truth to what Pollard advances. Indeed, consider my earlier Canadian-flag example. A majority of Canadians may agree with the interpretation of the maple-leaf flag as a long and episodic national struggle to gain a distinctively Canadian emblem. Yet, many citizens can (and actually do) dispute the value of this change. Has the adoption of the maple-leaf flag truly led to the progress of Canada? In what ways? For whom?

Clearly, imposing on the past certain value judgments raises a host of questions about historical interpretation. In every step of their inquiry, historians must make decisions in response to research questions, selection of events and evidence, acceptance or rejection of past moral beliefs, and so forth. The principle of evaluation of progress and decline adds up to the contested nature of this process because historians, even when confronted with the same events, do not all judge the direction of change in the same ways. Part of the problem is that, as of today, we still have no agreed-on standards in the history community to help judge the direction of change – assuming that there is possibly a direction.

Before the eighteenth century, questions of progress and decline were largely absent in history, as were those of historical time and consciousness. According to the theory of divine providence; God created the world and its creatures, all set in an orderly system. Because God ruled over human affairs and set the changes, individuals had in essence the responsibility to follow his commandments and prepare for the day of the Last Judgment. 'The whole movement of history [according to the Christian theory],' as Bury argues in his *Idea of Progress*, 'has the purpose of securing the happiness of a small portion of the human race in another world; it does not postulate a further development of human history on earth.'[23]

The whole reassessment of historical order and truth by eighteenth-century philosophers and historians, such as Voltaire and Condorcet, brought about important changes in the interpretation of history and progress. Based on the new conviction that rational history could lead to the emancipation of humanity, the concept of progress became more relevant to the study of human purposes and destiny. 'The unity of mankind's destiny,' Breisach contends, 'was no longer vouchsafed by the common descent from Adam and Eve but by the presence of reason in its every member, and its development bore no longer the marks of Divine Providence but those of the emancipation of rationality from error and superstition.'[24] If Christianity was, for the great nineteenth-century positivist thinker Auguste Comte, to be held responsible for presenting a sense of human progress by proclaiming the superiority of Jesus over Moses, he nonetheless blamed religion, including Christianity, for its 'obscurantism' and application of the theological method to human affairs.[25]

In an attempt to grasp the relational meaning of progress and decline since the Enlightenment, two contrasting 'stances,' or ways of representing how these concepts have been employed over time, should be considered: (1) oppositional; and (2) successional.[26] I believe these stances are very pertinent to the understanding of historical change considered as signifying concepts of progress and decline, because they illustrate how these concepts have evolved and influenced historical thinking. Below I review them briefly.

Progress and Decline as Oppositional

The first stance starts from the premise that, like the concepts of continuity and change, progress and decline are not only relational but also indispensable to one another. To talk about advances in certain human affairs (e.g., science, technology, or spirituality), the oppositional stance suggests that one necessarily assumes that changes signifying progress in some aspects of human affairs imply decline in other aspects. 'What seems for one group a period of decline,' Carr contends, 'may seem to another the birth of a new advance.'[27] In this sense, one concept would exist only by virtue of the other. The advance of diesel trains in the twentieth century, for example, necessarily brought with it the decline of steam trains as a mode of transportation. The same could be said of electric lighting, secular education, or women's rights. All these human advances in certain aspects of life inevitably led to decline in some other aspects (decline of the oil lamp, religious schooling, and paternalism and inequality). Progress and decline are thus not only relational but also mutually compatible, in that they can exist or occur at the same time in history. They are, for Koselleck, *oppositional concepts* of equal rank' because claims of decline can be compatible with claims of historical progress.[28] This does not mean that claims of progress and decline must be integrated in a unity but that for the same period or series of events set by historians it is possible to oppose claims of both progress and decline.

Perhaps the most illuminating example of this first stance can be found in U.S. historian William Cronon's examination of the 1930s drought that struck the Great Plains.[29] By juxtaposing an account of historical progress (*The Dust Bowl* of Paul Bonnifield) with one of decline (*Dust Bowl* of Donald Worster), Cronon demonstrates admirably well how the same historical subject, with the same historical sources and characters, may acquire totally different meanings and imply totally different conclusions, depending on the contemporary value judgments made by the historians. Consider, for example, the optimistic closing remarks of Bonnifield, 'The story of the dust bowl was the story of people, people with the ability and talent, people with resourcefulness, fortitude, and courage ... The people of the dust bowl were not defeated, poverty-ridden people without hope. They were builders of tomorrow ... Because those determined people did not flee the stricken area during a crisis, the nation today enjoys a better standard of living.'[30] Worster's interpretation, in contrast, presents a much bleaker picture of the period: 'The Dust Bowl was the darkest moment in the twentieth-century life of the southern plains. The name suggests a place – a region whose borders are as inexact and shifting as a sand dune ... The Dust Bowl ... was the inevitable outcome of a culture that deliberately, self-consciously, set itself [the] task of dominating and exploiting the land for all it was worth.'[31] In both cases, the authors deal with the problems and conflicts that the drought brought about for the local residents of the U.S. southern plains (Texas, Kansas, Oklahoma, and Colorado). Yet, the stories they tell lead to very different conclusions. On the one hand, Bonnifield focuses on the long-term successful struggle of the local farmers against a natural disaster affecting their whole farming culture and industry. On the other hand, Worster's account is about the arrogance of humanity and the failure of human beings to accommodate themselves to nature. Whose version of the events is best?

From an 'oppositional' point of view, there is no simple answer to this question, as both versions may occur to historians and be legitimated. Part of the problem is obviously their divergent (optimistic versus pessimistic) conclusions on the series of events they present. But conclusions, as necessary as they might be, are only one part of an historical narrative. It is, therefore, more than the conclusion that should inform people's evaluation of the stories they encounter. For Cronon, the historian's selection of where the story begins and ends in the *longue durée* of historical events 'profoundly alters its shape and meaning.'[32] If the beginning of the story of the Great Plains, for example, was shifted to encompass the Native past, the focus and meaning of the study would likely change. But aside from the length or duration of the historical sequence, the moral of it is also (and perhaps predominantly) shaped by the morality of the historians. As moral and political actors, Cronon maintains, historians commit themselves to understanding and judging the past fairly, but they do so within their own historical positionalities. 'Being American, being male, being white, being an upper-middle-class academic,' he concludes, 'I write in particular ways that are not all of my own choosing, and my biases are reflected in my work.'[33] In this sense, different positionalities would inevitably lead to different evaluations of the perceived direction of change, whether as one of progress, decline, or collapse. It is thus extremely important for people to judge the merit of an account (as one of progress or decline), knowing that historians do have their own moral perspectives and, therefore, make specific judgments of progress or decline opposed to other judgments and capable even of being put together in a synthesis with other, opposing judgments.

Progress and Decline as Successional

The second stance concerning progress and decline is precisely the opposite. An instance of one of these concepts cannot occur at the same time as one of the other. Faith in humanity, from this standpoint, means that one concept (progress) must inevitably be perceived as superior to the other (decline). This revolutionary idea emerged during the

Enlightenment. When philosophers conceptualized the modern idea of progress, they also enthusiastically spread the belief that progress is not only general but also continuous and desirable. Regression or decline ceases, for them, to be equal, or oppositional, to progress. 'Every regression, decline, or decay,' as Koselleck puts it, 'occurs only partially and temporarily.'[34] The consequence, for him, is that progress evolves in a unique direction in history: from its universalization to its reference as a guiding principle.

In the first phase, the idea of progress presented by Voltaire, Condorcet, and later by Kant, Buckle, and Acton became rapidly universalized to the whole Western world in the nineteenth century. It no longer referred to a delimited aspect of life (science, technology, art, or morality) but soon expanded to the whole idea of humanity. 'The subject of progress,' Koselleck observes, 'was expanded to become an agent of the highest generality, or one with a forced claim to generality: it was a question of the progress of humanity.'[35] In its second phase, progress became 'the historical agent,' in that it ceased to be a concept of study and turned into a leading agent in history, such as 'the progress of time,' 'the progress of Canada,' or more broadly 'the progress of history.' Finally, in its last phase, progress came to stand alone, as an end in itself. It came to be legitimated without being progressive or even set in succession or opposition to decline. It has become a political catchword that is largely employed rhetorically, notably by political parties in such forms as 'progressive conservative.' The existence and importance of this idea would be such that 'it has become difficult to gain political legitimacy without being progressive at the same time.'[36]

The consequences of this gradual shift are obvious and serious. First, progress and decline fell into an asymmetric relationship. Claims of historical progress and decline not only occur consecutively, but the decline takes place just partially and temporarily. From this point of view, decline turns out to be a stepping stone leading to further historical progress (such as in the popular French saying *reculer pour mieux sauter*).[37]

The second consequence of this development is the conceptualization of progress as a 'collective singular.'[38] By virtue of its universalization, progress now ties together and, perhaps more problematically, simplifies many human experiences, describing them by a single term, 'advance.' Because of this limiting situation, it is no longer possible to talk about the development of the divergent and manifold aspects of human life (scientific, technological, moral, artistic, and historical) (as

Cronon did with his competing stories of the Great Plains), but only of universal progress. 'Humans,' Koselleck ironically concludes, 'are [now] condemned to progress.'[39]

One of the most revealing examples of this view of progress was presented in 1770 by Louis-Sébastien Mercier in his book *L'An 2440*, which was subsequently published in English as *Memoirs of the Year Two Thousand Five Hundred*.[40] A veritable progressive thinker of his own time, Mercier envisaged what modern civilization (i.e., that of France) would be like in the year 2440. Human societies live in continuous harmony, rarely disrupted by war. Slavery is abolished, and the Pope has ceased to exercise a dominant influence over socio-political affairs. Cities are built on scientific plans, with adequate sanitary services and hospitals. Marriages are contracted only through mutual inclination, and dowries have been abolished. More interesting to educators, public education is now *de rigueur*. It plays a key role in promoting rationality, mutual exchange, better uses of language, and morality. School history has long been abandoned for its irrelevance. It has been replaced by subjects that give students true and useful ideas.

In his chapter on education, imaginatively entitled 'The College of Quatre Nations,' Mercier wrote, 'They formerly taught youth a multiplicity of knowledge that in no degree conducted to the happiness of life ... We [now] teach them little history, because history is the disgrace of humanity, every page being crowded with crimes and follies. God forbid that we should set before their eyes such examples of rapine and ambition. By the pedantry of history, kings have been raised to gods. We teach our children a logic more certain, and ideas more just.'[41] Mercier was never remembered as a creative Enlightenment intellectual, even in his own civilization of France. If, as Bury observes, it would be exaggerated to claim that he represented the soul of his age, he was assuredly 'one of its characteristic products.'[42] Progress was definitely a collective singular leading to the perfectibility of humanity.

5.2 Principles for Judging Change as Signifying Progress and Decline

Knowing how the relational concepts of progress and decline have been developed and disseminated helps us understand historical thinking. But it still does not address the earlier question of what criteria might be employed for judging the direction of change. How is it possible to assess the contrasting moral beliefs and conclusions of

Cronon's Great Plains stories if historians have no agreed-on criteria for making such evaluative judgments?

To this day, historians and philosophers debate the value of the concepts of progress and decline. For Collingwood, these concepts cannot be employed in meaningful ways in history. Because their use depends on a subjective point of view, progress and decline are irrelevant to historical scholarship, except perhaps in the generic sense of the unfolding of historical change. 'A change that is really a progress seen from one end,' he once argued, 'is no less really a decadence, seen from the other.'[43]

But more problematic to him was the fact that progress and decline could not do justice to the complexity of the past that historians investigate. Three reasons were provided by Collingwood. First, he believed that each historical event or period (what he called 'phase') is unique and thus cannot be compared with others as being relatively one of advance or regress. Human actors, he noted, 'found themselves confronted by a unique situation, which gave rise to a unique problem, or the eternal problem in a unique form.'[44] Thus, each event or period in history should be accepted on its own terms. These events cannot be compared or judged as being an improvement or decay over the other, because it would necessitate the comparison of totally distinct sets of circumstances and historical realities. 'Bach,' he observed, 'was not trying to write like Beethoven and failing; Athens was not a relatively unsuccessful attempt to produce Rome; Plato was himself, not a half-developed Aristotle.'[45]

Equally problematic for Collingwood was the fact that historians only study particular sequences of events and thus lack a clear direction for history as a whole. As I have already suggested, the inherent structure of the narrative, with its beginning and end, clearly shapes historians' interpretations of change. The result, for Collingwood, was the absence of an all-encompassing historical understanding of the past with its interrelations and various aspects of life, as in Braudel's *longue durée* of history. As Collingwood put it, 'So far as we can see history as a whole, that is how we see it; as a continuous development in which every phase consists of the solution of human problems set by the preceding phase. But that is only an ideal for the historian; that is what he knows history would look like if he could see it as a whole, which he never can. In point of fact, he can only see it in bits; he can only be acquainted with certain periods, and only competent in very small parts of those periods.'[46] Finally, Collingwood claimed that progress and decline could not be employed in meaningful ways within the realms of art, happiness, and morality. As different ages find and define happiness or morality in different ways, it is impossible for historians to judge events in these spheres of human life as those of progress or decline, without anachronistically imposing their own presentist values on the past. Using the concrete example of one's home, he asserted, 'Different ways of life are differentiated by nothing more clearly than by differences between the things that people habitually enjoy, the conditions which they find comfortable, and the achievements they regard as satisfactory. The problem of being comfortable in a medieval cottage is so different from the problem of being comfortable in a modern slum that there is no comparing them; the happiness of a peasant is not contained in the happiness of a millionaire.'[47] For Collingwood, the same would hold true for art. '[Because] a particular age has the task of realizing beauty in a particular way,' he argued, it cannot be assessed 'in terms of any other.'[48] Artists were not, for him, interested in progress, because their works were not about trying to improve or change what had been done. Their works were influenced by different ideals and aims and thus cannot be interpreted by a single teleology of improvement or decadence. 'There is development in art,' he concluded, 'but no progress ... every fresh work of art is the solution of a fresh problem which arises not out of a previous work of art but out of the artist's unreflective experience.'[49]

Collingwood's 'prudential' ideas of progress offer extremely useful advice for historians. Contemporary actors are often prompted to judge their predecessors' actions from a progressive teleological view of history. As Butterfield made it clear, by looking at the past exclusively in light of present-day standards 'historical personages can easily and irresistibly be classed into the men who furthered progress and the men who tried to hinder it.'[50] But, as useful as Collingwood's ideas might be, they do not necessarily equip contemporary actors with pertinent tools to evaluate developments in history. How is it possible to claim, as Wright does, that Western civilization is typical of failed societies at their zenith? How are historians, and ultimately society, supposed to judge conflicting pessimistic and optimistic views of humanity and orient themselves in what appears to be a critical moment in historical time?

At least three principles seem to have emerged for judging the direction of change in history. These principles do not in themselves tell historians whether or not events should be understood as signifying progress, but they can at least guide historians in making evaluative judgments. For practical purposes, I have named these principles as follows: (1) continuous application; (2) equal importance; and (3) prudential relevance.

Continuous Application

The first principle invoked in judging the direction of historical change deals with the application of such a judgment to the whole historical period in question. I have argued that historical interpretation involves the study of a chain of events (with a beginning and ending point in time) structured by colligatory concepts. Continuous application implies that the standards historians employ to judge the direction of change – as being for better or worse – must apply to the whole period. 'In order to establish that in some sequence there has been progress,' as Gordon Graham argues, 'we must not only invoke a principle of evaluation, but also show that the principle invoked has continuous application to the beginning and end of the sequence.'[51]

The first principle is meant to prevent historians from anachronistically imposing contemporary norms or concepts on the past that would fit only certain of the changes occurring during the period and, thus, predispose the historian to view events as moving in some single direction – usually one of progress. To go back to my earlier example of diesel versus steam trains, it would be totally unfair to proclaim progress in modes of transportation from the Middle Ages to today with the exclusive use of the railroad as an evaluative concept, since trains were not available until the nineteenth century. To make such a judgment, historians would need to either change the period of study (e.g., change occurring from the nineteenth to the twentieth century) or add other concepts that do have a continuous application to the whole period (e.g., canoe, boat, horse and buggy) and would more accurately reveal the direction of change. The rule is, therefore, to employ standards or concepts for judging the progress or decline of the past applicable to the whole period, and not exclusively to portions of it.

Equal Importance

The second principle for judging the direction of historical change refers back to the earlier discussion of progress and decline as concepts of opposition versus succession. I have argued that viewing instances of these two concepts as occurring successively led to the Enlightenment belief in continuous progress. From this point of view, the concepts of decline and progress no longer appeared to be oppositional but asymmetrical. Progress is followed by temporal regressions that are essentially catalysts for new or further progress. Yet, the problem, as I have stated, is that historians have been unable as yet to discover a way of '*stating* the belief in progress which will enable [them] to relate the different dimensions of values.'[52] In other words, there is still no agreed-on standard in the discipline to move legitimately from domain-specific progress to overall human progress.

Thus, to overcome this flawed asymmetrical view of historical change, historians must recognize the value of both progress and decline so as to allow for the oppositional treatment of the subject, that is, permit the study of the notions of both progress and decline, even if they do not wish to explore both. This principle does not mean, for example, that historians cannot claim that the determination to survive of the U.S. inhabitants in the 'dust bowl' during the 1930s led to progressive developments in their communities. Rather, it suggests that historians must consent to an oppositional treatment of the same events by different, but equally valid, evaluative standards. Historians may thus speak of progress in certain aspects of life (e.g., standards of living) while recognizing, or at least leaving open, the possibility of interpreting aspects of the same past and evidence as instances of decline (e.g., environmental).[53] 'In the elaboration and defence of progressivism,' as Graham observes, 'it very evidently matters a great deal which parts of the world and its history [historians] look at, and just whose progress is under consideration.'[54]

Supporting this view, Cronon contends that part of the implicit beliefs of historians, when they write historical narratives, is their anticipation of peer-review criticism. Knowing that different positionalities or criteria for judging historical evidence may lead to different interpretations, historians must necessarily absorb – or at least recognize – contradictory accounts in their own historical constructs in order for their work. Contingency, as opposed to certainty, appears to be the rule here. As Cronon puts it, with reference to historical narratives, '[the] stories we write ... are judged not just as narratives, but as nonfictions. We construct them knowing that scholars will evaluate their accuracy, and knowing too that many other people and communities – those who have a present stake in the way the past is described – will also judge the fairness and truth of what we say.'[55]

Prudential Relevance

The last principle is more ambitious and contested in history because it relies on the concept of historical empathy (see chapter 7). The notion of prudential relevance starts from the premise that the principle of evaluation must apply to the entire historical period historians set for their investigation (continuous application). But it goes further in that it requires that the standard be applicable or relevant to the historical actors themselves. To claim that there is progress or decline, historians must be able to show that the actors included in a series of events could have met or worked toward attaining the standard that the historians employ to judge their actions.

Clearly, this principle is far more complex and demanding. Historians, for example, cannot criticize medieval monasteries for not being comprehensive schools if they never tried or were never given the opportunity to be such. This judgment would be totally unfair to past actors. The idea here is for historians to judge the direction of change, knowing that predecessors had different codes of behaviour informing their decisions and actions – codes and behaviours not necessarily recognized or valued today. To successfully employ the principle of prudential relevance, historians must have the re-enactable evidence necessary to recreate the events from the actors' historically situated perspective, so as to evaluate their appreciation of the standard in question (to show its relevance) and the possibility of their working toward it. The following school example may help explain this third principle.

To claim that the present-day system of public education is more progressive than in the Middle Ages, historians would have to demonstrate that the standards they used to make this judgment could be applied to the whole sequence in question and that they would be relevant to their own contemporaries and to predecessors as well. In practical terms, this means that the standards (e.g., literacy) must have been known and valued by educators for the whole period under consideration. Predecessors must have used or been in a position to use the standards themselves and, if feasible, would see present-day developments as progress in education.[56]

Contemporary historians, from this point of view, cannot claim that public education is more progressive than in medieval times, simply because students now learn how to operate computers. This would imply that medieval educators could have worked to meet this standard in their own time and would see this present-day development as progress. Conversely, historians cannot blame these educators for ignoring standards that were not available to them back then (i.e., standards not *relevant*). This judgment would amount to a purely presentist imposition on the past, likely to lead moderns to see predecessors as inherently inferior. Yet, if historians still wish to consider computer skills as a standard for the period, they could only legitimately claim a major historical development in education, but not progress. 'In saying that history is development,' as Jeffreys cautiously observes, 'there is therefore no intention of implying a general tendency of things to improve.'[57]

The situation gets more complicated when historians have to evaluate whether the selected standard is indeed applicable to past actors, something often more complicated than my computer illustration. Historians such as Ignatieff, for example, can rightly claim, with supporting evidence, that there has been significant progress in human rights since the sixteenth century. The problem emerges when they have to show that the standard of 'human rights' was not only available, or relevant, to past people but also one that they would have valued themselves and worked to meet in their own time and under their own conditions. In these circumstances, it may turn out that only a few societies could support the claim of human rights progressive optimists.

5.3 Students and the Concepts of Progress and Decline

Established at the height of the nineteenth-century Industrial Revolution and Western theories of human progress, public schools have traditionally conveyed a progressive and 'Whiggish' history to younger generations, with generous emphasis on the stories of national heroes and the superior moral character of the nation. 'Presentation of ideals and heroes from other ages,' nationalist historian Trevelyan once wrote, 'is perhaps the most important among the educative functions of history.'[58]

Consistent with this view, several studies have shown the importance of progress in school curricula and history textbooks.[59] 'The idea that the evolution of history teaching had produced an anglocentric narrative grounded in Protestantism, in praise of parliamentary democracy and purporting that Britain was racially superior,' historian Peter Yeandle argues, 'is not necessarily misleading.'[60] While the imperialist notion of British superiority has gradually faded away in British and Canadian history classrooms over the last century, Shemilt has nonetheless found that many students continue to hold a teleological view of historical progress, with history seen 'as a one-way street that does not admit of multiple traditions or lines of development.'[61] In a narrative explanation of the history of medicine, for example, British students almost naturally connected the acceleration of scientific knowledge over the last century with the inevitability of medical progress, notably in the fight against cancer. During the interview phase of Shemilt's study, the following exchange took place:

> *Student*: We know where medicine will be in the future: there'll be cures for cancer, electric hearts, brains even.
> *Interviewer*: O.K. Are you saying that these things *might* happen? Or do you think that they will happen *for certain*?
> *Student*: For certain! It's the way it's got to go.
> *Interviewer*: Why has it 'got to go' this way? Suppose we run out of money for medical research? Suppose that World War III breaks out and people lose faith in science?
> *Student*: I'm not sure how long it'll take. It might get held up like you say, but it might be quick since history has speeded up since 1900.[62]

In another British school-history project, Husbands, Kitson, and Pendry recently found that teachers often have to struggle with students' inherent beliefs in progress. 'Pupils,' they insist, 'prefer to believe that things get better over time.'[63] One teacher in particular talked about his encounter with this very issue when teaching the Holocaust and the recurrence of genocides in modern history. 'They don't like it sometimes, because they want a study in development to be about progress, things getting better, and this isn't. This isn't all. Sometimes it seems a lot worse over periods of time, and it challenges this assumption nearly all of them have got, that life gets better.'[64] The situation in British schools is far from unique. Studies conducted in North America offer similar cases in point. In an analysis of U.S. school-history narratives, Barton and Levstik contend that two colligatory concepts seem to structure the dominant story of America's past as presented to students: freedom and progress. They argue that the eighteenth-century rhetoric of 'life, liberty, and the pursuit of happiness' still pervades every aspect of U.S. history, from classroom, to museum, to popular culture. Using James Wertsch and Kevin O'Connor's research on college students' views of the origins of the United States, they conclude that almost every essay referred systematically to what they call the 'quest-for-freedom' narrative.[65] Explanations revolved almost entirely around the inherent will of a persecuted people to fight colonial oppression and acquire personal and collective freedom. In a related study, one student said that the U.S. Revolution is important because previously 'we didn't have our rights, we weren't free' and without it 'we wouldn't have freedom.'[66]

Furthermore, beliefs in the quest for freedom are closely related to the idea of progress. The westward expansion and the railroad, industrialization, the Emancipation Proclamation, and the women's and civil rights movements, along with developments in science and technology over the last century, all serve, for students, to provide unmistakable evidence of the inevitability of U.S. progress. Equally interesting is the perception among students not only that progress and decline are successional but also that the latter is essentially the basis for further U.S. progress. The Great Depression, for example, is often depicted as a history lesson useful to teach Americans that the United States was not 'the god of all countries,' and the Vietnam War 'taught us ... that we shouldn't go slowly into a war.'[67]

The recent French Canadian study by Létourneau and Moisan offers very different findings with regard to students' views of progress. Unlike their U.S. counterparts, young francophone Québécois cannot count on the political development of their society to establish a progressive narrative of their nation, as Québec is still a province of Canada. From the time of the British conquest of New France (1759), the historical experience of Québec has been, according to students, 'nothing but the expression of a conflict between archetypal francophones and anglophones.'[68] The result, for Létourneau, is that Québec students have developed a 'nostalgic and melancholic' history of their society that fails to follow the dominant tenets of the progressive narratives of French or North American nations. For him, school-history programs and teaching – along with a nostalgic collective memory, still vivid in political discourse and other *lieux de mémoire* (e.g., historically oriented movies, books, commemorations) – sustain and even reinforce many of the ideas presented in Québec students' non-progressive view of their history. But perhaps more fundamental to this explanation is the fact Québec students typically use a specific political agenda (national sovereignty) as a standard to evaluate the unique development of their society. If students were using 'citizenship rights,' 'collective affirmation,' or 'socio-economic prosperity' as standards to evaluate the direction of their collective history, their accounts of the past would likely provide different results.

Seixas and Clark's recent analysis of BC students also offers intriguing results from Canada.[69] As part of a regional contest on national history in 2001, student volunteers (grade 11) were asked to write a position statement on a controversy that struck the provincial legislature that same year. Displayed in the rotunda of the BC legislative assembly were four historical paintings, representing four qualities seen as necessary for the establishment and progress of civilization (courage, enterprise, labour, and justice). These paintings from the 1930s became the centre of a debate. First Nations people were largely offended by the colonialist paintings, notably the mural of 'labour,' which depicted bare-breasted Aboriginal women helping to build Fort Victoria under the supervision of white British men. The advisory panel that the provincial government set up to review the situation subsequently presented to the public with five possible options: maintain the murals as they are, maintain the murals with the addition of other materials, alter the murals, cover the murals, or remove the murals. Taking the panel's recommendations as an historical case study, the Canadian contest included a question asking for students' suggestions for ways of resolving the issue.

The analysis of students' responses is extremely interesting and pertinent to our understanding of the concepts of progress and decline. Because the purpose of the murals was to celebrate the establishment and progress of British civilization on the west coast, their evaluation necessarily entails an understanding of the relational concepts of progress and decline in BC history. Of the fifty-seven contest responses analysed, eighteen indicated that 'we have a responsibility to respect the past, regardless of whether we endorse the perspectives represented in its visual remains.'[70] These students recommended, therefore, maintaining the murals, either in their present location or in a museum for display. Yet, twenty-nine students suggested, instead, destroying or removing the murals, as they clearly represented a colonial tradition that hindered 'the move toward a more just society in which every member enjoys equal respect.'[71] More interesting were the eight students whose responses to the controversy indicated what Seixas and Clark call a 'modern type of historical consciousness.'[72] While these students proposed preserving the murals, they explicitly distanced themselves from the views and beliefs held at the time of the murals. These responses were, in some ways, consistent with my earlier discussion on progress and decline as concepts of opposition. Instead of viewing the four paintings as anachronistic representations for a modern progressive society, they considered them as objects of 'historical significance' and a 'teaching tool' for understanding changes in BC history.[73] In this sense, the paintings presented a discontinuity with the present but not inevitably or exclusively in a direction of progress or decline, as so many students suggested.

Teaching Standards of Progress and Decline

There is clearly no simple approach to understanding the direction of change in history. Students are exposed to a variety of sources of information about the past that use the nation, technology, science, or even civilization for specific moral claims. Presenting collective history as stories of inevitable freedom and progress seriously limits students' ability to critically evaluate the direction of historical change. 'In an era when the meaning of memory is openly debated,' Seixas and Clark claim, 'preparing students to engage in those debates assumes center stage.'[74]

Yet, part of the current educational problem is the limited focus of history curricula and learning materials on the study of progress and decline. If curricular objectives and textbook activities are often framed by such concepts (usually emphasizing progress), they are rarely presented as procedural concepts to be employed by students in judging the direction of historical change. Consider, for example, the introductory note of the overall rationale for a grade 10 course on twentieth-century Canadian history for applied-level students (written in 1999): 'This course traces Canadian history from [Prime Minister] Wilfrid Laurier's pronouncement that the twentieth century belongs to Canada to the United Nations' recognition of Canada as one of the best countries in which to live.'[75] While students are encouraged to study various individuals, communities, and changes in Canadian history, the introductory note (on Laurier and the United Nations) clearly structures the direction of the course for teachers. Implicit in the rationale is the belief that Canada not only changed over the period but also did so toward something better, which is encapsulated in the progress suggested by Laurier at the turn of the century. How are teachers and students supposed to conceptualize changes during the twentieth century in these circumstances? What influences do the current curriculum expectations have on students' understanding of the past? And of their future?

One way of addressing these questions would be to have teachers engage their students in the use of evaluative criteria in the study of the past (e.g., continuous application, equal importance, and prudential relevance) to allow for critical analysis of change in history. Unlike the British conceptualization of 'progression in historical thinking,' the criteria presented here should not be seen as entailing systematic progress toward sophisticated thinking about the past. In fact, the very idea of progression suggests that teachers and students are aware of the goals set by the researcher and are also working to achieve them. Yet, I have argued that this imposition on students' historical thinking could be highly misleading. Students, and their teachers, could be working with different (and possibly equally valuable) standards not recognized by the researcher. Therefore, we cannot blame them for their lack of progression if they never worked to meet the standards in question (prudential relevance). As a result, the three standards outlined here should be seen, more modestly, as complementary features of the teaching approach presented in the previous chapter, focused on chronological thinking and synoptic judgment.

First, it is important that students understand the chronology of the historical events and employ evaluative concepts that apply to the entire period. If students typically ascribe significance to the past according to their present-day questions, interests, or values, they must nonetheless avoid imposing on the events they study present-day standards not relevant to the whole period. This may seem a simple step in historical thinking, but it is often omitted or ignored.

To claim, for example, that there is overall progress in Canadian history during the twentieth century, one has to show that the standards used to make this evaluative claim apply to the whole of the twentieth century. Using the popular and largely accepted idea of Canada as 'the peacekeeping country of the world' as a standard, for instance, would be totally unfair to the history of the twentieth century, as the very concept of peacekeeping was invented only during the Cold War (by Lester B. Pearson). It thus misrepresents completely the first half of the period, as well as Canada's other military development, training, and efforts, notably during the world wars. As Granatstein recently put it, 'Canadians do not realize that the major reason the Canadian Forces have proven themselves capable of peacekeeping is that the nation trains its men and women for war.'[76] For him, not only is the concept of peacekeeping fallacious to describe Canada's historical progress, but a more accurate study of its development actually shows a significant decline in Canada's military support, strengths, and capacities during the twentieth century.

For all these reasons, it might be useful for teachers to have students consider the following questions when they wish to create and employ standards to judge historical change as of better or worse:

• Does the principle invoked have continuous application from the beginning to the end of the relevant period in history?
• Does the principle represent aspects of the past included in the period or events in question?

Second, students should be presented with events or case studies showing the value of, or support for, both progress and decline and thus allow for considerations of opposing perspectives on the past. '[The] narrative of freedom and progress,' Barton and Levstik contend, 'like all narratives, is a human construction rather than a mirror of reality.'[77] Therefore, it is important that students do not engage in merely intuitive historical practices that lead to the optimistic misrepresentation of humanity as inherently better now than in previous times. All advances in some aspects of human life inevitably lead to decline and possibly collapse in other aspects.

To favour a better appreciation of progress and decline as mutually compatible concepts and thus allow for oppositional treatments and perspectives on the past, teachers might find the following questions worth considering:

• Does the standard for progress or decline allow for oppositional treatment of the sequence of events in question?
• Have things progressed *and* declined during the same period? In what ways? For whom?
• Could the standard be generalized to overall human development? With what reservations?

Finally, students should learn to judge the past in terms of progress and decline, employing standards applicable and relevant to the past actors themselves. This last step adds another layer to the evaluative claims made by students. They should not only employ standards to judge events or cases applicable to the whole period but also avoid imposing such standards anachronistically on past actors (e.g., computer skills) to create a 'straw man' or make history support present-day claims of progress. This step is more complex and challenging because it requires that students recreate the sequence of events so as to mentally see – to imagine – whether the standards they employ were recognized and valued by predecessors as well. This empathetic task demands that students use their historical imaginations and contextualize the sources – something discussed in chapter 7.

To claim, for example, that Canada advanced in such a way during the twentieth century as to be considered 'one of the best countries in which to live,' students would have to use relevant standards and show that predecessors were working during the period to meet them and potentially aiming at making Canada one of the best countries. Taking the Declaration of Independence as an example, Appleby, Hunt, and Jacob contend that the progressive view of the Declaration as an instrument for securing the inherent rights of the U.S. people is misleading. 'Few people,' they argue, 'had earlier thought that these separate societies could or would want to unite as a nation; fewer still would have named an abstract philosophy of natural rights as the reason for their union.[78]

Clearly, this last step in judging the direction of change is intellectually demanding, as well as disputed, because it requires extensive content knowledge, as well as experience with historical inquiry and empathy. To guide students in this practice, the following questions might serve as basic elements:

- Is the standard for progress or decline relevant to the whole period in question?
- Were predecessors aware of, and interested in meeting, this standard? According to what source or sources?
- Were predecessors working to meet the standard?
- Would predecessors, using the same standard, recognize present-day developments as those of progress or decline?

5.4 Conclusion

Students, teachers, and the public, no less than historians, are engaged in complex relations with the past. They not only ascribe significance to diverse and sometimes competing aspects of it but also structure their understanding by assigning some direction and value to it. As things have changed, have they improved? Making evaluative judgments about the past is a difficult and contentious practice. Part of the problem is the lack of agreed-on standards in the discipline to make such judgments. Since the Enlightenment the widespread secular belief that replaced faith in divine providence has favoured the inevitability of human progress, notably because of rapid and triumphant developments in science and technology. Yet, this understanding is deceptive, as it misrepresents the relation between contemporary and historical perceptions of progress and decline.

To help educators and students face these complex issues as they engage in the interpretation of the past, I have presented a set of three principles: continuous application, equal importance, and prudential relevance. These principles do not, in themselves, indicate the direction of historical change. More modestly, they are analytic principles with which contemporary actors may evaluate the past without naively imposing current standards, too often attesting to a progressive present-day teleology.

School history in the Western world has traditionally endorsed a progressive view of the collective past, with all the consequences that such an optimistic philosophy entails. It would be too easy to blame past and even present-day students (and educators) for paying no attention to the contested nature of progress in human history. Such an evaluative judgment would be premature and inappropriate. To claim that students should have thought differently about progress and decline, it would be necessary to demonstrate that these young people were actually in a position to engage in practices that historians now recognize as improvement. In most cases it would be impossible to find hard evidence to support that allegation. What would be more appropriate in the present circumstances would be to recognize that generations of students confronted conditions that may have not permitted them to view the world differently. This does not excuse them for what students did or did not do, but it may put a stop to the current tendency of seeing past actors as inherently inferior and ill-advised. To go back to my introductory comments, one may wonder, in light of this discussion, whether Malthus was fundamentally wrong in his pessimistic thinking. Was he really mistaken or simply ahead of his time?

6 How Do We Make Sense of the Raw Materials of the Past? – Evidence

> We accept memory as a premise of knowledge; we infer history from evidence that includes other people's memories. Unlike memory, history is not given but contingent: it is based on empirical sources which we can decide to reject for other versions of the past.
>
> – David Lowenthal[1]

As part of the global war on terror, President George W. Bush confidently addressed the UN General Assembly in September 2002. In his controversial President's remarks, he declared to the international community that despite UN sanctions, Iraq under Saddam Hussein represented a dangerous and immediate threat to the stability of the Middle East, the United States, and ultimately the entire world. Saddam Hussein's use of weapons of mass destruction (WMD) over the last decades was, for President Bush, the chief reason to lead a 'coalition of the willing' that would disarm him promptly.

> We know that Saddam Hussein pursued weapons of mass murder even when inspectors were in his country. Are we to assume that he stopped when they left? The history, the logic, and the facts lead to one conclusion: Saddam Hussein's regime is a grave and gathering danger. To suggest otherwise is to hope against the evidence. To assume this regime's good faith is to bet the lives of millions and the peace of the world in a reckless gamble. And this is a risk we must not take.[2]

President Bush was not alone in his crusade against the 'axis of evil.' Following an assessment by the United Nations Monitoring, Verification, and Inspection Commission (UNMOVIC) in January 2003, Secretary of State Colin Powell asserted in an address to the UN Security Council, on 5 February of the same year, that sources unmistakably indicated Iraq had reconstructed its nuclear weapons program, along with its programs for biological and chemical weapons and an entire fleet of vehicles capable of delivering these weapons. He declared,

> What you will see is an accumulation of facts and disturbing patterns of behavior. The facts on Iraqis' behavior – Iraq's behavior demonstrate that Saddam Hussein and his regime have made no effort – no effort – to disarm as required by the international community. Indeed, the facts and Iraq's behavior show that Saddam Hussein and his regime are concealing their efforts to produce more weapons of mass destruction ... My colleagues, every statement I make today is backed up by sources, solid sources. These are not assertions. What we're giving you are facts and conclusions based on solid intelligence.[3]

Four years after these firm declarations, and inconclusive UN- and U.S.-led inspections of Iraqi facilities and military equipment, Iraq's program for WMD has proved to be highly hypothetical – even fabricated. Even the two apparent 'biological laboratories,' found in the summer of 2003 and reported around the world as 'hard evidence' of mobile germ warfare labs, turned out to be simple military trailers used by the Iraqi army to produce hydrogen gas for artillery weather balloons. The situation was such that Dr Hans Blix, leader of UNMOVIC in Iraq, did not hesitate in November 2003 to blame the British and U.S. governments for advancing political claims and promoting military interventions backed only by weak intelligence.

> [These governments] had the difficulties of interpretations. Satellite images are very objective. But the satellite team don't tell you what is under the roofs. President Bush was able to say in the autumn of 2002 that they had seen how some nuclear installations had been recently extended, and he said, 'I don't know what more evidence is needed.' Well, sorry, they didn't see what was underneath ... But I don't think that they could have sold the war to the public by simply saying that we are uncertain. They sold it on the ground that we know for certain that there are weapons of mass destruction and that they are close to getting a nuclear weapon – they can get it soon.[4]

Even Secretary of State Colin Powell had no choice but to admit in

April 2004 that the information used in his rallying speech of February 2003 'appears not to be ... that solid,'[5] thus acknowledging publicly the failure of his government to support claims for military intervention with solid evidence. 'The truth,' Deputy Secretary of Defense Paul Wolfowitz bluntly recognized later, 'is ... that we settled on the one issue that everyone could agree on which was weapons of mass destruction as the core reason.'[6] As the Carnegie Endowment for International Peace states in its report *WMD in Iraq*, the critical situation that led to the war in Iraq is far from unique in the history of international conflicts but raises important questions for twenty-first-century interventions: Did the Iraqi apparent WMD threat to the United States and (or) global security justify unilateral military intervention? Did intelligence services and governments misrepresent what was known or unknown, to promote their political agenda? And, ultimately, could democratic states engage their citizens in war without defensible evidence justifying doing so?

The collection of, reference to, and use of evidence are fundamental to any authority, from that of teachers, to that of politicians, to that of professional historians. The 'struggle with the evidence,' to paraphrase French historian Marc Bloch, remains key to getting the facts right, establishing new knowledge, or engaging fellow citizens in collective ventures. Evidence 'is ground for belief.'[7] Only with evidence can people reasonably approve or disapprove a particular claim or conclusion. Without it, everything becomes relative and a matter of one's faith – my belief is as good as yours. 'Facts are stubborn things,' John Adams famously claimed in his defence of the British soldiers involved in the Boston Massacre of 1770, 'and whatever may be our wishes, our inclinations, or the dictates of our passions, they cannot alter the state of facts and evidence.'[8]

The introduction of a meticulous and critical approach to evidence of the past was Ranke's first principle of scientific history. To this day, it remains one of the key elements distinguishing the discipline from literature or antiquarianism. Yet, evidence does not easily find its way into the history classroom, being often lost in transit through the archives, historians, publishers, bureaucrats, and teachers.

Typically, two general justifications have been offered for the use of evidence in history education: public analysis of knowledge and the understanding of historical knowledge. I have illustrated in the introduction to this chapter that reference to evidence can hardly be avoided in public affairs, even if this process may imply a deliberate subordination of sources to predetermined objectives, such as those of political partisanship. The intellectual ability to collect, process, analyse, and cross-reference evidence is crucial to an informed citizenry. As part of its contribution to citizenship education, school history can favour the development of the attitudes and skills of democratic reasoning, using past or contemporary evidence. 'To use history to understand the present or to solve modern problems,' Barton and Levstik claim, 'students must be able to analyse the creation of historical accounts so that they will be able to determine how well supported a claim is by the available evidence.'[9]

But there is also a second, disciplinary justification of evidence in history education: understanding historical knowledge. 'Historians,' Husbands observes, 'only have access to the past via its remains: we cannot, therefore, acquire any historical understandings without addressing historical evidence.'[10] Indeed, like astronomers scrutinizing distant stars, historians study places and subjects that are generally beyond their own observation. Because these cannot be observed or experienced directly, any knowledge of the past has therefore to be mediated by what has survived into the present: relics and records. Yet relics and records, despite coming from the past, remain largely silent until historians start to question them and create some interpretative answers. Relics, as C.R. Cheney admirably put it, 'like the little children of long ago, only speak when they are spoken to, and they will not talk to strangers.'[11]

In this chapter, I analyse how historians make sense of the past using evidence. First, I explain the need to develop research questions and select relics from the past according to these questions. Then, I discuss the problems and limits of evidence in historical inquiry and the necessity of evaluating critically the sources employed in terms of both external and internal criticism. In the last section, I look at the challenges of engaging students in the collection and evaluation of sources and propose an approach based on four interrelated steps (research questions, collection and selection of evidence, analysis, and interpretative answers).

6.1 From Relics to Evidence: The Necessity of Questions

What relics and records of the past should be selected for study? On what grounds? These simple questions have been central to the work of historians since the time of Ranke. 'Only by comprehensive historical investigation,' Ranke argued, 'can we aspire to a divining perception of the deeply hidden, all-embracing spiritual laws.'[12] The claim made by Ranke is straightforward: historians can know the past ('what actually happened') only if they study the sources originating at the time of the events under consideration. These 'primary sources' of the past were, for him, the most important pieces of information surviving into the present. Historians' truthful re-creation and explanation of what happened would only be possible if their investigation relied primarily on what was left behind (relics and records), and not on what could be inferred directly or indirectly from the original authorities (i.e., the 'secondary sources').[13] But the traces left behind by human actors have their own intricacies. They appear in various forms, shapes, and locations. In many ways, everything resulting from human action could be considered a trace or evidence of the past. A distinction between evidence-as-relic and evidence-as-record might be useful here.[14]

On the one hand, relics such as potteries, ships in decay, bones, arrowheads, and castles are traces that have survived into the present and wait to be questioned and analysed by historians. It is only when historians select and question them that such traces become historical evidence. Records, on the other hand, are pieces of information such as letters, diaries, photographs, and books that provide historians with some evidential arguments about the past. Like relics, they may also originate at the time of the event, but they are not as mute because they do provide historians with some first-hand information in visual or print form. As useful as records might be, they must nonetheless be analysed carefully because they do not always expressly reveal what happened. A personal or confidential letter, for example, can expose historians to a first-hand account of a particular situation but may conceal information or express it in a way foreign to contemporary historians.

Despite all these problems, some more fundamental than others, relics and records are central to the historian's craft. They are, with secondary sources (which exist only by virtue of the primary), the raw materials historians have for crafting their work. As Husbands observes, the primary sources 'are not, in themselves, "history," or "the past," but they provide one basis for constructing historical knowledge.'[15] Yet, historians know very well that it is practically impossible for them to study everything about the past under investigation, even if such evidence may appear to be sparse. They must necessarily be selective in their own investigations, as evidenced in my earlier discussion of historical significance (chapter 3). Whereas certain historians maintain that contact with the evidence precedes the formation of questions and topics for inquiry, many others believe that the analytic process for getting at and selecting evidence emerges from the questions historians have about aspects of the past. Although both (the evidence-based and the question-based) methods are possible in history, the second one is not only the common-sense approach to historical investigation but also the one that 'corresponds to most people's idea of research.'[16] As Dewey, strong advocate of inquiry-based strategies in education, once declared, 'anything that may be called knowledge, or a known object, marks a question answered.'[17]

In support of this view, it could be maintained that a great deal of historical inquiry has indeed attempted to answer specific questions about the past, including the nature of history itself (e.g., E.H. Carr's *What Is History?*). Historical research, from this question-based standpoint, becomes a sort of problem-solving approach applied to past actions and events. Collingwood suggested that every generation of historians must rewrite history, not so much because new evidence has emerged from the past, but because 'every new historian, not content with giving new answers to old questions, must revise the questions themselves.'[18] In other words, because historical investigations depend on questions, different questions may lead historians to different inquiries, evidence, and histories. For the same past, there can be more than one possible and defensible account of what happened – something completely overlooked by Ranke.

6.2 Problems and Limits of Evidence

This understanding of the manifold nature of historical inquiry is complex. The pitfalls in selecting and using historical evidence are many, and the methods of selecting evidence are often unknown to laypersons. It is thus necessary to be astute not only in selecting a significant topic and asking appropriate questions about the past but also in assessing the selected evidence. Historians must listen attentively to the possible voices coming from the sources, keeping in mind that sources, notably relics, do not talk to strangers and only speak when they are spoken to.

Initially trained as a philologist, Ranke was well aware of the problems and nuances of sources in historiography. He thus conscientiously alerted his colleagues to the necessity of being extremely careful in selecting and critically examining the sources. Historians must first root out forgeries and falsifications, and then test sources for both the internal consistency of each source and its consistency with other sources. Following Ranke, various history education scholars have offered their own particular sets of habits of mind (or 'heuristics') to be employed by novices engaged in source analysis. In 1909, for example, Fling developed an historical method based on a series of related steps (or questions) that he used with his own students to study past sources and construct warranted interpretations: genuineness (Is the document authentic? How can we tell?), value of the source (Is this a correct record of the facts?), localization (Who wrote it? When? Where?), affirmation (How does the source prove the facts? How does it compare with other sources), and interpretation (What is the overall affirmation of the source? What other affirmations or assertions can be made from the source? With what reservations?).[19]

More recently, Dickinson, Lee, Wineburg, Barton, and VanSledright, to name but a few, have also proposed related source heuristics to encourage the critical evaluation of evidence and thereby initiate students into historical investigation. A review of these various methods suggests at least four interrelated steps (or stages) in evaluating selected evidence: (1) identification; (2) attribution; (3) contextualization; and (4) corroboration. For conceptual purposes, I have regrouped these steps into two broader categories: external criticism and internal criticism.

External Criticism

One of the first tasks when historians evaluate selected evidence is to study carefully its nature and origin, that is, to analyse critically the source itself, not its content per se. Two related steps are *de rigueur* when one considers external criticism. First, it is necessary to *identify* the source by asking a number of key questions to clarify its nature. What type of source is it? What is its physical appearance? When was it created? Has the source changed over time? How does it come to be here?

I have already noted that sources can be distinguished as *primary* and *secondary* (or derivative). Yet, this distinction, fundamental though it is to the work of historians, is highly problematic. If primary sources are those most immediately related to the past, it is naive to believe that they are inevitably the purest pieces of evidence. Like secondary sources, many primary sources are inaccurate, as they could be either eye-witness accounts based on partisan perspective or relics purposely designed or forged to mislead people (then or now). Perhaps one of the most infamous fraudulent relics in the history of science is the 'Pilt-down man,' discovered in the Piltdown quarry in Sussex, England, in 1912. The Piltdown man (or *Eoanthropus dawsoni*) was discovered by archaeologist Charles Dawson, who believed he had found the 'missing link,' a skull representing a mixture of human and ape, with the noble brow of *Homo sapiens* and a primitive jaw. Although the initial reaction to the finding in the scientific community was mixed, British palaeontologists were enthusiastic about the discovery. It took over 40 years, and advanced scientific testing, to finally discover that the Piltdown man was a deliberately forged fossil made up of human, orang-utan, chimpanzee, and even hippopotamus bones and teeth from various ages. According to Michael Hammond, who studied the case in the 1970s, a key reason why the hoax convinced scientists for such a long time was that it fit in well with the evolution theories of the period, notably in England.[20]

Further complicating the distinction between primary and secondary is the fact that some sources are both primary and derivative. The *History of the Peloponnesian War*, for example, is clearly a secondary account of the war, written during and after the conflict (which took place during 431–404 BCE) by Thucydides. Yet, for whoever is interested in the history of antiquity and Greek politics (the *polis*), Thucydides' history is one of the most valuable primary sources of the time. Thus, the origin and proximity of a source to the events it depicts do not automatically and permanently situate it in one or other of these mutually exclusive categories. Whether a source is primary or secondary all depends on its historical context and the use made of it by historians. Put simply, in some instances the same source may be considered primary; and in another instance, secondary. Primary and secondary sources are, from this point of view, necessary to the craft of historians, but their label or initial proximity to the period cannot be taken simply at face value. If both types of sources can be (and often are) relative and incomplete, they each uniquely contribute to better answering the questions asked by historians.

The second heuristic step when one is engaged in external criticism involves a meticulous analysis of the construction of the source by *attributing* it to its author or authors. Two key questions should guide this inquiry. Who produced the source? And for what purpose? With respect to the intentions of their authors, sources can be divided into two types: those unintended and those intended for posterity. The first

category, called by Bloch 'evidence of witnesses in spite of themselves,'[21] refers to sources that have survived but were not produced
intentionally for posterity (e.g., pottery, minutes, and diaries). They are,
in a way, private sources of information produced or recorded by people during the period. These sources may be artifacts, personal correspondence, private letters, or diaries providing external readers a first-
hand account of confidential dialogues or personal reflections on issues
or relations. They are not 'filtered,' so to speak, by the 'external' requirements of being published or of being read by a larger audience,
although diaries and minutes can sometimes be intended for the public.
These sources unintended for posterity are generally regarded by historians as extremely rich and compelling, as they may (and often do) provide contrasting views and opinions.

Yet, they also have their own intricacies. If their authors did not necessarily want to preserve them for posterity, and far less for historical
research, they still reflect their authors' unique perspectives. Unintended sources were produced for clear purposes (e.g., to record personal thoughts as a sort of *aide-mémoire* or to communicate or exchange
private information with loved ones) often unknown to historians. Cor-
respondences, for example, are written to a particular reader and thus
imply a private dialogue not necessarily shared in the available documents. In the same way, artifacts such as a Native arrowhead can be
extremely silent on their origin (European, Aboriginal?) and purpose
(hunting, fighting, ornament?).

However, the author may have little genuine understanding or direct
experience of the event, writing personal notes from hearsay, or diverse
sources could provide contrasting views of the event because of each
author's unique participation in it. War diaries are typical. For the same
battle, soldiers, depending on their perspective and position, have frequently reported very different accounts of what happened. Historian
Stephen Ambrose, for example, collected over 1,400 different soldiers'
accounts of D-Day to write his book *D-Day: The Climactic Battle of World
War II*. One U.S. veteran, Private Felix Branhan, expressed the difference of perspective in these terms in the book: 'Each one of us had our
own little battlefield. It was maybe forty-five yards wide. You might
talk to a guy who pulled up right beside of me, within fifty feet of me,
and he got an entirely different picture of D-Day.'[22] This conclusion is
shared by another World War II veteran, Lieutenant Sidney Salomon,
who, 'up until noon D-Day ... thought the invasion was a failure and ...
wondered if we could make a successful withdrawal and try the invasion some time again in the near future.'[23]

Hence, it is important for historians to keep in mind that the private nature of the source, however sincere and vivid it may be, does not automatically make it reliable for historians. On the contrary, unintended sources can sometimes blur a complex situation simply because of the unique historical language used in the text, the concealed and intimate dialogue between the authors (in the case of correspondence), or the totally different perspectives on the same event. Equally problematic, print materials present only the voices of literate individuals, more likely found in the middle and upper classes of society, not the 'silent' voices of the illiterate. Finally, recent findings suggest that those who keep diaries – a practice dating back to medieval times – would be atypical persons who are more likely to 'suffer from insomnia, headaches, [and] social dysfunction.'[24]

But sources can also be purposely created by authors for the benefit of posterity. Unlike unintended sources, these tend to be more official and accessible because institutions, rather than chance or private interest, contributed to their creation and survival. Historically, the state and the Church were (and in many ways continue to be) the most important source-keeping institutions in the West. It is no surprise, therefore, that historians typically consult them in their search for and collection of evidence from the past. Unlike unintended sources, evidence left for posterity unveils a public or official character. Parliamentary speeches, ministerial memoranda, cabinet minutes, state statistics, provincial or local regulations, to name but a few, were all recorded with the intent of leaving evidence for the future. The same could be said of Church records, newspapers, memoirs, or business records. The authors of these sources were not only recording information for themselves but doing so for publicly acceptable motives that may even be accepted today, although historians must treat these sources extremely carefully.

Though they can fit either the primary or the derivative categories, or both, their authors included only what they considered relevant for the public or posterity: what politicians wanted to reveal or conceal, what journalists could access and legitimately convey to their readers, what editors thought would be marketable, and so on. Historians, therefore, must analyse carefully the official intents of their authors, keeping in mind that external factors (reading accessibility, market, propaganda, censorship, etc.) may have shaped the way such evidence was presented. It is thus necessary to meticulously study the author's and (or) publisher's credentials and motivations and go behind the official words or phrasing of the text. A recent article published in the *National Post* (a Canadian newspaper) illustrates this sourcing difficulty. Using a story from the British news agency, Reuters, on 14 September 2004, the newspaper purposely altered the phrase, 'the al-Aqsa Martyrs Brigades, which has been involved in a four-year-old revolt against Israeli occupation in Gaza and the West Bank,' to read, 'the al-Aqsa Martyrs Brigades, *a terrorist group* that has been involved in a four-year-old campaign of violence against Israel.'[25] Reuters rapidly informed the *National Post* of this unusual and unacceptable journalistic practice of changing the original wording of a news *communiqué*. Yet, defending its editorial policy, the *National Post*'s Kelly McParland responded in the following terms: 'I know something about this situation, because I'm the one who changed the wording. The reason was simple. The original story didn't come close to conveying to readers what al-Aqsa is really all about ... From the point of view of the wire services, it's possible to understand why they would be wary of demonizing organizations as transparently deserving of it as al-Qaeda or al-Aqsa. The wires ... have to operate in dozens of countries, transmitting copy to subscribers in dozens, maybe hundreds, more. That's a lot of differing cultures to keep happy, and so they strive to find words that are the least likely to offend.'[26] The blatant response of the *National Post*'s McParland is telling: newspapers are entitled to deliberately modify the wording of a news agency's story to reflect the ideology of their editors and subscribers, even if the modifications can cause serious political or epistemological imbroglios about the changes themselves. Clearly, there is a lot at stake with this type of reasoning, which only amplifies the necessity of a critical examination of sources.

With the advancement of communications and computer technology, electronic sources create an additional challenge for historians – so much that one historian recently acknowledged the growing need of 'digital literacy' for history students.[27] Millions of print materials (past or contemporary) are now available on the Internet, raising several research and archival questions, notably those of reliability and long-term accessibility. Digital sources, as David Trask puts it, are no longer 'grounded in space and time and are therefore immune to many of the traditional validation tests that could establish their "authority."'[28] If digital collections from museums and public archives now allow researchers, and even schools and the public, to access more rapidly and comprehensively (virtually anywhere around the world in any language) archival materials from their own office computers, other forms of electronic sources are more problematic. Electronic newspapers and magazines are, for that matter, extremely vulnerable.

The low barriers to electronic publication have resulted in a multiplicity of private websites presenting 'official' information that could in fact easily serve as a deceiving *trompe l'œil* for historians or any reader. Many Internet sites (e.g, *Wikipedia*) do not hold to strict professional or ethical standards for their content or simply lack any official authorship. It becomes, therefore, tremendously difficult for historians to critically analyse the reliability of the source and the attribution of its content, as so much is made available easily and fraudulently in electronic form. 'This lack of control,' Thomas Dynneson, Richard Gross, and Michael Berson conclude, 'makes the Internet a poor research source for those who are ill-equipped to critically analyze sources of information because information can be invented, rapidly changed, or deleted.'[29]

One of the best pieces of advice to offer teachers about these new types of sources is to rigorously supervise students' experiences and access to electronic materials by prescribing some valid sites already recognized for their reliability (e.g., national archives). These tend to be websites with official electronic addresses (Uniform Resource Locators – URLs) with domain suffixes such as *.gov* (U.S. government agencies), *.org* (official or non-commercial organizations), or *.edu* (U.S. educational institutions) or international domain suffixes, such as *.ca* (official Canadian sites, including governmental and educational institutions). Given the growing number of electronic sources and the poor reliability of Web search engines, some professional organizations also monitor and evaluate websites for their content reliability and educational usefulness; these include www.medialit.org, www.media-awareness.ca, www.webquest.sdsu.edu, and www.historymatters.gmu.edu.[30]

There seems also to be, so far, no clear policy or procedure for storing electronic sources for posterity. Sources deliberately recorded on read-only CDs, DVDs, or microfilms (such as databases) pose fewer problems, as they can always be physically stored, archived, and retrieved. Yet, most Internet sources, including official governmental websites, do not have clear archival procedures known to users. In some cases, research tools are available for detailed archival research, but many sites allow retrieval for a short period only (e.g., seven days). Equally challenging for historians, there is no clear rule on the archival location of these electronic sources. The original electronic addresses are sometimes changed or the document simply removed without notice for reasons of storage, thus resulting in major difficulties for other scholars retrieving such documents. So far, most publishers and editors, as well as the leading style manuals, in academic circles appear to be following the same rule for using and referencing such electronic sources. The Web location of the source (the URL) must be clearly and explicitly identified, along with the author (if available) and date when the file was retrieved electronically.[31] Some users may even take the extra precaution of printing a hard copy of the source with the Internet link and date of access, thus providing a copy for future use and reference. Unless changes are made to the current policies and procedures for archiving and protecting electronic sources, notably, electronic periodicals, current and future evidence produced exclusively on electronic platforms will be extremely difficult for historians to investigate.

Internal Criticism

Although necessary, the external criticism of a source is only one (preliminary) step in assessing historical evidence. The second task is to study carefully the content of the source to establish its (1) internal validity; and (2) reliability. As for the first step, two interrelated moves are essential: contextualizing and corroborating the source.

Once the historian has established the specific type of evidence and the author of it, he or she must analyse its meaning carefully, asking a variety of questions to contextualize the source. What was the author's perspective? What was the historical context? What was the meaning of it for the author? These questions are extremely important but difficult to answer definitely, even for professional historians, because they generally lack direct access to authors. The meaning of the source can only be inferred by historians through the mental act of empathic understanding, a complicated mental process dealt with in chapter 7. It implies reading and understanding the source in its historical context. Historians must, therefore, acquire not only some form of linguistic fluency (if a print or oral source) but also 'a command of the historical context which will show what the words actually refer to.'[32] It is easy to miss the overall meaning or subtle nuances of the evidence if historians do not pay close attention to the reading of it and the appreciation of its particular context.[33] 'The problem,' as Stanford observes, 'is to grasp not what [sources] mean to us, but what they meant in the cultural context in which they were written.'[34] In the *Annales*, French historians Marc Bloch, Fernand Braudel, and Lucien Febvre referred to this historical uniqueness as the *mentalités* of historical actors, that is, the implicit set of mentalities and beliefs that individuals hold in society.[35] These 'mentalities' are often concealed in the language used in the period and not necessarily found or expressed in its modern equivalent.[36]

Perhaps the following example of a piece of nineteenth-century evidence can illustrate the critical issue facing historians when trying to contextualize sources. On 6 July 1885, Prime Minister John A. Macdonald addressed the House of Commons on the question of Métis leader Louis Riel, on trial for high treason. In what could be construed today as a lengthy vitriolic speech, he talked about Aboriginal and Métis peoples in these terms:

> Why, Sir, I have come to this House again and again and stated the case of the Indians. I have said it was a case of hardship, and we could not, as christian men, allow them to starve. We have done all we could to put them on themselves; we have done all we could to make them work as agriculturists; we have done all we could, by the supply of cattle, agricultural implements and instruction, to change them from a nomadic to an agricultural life. We have had very considerable success; we have had infinitely more success during our short period, than the United States have had during twenty-five years. We have had a wonderful success; but still we have had the Indians; and then in these *half-breeds*, enticed by white men, the *savage instinct* was awakened; the desire of plunder – *aye*, and, perhaps, the desire of scalping – the savage idea of a warlike glory, which pervades the breast of most men, civilised or uncivilised, was aroused in them, and forgetting all the kindness that had been bestowed upon them, forgetting all the gifts that had been given to them, forgetting all that the Government, the white people and the Parliament of Canada had been doing for them, in trying to rescue them from *barbarity*; forgetting that we had given them reserves, the means to cultivate those reserves, and the means of education how to cultivate them – forgetting all these things, they rose against us. Why, Sir, we are not responsible for that; we cannot change the barbarian, the savage, into a civilised man.[37]

It is too easy for an offended reader of the twenty-first century to dismiss Macdonald as a rude British Canadian racist and white supremacist who felt deeply betrayed by the rebellious actions of Louis Riel and his Métis insurgents, given 'all the kindness' the Canadian government had offered them. But a command of historical context for this document should lead historians to ask what these words, and the political rhetoric employed, meant to Macdonald and the members of the House of Commons in 1885. A sophisticated answer would necessarily require an '*intra*textual evaluation' of the excerpt as part of the complete document itself, with philological consideration for words such as 'aye,' 'half-breeds', and 'savage instinct.'[38] It would also entail a careful historical consideration, and ultimately appreciation, of Macdonald's cultural, political, and social milieu. In other words, it is not sufficient for a contemporary reader simply to condemn Macdonald for words and ideas that are against twenty-first-century moralities, from which deviance is *la fin du monde*. Critical readers need to understand how and why Macdonald would express these ideas in his speech and in the social context of the time. 'Students who have been *properly* introduced to Western civilization,' Daniel Gordon observes, 'will know that inequality has not only been a fact but also a norm throughout most of history.'[39] As disturbing as it may sound, Macdonald was indeed a man of his own time.

But the historians' interpretative task should not stop there. They also have to study the meaning of the document *for them* in the present, knowing with hindsight what the piece of evidence meant for Macdonald and his contemporaries, as well as studying the legacy of Macdonald's policies for Aboriginal and Métis relations. In this sense, the selected evidence from Macdonald's past only makes sense because it forms a temporal bridge between Macdonald and historians' selection of, interest in, and writing about him. Otherwise, the remarks of Macdonald would have no relevance to people's understanding of the past. The evidence is thus something necessary for people in the present to give meaning to the past, not something necessary for the past itself.[40] Thus, Canadians cannot understand today how federal authorities mistreated Aboriginal and Métis peoples, and why they are asking for collective redresses – such as recognizing officially Louis Riel as a Father of Confederation – without both placing this selected piece of evidence in its historical context and adding their own contemporary meaning.

Although necessary to historians' critical evaluation of sources, the contextualization of evidence brings with it another set of questions: Is the source reliable? How is it consistent with other related sources? What factors could account for these similarities or differences? What other sources could corroborate or support it? No historical source can be employed by historians as evidence until they establish its internal reliability. I argued in the previous section that even primary sources must be carefully scrutinized by historians because immediacy with the events or actions in question does not eradicate the possibility of forgery or viewpoint. Primary sources must be analysed for their validity and accuracy. This is the '*inter*textual evaluation' of sources, that is, how selected evidence is assessed for its reliability by comparing it with other related (primary or secondary) sources.[41]

It is always difficult and tentative for historians to know whether the author of a source was in a position to faithfully appreciate the situation. Is the information accurate or simply what the author wished it to be? Was the author alone in his or her point of view, or is it corroborated by other sources? Equally important, is the author of the source consistent, or contradicting him- or herself later in the source or contradicting a related source of the time?

Although there is no magic formula for ruling out every possible factor affecting the reliability of historical evidence, historians have typically adopted an approach resembling the cross-examination of witnesses in courtroom investigations. Having selected the necessary or available sources on 'the case' and having considered their internal consistency and meaning, historians engage in corroboration, that is, a complex comparative evaluation of the facts presented and claims made in one source with those made in other, related sources. Because the reliability of sources is not fixed but contingent and always depends on the questions asked, historians can judge the content or meaning of the source only by cross-examining it with other sources. Moving from the role of 'investigator' to that of a 'judge,' the historian therefore examines various and possibly contradictory sources before making a final judgment. As Collingwood observed, no source and no author can be accepted as authoritative in this process: 'As soon as it became understood that a given statement made by a given author, must never be accepted for historical truth until the credibility of the author in general and of this statement in particular had been systematically inquired into, the word 'authority' disappeared from the vocabulary of historical method, except as an archaistic survival; for the man who makes the statement came henceforth to be regarded not as someone whose word must be taken for the truth for what he says, which is what was meant by calling him an authority, but as someone who has voluntarily placed himself in the witness-box for cross examination.'[42] It can be inferred from Collingwood's statement that the corroborating step of internal criticism necessitates (1) the selection and inclusion of other, related sources that support or challenge the initial one; and (2) a careful cross-examination of the various historical facts and claims made by each authority.

But the courtroom analogy is incomplete.[43] The 'witnesses,' the primary sources for historians, cannot (and should not) always be cross-examined exclusively with other witnesses. It is necessary for historians to study various sources from the same author to assess the consistency and complexity of this person who created the primary source and to find reasons for possible contradictions. Wineburg, for example, presented history teachers with a set of sources containing contradictory statements from Abraham Lincoln on slavery. Although a quick review would have led the teachers to believe that Lincoln was a hypocritical politician, a meticulous cross-evaluation reveals more nuanced findings. Both the unique contexts of the documents (electoral speeches for different audiences, private letter to a friend later in his life) and the complexity of the character himself render that initial conclusion too simplistic.

Historians must, moreover, compare the primary sources not only with other, related primary sources ('witnesses') of the time but also with secondary sources that may offer different interpretative answers to the same initial questions of historians. The examination of Wineburg's selection of sources from Abraham Lincoln, for example, also included the 'voices' of several interpreters of Lincoln, that is, historians who wrote about him and about slavery. These secondary sources may not always clarify the reliability of the primary sources per se, but can surely help historians in their selection of trustworthy sources. As Collingwood contended, 'As a rule, where he [the historian] has many statements to draw upon, he will find that one of them tells him what another does not; so both or all of them will be incorporated. Sometimes he will find that one of them contradicts another; then, unless he can find a way of reconciling them, he must decide to leave one out; and this, if he is conscientious, will involve him in a critical consideration of the contradictory authorities' relative degree of trustworthiness.'[44] This critical task of selecting and leaving out sources can be accomplished only with the right kind of historical knowledge. The corroboration of sources using the interpretations of historians can play an important role in the appropriation of this knowledge, particularly for novices.

6.3 Students and the Use of Evidence

Knowing that historical knowledge depends on the critical use of evidence is key to historical thinking, but it does not address the issue of students' engagement in this process. Until recently, it was far from clear in the educational community whether students had the intellectual capacity to grasp the complex nature of historians' sources and the grounds for knowledge claims about the past. For example, following the lead of Piaget's categories of intellectual development, British scholars E.A. Peel and Roy Hallam established in the early 1970s that most students (even at the high-school level) could not engage in source analysis and questioning. After studying one hundred students' responses to analytical questions on several history passages, Hallam found they answered only two questions at the highest, 'formal operational,' Piagetian level.[45] These psychological findings were also supported by other related studies during the period.[46] Even British historian Elton offers a bleak picture of what could be accomplished in class with 'immature' students: 'The well-known fact that "serious" history requires some maturity weighs inescapably upon those who have to teach the altogether immature; and all that I would wish to say about those earlier years may be summed up in one phrase – *concern* and *amusement*. There are some children whose inclination is fixed upon the past: they pose no problems. The rest – the great majority – should be excited by stories and descriptions distinguished from other similar tales by being about real people.'[47] Yet, the belief that students cannot engage seriously in historical inquiry has been challenged in recent decades. Echoing Bruner's earlier claim that any academic subject could be taught effectively to any child and at any stage of intellectual development, some European and North American research now suggests that students can read and use historical evidence, provided they are taught appropriately to do so. In England, where the use of evidence has been part of the curriculum since the 1980s, results are encouraging.[48] Booth, for example, has demonstrated that British high-school students could use factual details from sources (e.g., photographs) to answer specific questions and make some inferences from them.[49] His colleague, Hilary Cooper, comes to similar conclusions, noting the limits of Piagetian theory for conceptualizing learning progression in history education.[50] Shemilt's seminal works on students' historical thinking also address the question of evidence. 'The majority of control pupils studied,' he writes in his study *History 13–16*, 'thought that History dealt with facts and not with evidence.'[51] Faced with this critical situation, Shemilt proposed to map out what he referred to as four progressive stages in the conception of the nature of history. These stages, he argues, could serve to exemplify the nature, degree, and range of ideas as found in the school: historical knowledge is about (1) uncontested facts; (2) a sequence of events (but no clear idea of connection); (3) explanations of facts; and (4) the critical study of evidence.[52]

More recently, Lee and Ashby found that when facing conflicting evidence, students (ages 7–14 years) can understand that selection and interpretation of available sources could lead to different accounts of the past. They also established that (1) at any given age, students' levels of historical thinking vary widely; (2) progression in historical thinking is not necessarily constant and equal in all aspects (that is, students can understand certain concepts more rapidly than others); (3) age can be a factor in students' historical development; and (4) students tend to have better historical understanding when taught history as a distinct school subject.[53]

In Canada and the United States, several studies have also addressed the issue. VanSledright, for example, spent four months in 1999 teaching U.S. history in a grade 5 social studies class in a mid-Atlantic state. His goal was to teach students 'investigative practices closely linked to the ones historians use in order to effectively build among students the cognitive capacity to understand what happened in the past.'[54] Using sources from a number of key historical cases (Boston Massacre, Jamestown Starving Time, Battle at Lexington Green), VanSledright determined that his students (ages 10–11 years) could effectively and passionately engage in historical investigation when offered adequate time and opportunity. However, their deficient prior knowledge of the discipline significantly hampered their critical use of historical evidence. Faced with conflicting (e.g., British versus U.S.) views of history, many students did not hesitate to condemn sources as inherently biased and untruthful and thus preferred to espouse the epistemological position of the dominant, patriotic interpretation of collective memory, a point of view later challenged in class, as the study progressed.

VanSledright's findings are consistent with the studies conducted by Barton, Grant, Levstik and Smith, Mayer, and Wineburg in the United States, and Seixas, Martineau, and Lévesque in Canada.[55] In all of these studies, the authors conclude that unless students are exposed *gradually* and *persistently* to the practice of investigating the past using sources, sporadic attempts (for a lesson or two) seem to have limited impact on their historical learning. 'Teaching children to think historically,' VanSledright concludes, 'is a slow, arduous process. The more novice the student, the more time and intensive energy it takes.'[56]

One of the problems found in these studies may well lie with the fact that history and social studies curricula, supporting textbooks, and official testing programs typically fail to engage students in the critical reading and writing of history. As Barton found in his comparative study of U.S. and Northern Ireland elementary students, a major difference between the two groups is the early and systematic exposure of British students to historical questions and evidence.[57] In the United States, he argues, the focus is still too much on the transmission and assessment of the substantive (content) knowledge of history, sociology, and like social sciences, and not the teaching of procedural knowledge. In many ways, the same is true of teaching in Canada.[58] While there is growing interest in using and assessing historical evidence in history classrooms, research suggests that teachers' knowledge of history (or of the use of evidence) is not a sufficient condition for successfully introducing students to the contentious nature of historical research. In the late 1980s, for example, the Bradley Commission concluded that 'teaching history requires more than knowing history [as a discipline] because a third party, the learner, is always present.'[59] Learners not only have beliefs, preconceived notions, and experiences but also bring to class all the historical, ancestral, and societal background that has (often unconsciously) contributed to shaping their ideas about the past. It is with all this 'baggage' that learners will filter and reconstruct the information learned in class. The Bradley Commission referred to this complicated process of thinking about the discipline, the learner, and pedagogy as the 'transformation' of history.[60]

But what might this transformative process of using evidence in teaching historical thinking to youngsters look like? How would teachers go about teaching like this in class? Although past and recent international studies have attempted to examine these questions, it is still not entirely clear how history teachers could realistically and effectively use evidence in their classrooms. So far, the result has typically been an imaginative *bricolage* of techniques, which too often turn out to be well tailored to classroom practice but highly ineffective in conveying the complexity and constructedness of historical claims. The 'bias detection' approach to sources is typical.[61] Suggesting that the author of a source inherently holds a personal opinion that is biased inevitably leads students to a simplistic dichotomy of truth and deceit and to the naive epistemological position of widespread suspicion of any historical evidence. To invoke bias as a criterion to assess sources and their authors is to suggest that there must be truthfulness 'out there' waiting to be discovered – an argument already made in chapter 2. It is as though teachers were saying 'if only they were to tell the truth, then we could get to what really happened.'[62] 'The very idea of bias,' Partington argues, 'presupposes the possibility of a straighter course for a bowl or for an explanation.'[63] Bias detection can undeniably provide a form of critical thinking, but it renders the analysis of historical evidence and accounts of the past unachievable, simply because authors of sources may be presenting positions that appear to contemporary readers as exceedingly unfair or prejudiced but, in reality, were legitimate in the historical context of the time (i.e., as discovered through empathic contextualization).

As result, I am offering below an approach to historical evidence using the works of Husbands, Lee, VanSledright, and Drake and Brown. Building on my earlier inquiry-based teaching model (chapter 2), this far-from-revolutionary approach to evidence encompasses four pedagogico-disciplinary steps: (1) developing research questions; (2) collecting and selecting evidence; (3) analysing evidence; and (4) developing interpretative answers.

Developing Research Questions

In previous chapters, I argued that one way of uncovering the past is to reconsider course planning. Teachers should frame course, unit, and lesson plans as those of modest and realistic historical inquiries, keeping in mind that this method for teaching does not have to frame every lesson or subject. Indeed, children are not historians, and it is unrealistic to insist that they learn and test every aspect of the past with reference to the methods of historical research.[64] Because the questions or cases to study are virtually unlimited, it is important to delimit what can be achieved in a given course or unit of study. As the goal is ultimately to facilitate understanding and to render the past more engaging and intelligible, it is thus important to know about the rationale and objectives of the course, as well as about the student body (students' prior knowledge, learning difficulties, etc.), and to understand the requirements of the classroom environment to support the desired learning. Otherwise, what may initially appear to be on paper an engaging and stimulating exercise could turn out to be an inconclusive and highly frustrating experience for students, particularly if they have not been initiated into historical thinking and writing earlier in their school lives.

Hence, based on the identified learning objectives of the course or unit of study, teachers could develop one or a set of research questions (essential questions) to frame a 'case' for students to investigate. These questions must not only be at the heart of the discipline and the course of study (i.e., not trivial tasks) but also be drafted in a thought-provoking language accessible to students. Perhaps more importantly, they should elicit historical reflection, research, and investigation and not lead to simple yes-or-no answers. To generate these questions, it is important for teachers to have an holistic view of the course of study (by framing content around certain colligatory concepts) and to use curricular objectives and textbook content as potential answers or outcomes to inquiry questions.[65] For example, if an expectation of the Canadian curriculum is for students to 'understand the conscription crisis during World War II,' then the lesson or unit could be framed as an inquiry around the colligatory concepts of 'French–English relations' and 'Canada and conscription,' with a research question such as Why did Prime Minister Mackenzie King hold a plebiscite on conscription in 1942? Alternatively, teachers could focus more explicitly on the result of the political decision by asking students, Was Prime Minister Mackenzie King right to hold a plebiscite on conscription in 1942, despite strong French Canadian opposition to it?

The initial step of framing these questions is crucial, as the entire activity itself (its significance, duration, sources, and assessment) would depend on what the teacher has initially identified. Not every question would be appropriate for a given evidence-based inquiry. Only those should be considered that would lead students to investigate the relevant content and to achieve deeper and more enduring historical thinking.

But research questions can also elicit specific levels of reflection (e.g., require specific evaluation or choice between options) or simply focus on shorter periods and specific events in history – what Wiggins and McTighe call 'topical questions.'[66] The use of research questions to teach specific levels of thinking might be more successful with novices, as such questions call for a circumscribed analysis of events in history. A research question on the speech of John A. Macdonald in the House of Commons on 6 July 1885, for instance, could lead students to a more specific and less time-consuming activity than one on the entire Rebellion of 1885. Yet, in both cases, students would have to become involved in source-based investigation and analysis.

Collecting and Selecting Evidence

Having defined the case through the design of research questions, teachers could next engage in the complicated task of locating and collecting the necessary sources for students to use in class, including background sources of information on the cases for students to familiarize themselves with the historical inquiry and context. Given the need for time management and practicality, it might be preferable (at least initially) to have teachers accomplish the task, as it requires the consultation of archives, libraries, or web-based digital collections. Because general and background resources typically offered to teachers and students in textbooks, learning guides, and school libraries rarely reference or include the primary sources themselves, teachers must inevitably dig for them – an exciting but demanding process to accomplish with thirty inexperienced students.

Teaching students the techniques of collection and selection of sources for evidence-based research requires serious thinking and planning on the part of teachers. The initial question must not only focus the study but also prescribe the type of activities to be performed by students. Therefore, the sources rendered available to them must clearly support the task, that is, further historical thinking – and not necessarily professional historical-knowledge production. Being an act of interpretation and judgment, the selection of significant sources by teachers would in many ways determine the intellectual direction of students. Faced with this situation, teachers may find the following list of questions, adapted from Drake and Brown, useful in planning inquiries and, more specifically, in searching and selecting evidence:

- Is the source essential to the task (research question)?
- Does the source relate to – support or contradict – other essential sources?
- Does the source contribute to deepening students' historical thinking?
- Is the source appropriate cognitively for students?
- Does the source favour multimodal (multiple-senses) learning?
- Will the source be of interest to students?
- Can the source (if a print source) be edited or translated for clarity and pedagogical convenience?
- Would the edited version retain its original meaning? What would be lost?

Analysing Evidence

Because students are not professional historians, it is not feasible to assume that, confronted with conflicting primary sources, they would intuitively engage in the critical evaluation of the evidence. It is thus pedagogically pertinent to guide students in the set of heuristics presented in section 6.2. In school history, as Drake and Brown contend, 'intellectual enjoyment and engagement are the products of a co-investigation involving *both* teachers and students.'[67] Facing many sources with conflicting views on an issue, some possibly in an inaccessible language, students could easily be confused and irritated. As Roland Tharp and Ronald Gallimore insist, 'until internalization occurs, *performance must be assisted.*'[68] Students differ not only in capacities but also in interests, self-esteem, creativity, and reading strategies.

But before (or while) students get to the source work, it is important to keep in mind that they should have a reasonable understanding of the subject matter of the inquiry if the study of the sources is to be a valuable learning experience. Students can only acquire some understanding of the sources if they have some prior knowledge of the historical period, notably through chronological thinking and synoptic judgment.[69] The key question to bear in mind here is 'What do students need to know and understand to successfully address the research question?'

Developing Interpretative Answers

The final step of the inquiry is to have students construct an evidence-based argument to offer a defensible answer to the research question. 'If we are asking historical questions,' as Husbands observes, 'we have to allow them to learn to offer historical answers.'[70] As inconclusive as the evidence and answers to the previous steps of an evaluation might be, the development of an argument represents one of the deepest and most sophisticated ways of historical thinking. In their conceptualization of evidence use in the classroom, Dickinson, Gard, and Lee contend that the 'use of evidence for interpretation and histories' is the highest level of understanding of the past.[71] It not only requires students to understand how historical knowledge claims are based on evidence but also engages them in the complex interpretation of *some* evidence. Put simply, the exercise of creating an argument forces students to face the necessity of pulling the sources apart and then putting them together in a coherent and personally meaningful way.

Yet, there is no clear pedagogical model in the literature explaining how students can successfully construct an historical argument that is both coherent and meaningful to them.[72] Teachers have often pointed, with good reason, to the difficulties of the task. To go back to the example of Prime Minister Mackenzie King's conscription plebiscite of 1942, students' interpretative answers require a high level of historical knowledge and thinking. The reconstruction of the problematic situation by students can be entirely misleading if they fail to understand the context of the time and the character's intent, if they misjudge historical evidence, or if they base their argumentation primarily on their prior beliefs and contemporary views of the situation. More problematic is the selective use of conflicting evidence by students to arrive at an answer they have already decided on, a situation possible when novices are introduced to sourcing and evidence-based argumentation with limited sources. As VanSledright found in his own study, '[the] jump from initial trust in the general veracity of accounts to concluding that people are prevaricating in one form or another raises again the question of what young children learn when you expose them to the referential illusion and reveal the inner interpretive machinery of doing history.'[73] In the face of inconclusive evidence, students may simply abdicate, concluding that the 'real truth' could never be achieved. Clearly, their ability to develop a reasonable evidence-based interpretation is replete with sourcing and evaluative challenges that must be overcome with steady guidance from knowledgeable teachers.

But aside from these sourcing and interpretative pitfalls is the structure of the interpretation itself. I have argued in previous chapters that narrative is a fundamental element for structuring and conveying historical scholarship. Unlike a chronicle, the narrative sorts out, organizes, and groups selected historical events in a specific sequence (with causal relation and colligation), which gives it a certain logic, coherence, and meaning (with a beginning, middle, and end). But this form of expression, used by historians, is also familiar to students, as they are frequently (some would even say *naturally*) exposed to various types of narrative in the classroom and outside (e.g., novels, cartoons, films, textbooks, and family stories). Bruner, for example, claims that children are cognitively well equipped to learn, comprehend, and even create stories, whether or not they are fictional. These abilities, he argues, are soon emphasized, developed, and even perfected as children grow up in their cultural community. As he puts it, 'I have wanted to make it clear that our capacity to render experience in terms of narrative is not just child's play, but an instrument for making meaning that dominates much of life in culture – from soliloquies at bedtime to the weighing of testimony in our legal system ... Children, I think, are predisposed naturally and by circumstance to start their narrative careers in that spirit. And we equip them with models and procedural tool kits for perfecting those skills. Without those skills we could never endure the conflicts and contradictions that social life generates. We would become unfit for the life of culture.'[74] Having students use narrative to develop interpretations of the past would thus be an effective method for teaching history because it would draw on their own expertise, as well as on other concepts of the discipline, such as continuity and change. Supporting this view, James Voss and Jennifer Wiley, for example, found in their study of students' responses to textbook and historical texts on the Irish potato famine that students' writing a narrative explanation improves understanding, because they have already mentally developed narrative representations of the content presented to them in the experiment. 'When they are then asked to write a narrative essay on the subject,' Voss and Wiley contend, 'a type of resonance occurs, making the task somewhat easier and reducing the amount of processing required.'[75] Other studies have also confirmed that students typically prefer narratives to other types of texts and modes of expressions, although the reasons for such preference seem to vary.[76]

But the narrative should not be considered the only possible or affordable tool to present their interpretations. In the first place, the familiarity of students with narratives may blind them to the very fact that as powerful as they might be, they are only literary constructs and, as such, do not present authentic windows of the past. Furthermore, Voss and Wiley also found in their study that students who write argumentative essays, as opposed to stories, are more likely to have a deeper understanding of the issue and the content. The reason they offered for this finding is that essays require more deliberate mental processing than narratives. Therefore, students would be less likely to follow their natural pattern of creating self-contained, chronological stories and tend rather to engage in the 'deliberation and processing that are not present in the narrative.'[77] Their results also indicate that students who choose the argumentative essay write a greater number of 'transformed sentences' (original sources reorganized in their own language) and 'greater proportion of correct inference verifications.'[78] These findings suggest, for them, 'that individuals, to understand or make sense of events, are predisposed to place them in a chronological, narrative form and that writing an argumentative essay requires deliberation or processing that are not present in the narrative.'[79]

Voss and Wiley's research findings are fascinating from a cognitive and instructional points of view. Yet, more studies are needed in this area to determine the influence of narrative and other forms of expression (expository, persuasive, and descriptive) on students from different age groups, genders, ethnicity, and national and cultural backgrounds. Pietro Boscolo and Lucia Mason, for example, found in their experimental study of writing as a learning tool for history with grade 5 students in Italy that those who use writing as a learning strategy (for note-taking, commenting, reflecting personal ideas, expressing doubts, and synthesizing) are more likely to develop elaborate historical explanations and more sophisticated understanding of the subject matter and the discipline than those who learn history without this strategy.[80] The authors conclude by arguing that 'the study provides further evidence that writing can be effective in building new knowledge in complex domains.'[81]

6.4 Conclusion

The use of evidence to answer research questions and ultimately engage in reconstructing the past is a long and demanding process. Students are not educated in a school-history environment that elicits their own thinking about the past, nor does it put students in a situation to collect and select sources and thus struggle with issues of historical meaning and interpretation. The result is that many do not consider knowledge of the past as being the result of human constructs based on the critical use of evidence. History is understood as the straightforward acceptance or rejection of authoritative, binary stories presented to them as self-evident by teachers, textbook authors, historians, or other authorities. Students, as Barton reminds us, '[act] as though knowledge of the past [exists] independently of evidence.'[82]

Yet, it would be unrealistic and ill-advised to assume that historical thinking inevitably engages students in disciplinary activities as performed by professional historians. Disciplinary inquiries, as embedded within a community of experts, cannot be directly 'transplanted' to the world of school history. As Robert Bain acknowledges, 'teaching history is more complicated than either transmitting historical facts or engaging students in history projects.'[83] As of yet, students do not live in an environment that sustains disciplinary practice, with its shared procedures, standards, and knowledge. It is, thus, a *folie de grandeur* to believe educators can make students accountable to the same scrutiny as professional historians.

For that reason, the place of evidence in the classroom must be different from its place in the craft of historians. 'Unlike historians,' Husbands argues, 'school pupils will not claim to generate "new" public knowledge from the study of (selected) historical evidence; they will generate new *private understanding*.'[84] From this very legitimate perspective, evidence should be included in classroom instruction not so much because it will lead novice students to become professional historians but because of its potential for fostering historical thinking and learning. 'Without an understanding of what makes an account historical,' Lee concludes, 'there is nothing to distinguish such an ability from the ability to recite sagas, legends, myths or poems.'[85]

7 How Can We Understand Predecessors Who Had Different Moral Frameworks? – Historical Empathy

We cannot simply replicate the thought of the past. The student of history knows that he is not the historical actor; he cannot think just as Theodosius did, since he knows he is not Theodosius. There is no reason at all, however, why the student should not seek to place himself in Theodosius's position and to seek to rethink the possibilities of that situation as closely as is possible to the way Theodosius did. The objection would only carry weight if we confined ourselves to the thought of the historical actor and saw this as a sufficient as well as a necessary condition for historical understanding.

– Geoffrey Partington[1]

In his poignant and final book on the Holocaust, *The Drowned and the Saved*, Primo Levi recalls his and fellow Jewish experiences of the concentration camps – the so-called *Lager*. Stripped of their belongings, clothes, and even identity and separated from their loved ones, Jews were precipitated into an inhuman world, horrible – deadly. The concentration camp system, as Levi observes, 'has as its primary purpose shattering the adversaries' capacity to resist.'[2] The isolation, the shaving off of all hair, the outfitting in rags, the rudimentary sanitary conditions, the beatings, the cold, the illness, the rationing, the hard labour, the fatigue, and, perhaps more dreadfully, the daily struggle against inevitable death in the gas chambers made the very idea of rebellion, escape, or even resistance illusory. 'What sense, what use,' Levi asks, 'would it have been to open the gates for thousands of individuals barely able to drag themselves around, and for others who would not have known where, in an enemy country, to look for refuge?'[3]

In the camps, as Levi recalls, the oppression was so extreme, and enforced with such military efficiency, that anger, indignation, and moral and physical strength – the driving forces of resistance, rebellion, or escape – were pushed to an extremely low level, so low as to deteriorate both the body and the mind. 'The typical prisoner, the one who represented the camp's core, was at the limits of depletion ... He was a rag of a man, and, as Marx already knew, revolutions are not made with rags in the real world but only in the world of literary and cinematic rhetoric.'[4] In this context, escaping or even rebelling was an extremely rare thought to entertain, notably among the experienced prisoners (surviving more than three months in the camp was remarkable), even if the 'final solution' appeared to them as inevitable.

Yet, the contemporary views on survival and escaping as a moral duty at all costs, promoted in popular culture and even in war conventions, render the very notion of Jews' weakened strength and depressed morale in the camps difficult to imagine – to accept. 'The typical prisoner,' as Levi comments, 'seen as a man of integrity, in full possession of his physical and moral vigor, who, with the strength that is born of despair and ingenuity sharpened by necessity, flings himself against all barriers and overcomes or shatters them [is a] schematic image of prison and escape [that] bears little resemblance to the situation in the concentration camps.'[5]

So it is no surprise that decades later, when confronting a class of grade 5 students, Holocaust survivor Levi could not evade the inevitable questions: Why did you not escape? Why did you not rebel? Why did you not avoid capture beforehand? Beyond students' indignation and sympathy for the personage, few were convinced by Levi's explanations. One student in particular asked him to draw on the blackboard a sketch of the camp with the watchtowers, gates, barbed wires, and power station. After a brief analysis of the situation and a few more clarifying questions, the student then presented Levi and the class his obvious escape plan: 'Here, at night, cut the throat of the sentinel; then, put on his clothes; immediately after this, run over there to the power station and cut off the electricity, so the search lights would go out and the high tension fence would be deactivated; after that [you] could leave without any trouble ... If it should happen to you again, do as I told you. You'll see that you'll be able to do it.'[6] For Levi, this student's intuitive understanding of the concentration camps, and of the whole notion of the Holocaust, illustrates very well the gap that now exists between 'things as they were "down there" and things as they are represented by the current imagination fed by approximative books, films, and myths.'[7] Humans' difficulty (or perhaps inability) to appreciate the experiences of others in the distant past represents, for Levi, a crucial impediment to genuine historical understanding. 'We are prone to assimilate them to "related" ones,' he ironically contends, 'as if the hunger in Auschwitz were the same as that of someone who has skipped a meal.'[8] Faced with this critical situation, Levi saw no choice but to invite historians to foster young people's historical thinking and empathy. As he put it, 'it is the task of the historian to bridge this gap, which widens as we get farther away from the events under examination.'[9]

The experience of Levi with elementary students illustrates all the complexities of connecting with the distant past. The 'smart' student was quite passionate about his subject. He asked questions and used his experiences to create a plausible solution to the escape problem that so many Jews seemed to have missed during World War II. Yet, although the student's solution was imaginative, it raises a host of problems with regard to people's ability to imagine, experience, and interpret the world through different belief systems, notably those of past societies. Investigating the past and constructing defensible solutions to historical problems inevitably involve asking such questions as these: How was it different back then? How could human beings act differently, with different beliefs, values, and experiences? How can we, as contemporary actors, imagine, experience, and entertain the views and ideas of others? With what reservations? Under what conditions?[10]

This chapter looks at the concept of historical empathy. Using the influential work of Collingwood on history as a study of the thoughts of past actors (section 7.1), it discusses empathy on the basis of three interrelated concepts employed in the discipline: historical imagination, historical contextualization, and moral judgment (section 7.2) and then considers students' ability to appreciate the past through historical empathy in light of this account (section 7.3).

7.1 Historical Thought ... and Imagination

Ranke, in his nineteenth-century historicist attempt to establish a scientific history, believed that historians could only reconstruct the past accurately if they understood it as the people who lived in it. The past, in his view, could be judged by historians only on its own terms. While reading *Quentin Durward*, he came to realize that Sir Walter Scott's historical novel contained obvious inaccuracies. The British past he described could not, for Ranke, be accepted, given the evidence available at the time. He wrote, 'I was also offended by them [the inaccuracies]. Among other things it distressed me that in *Quentin Durward* he treated Charles the Bold and Louis XI in a manner quite contrary to historical evidence.'[11] A true believer in science, Ranke was convinced that historical writers could not play half-tricks on the dead, even if their works were purely imaginary. For him, the construction of the past depends on the historian's interacting with the sources of the time. Imagination, sympathy, or shared feelings could not be allowed free rein. Accounts, as emotionally powerful as they might be, had to be supported by the necessary evidence.

But Ranke never clearly explained how historians had to (or could) recreate the past as it 'actually happened' for those who lived in it. It was only in the twentieth century, notably in the works of Collingwood, that some responses were provided to the question of the imaginative reconstruction of the past. I have noted, in previous chapters, that because the past can no longer be accessed, historians' re-creations are influenced not only by the relics and records they select but also by the perspectives and beliefs of the present in which they find themselves. 'All history,' as Collingwood famously – and contentiously – argued, 'is the history of thought.'[12] In his view, the craft of historians is an activity of thought because the past could only be known to historians by 'rethinking the same thought which created the situation we are investigating.'[13] The whole process of historical research would thus be tied to the power of the historians' minds to rethink, or re-enact, the thought of historical actors, as based on the selected evidence. As Collingwood argued, 'Historical knowledge is the knowledge of what mind has done in the past, and at the same time it is the redoing of this, the perpetuation of past acts in the present. Its object is therefore not a mere object, something outside the mind which knows; it is an activity of thought, which can be known only in so far as the knowing mind re-enacts it and knows itself as so doing.'[14]

But how do historians get to re-enact, or rethink, the states of mind of past actors? What kind of machinery or sorcery would be necessary to do so? For Collingwood, the inquiry into the thinking of historical actors, although logically impossible, could be rendered more or less feasible through what he called the 'historical imagination.'[15] 'Every present,' he observed, 'has a past of its own, and any imaginative reconstruction of the past aims at reconstructing the past of this present, the present in which the act of imagination is going on, as here and now perceived.'[16]

Collingwood's idea of the imagination did not go unnoticed; it led to much controversy in the history community. Many philosophers and historians accused him of turning historical interpretation into a fanciful, intuitive methodology of attempting to explain the past, using the irretrievable experience of the minds (or the 'inside') of past actors.[17] 'We can know *why* somebody did something,' Patrick Gardiner contends, 'just as "directly" as we can know *what* it was that he did. There is no inference to unobservable "interior" mental events.'[18] A close review of Collingwood's ideas suggests, however, that despite some inconsistencies in his writings he did not base his notion of the imagination on fanciful intuitions about the insides of past minds.[19] Rather, his methodology explicitly focuses on inferential judgments from the evidence.[20] The historical imagination would, therefore, only be valuable if historians had access to evidence sufficient to carry out the re-enactment, to make their inferences. Making a comparison between the novelist and the historian, Collingwood argued, 'The novelist has a single task only: to construct a coherent picture, one that makes sense. The historian has a double task: he has both to do this, and to construct a picture of things as they really were and of events as they really happened. This further necessity imposes upon him obedience to three rules of method, from which the novelist or artist in general is free ... First, his picture must be localized in space and time ... Secondly, all history must be consistent with itself ... Thirdly, and most importantly, the historian's picture stands in a peculiar relation to something called *evidence*.'[21]

To delineate Collingwood's notion of historical imagination, three contrasting portraits or characters, initially developed by Shemilt, may help conceptualize and clarify what historians' imaginative re-enactment is and is not: the psyche-snatcher, necromancer, and time-traveller.[22]

The first portrait (the psyche-snatcher) represents the historian as a 'stealer of souls' who relives the thoughts, feelings, and actions of his or her subjects. Rather than simply re-enacting what the actors have done, the psyche-snatcher will exercise his or her own prerogative as the actors themselves, losing his or her own identity to mentally become the subjects in question. Imagining Caesar's crossing the Rubicon, for example, would imply for the psyche-snatcher telling 'what the great man would have thought had he had occasion to rehearse formally his reasons or to explain himself after the event.'[23] Clearly, this first position has serious historical implications. It first assumes that there is no boundary between now and then. Direct access and hence continuity between past and present realities would allow contemporary historians to get into the minds of past actors without temporal problems. Questions of presentism, societal beliefs, moral judgments, and contexts would be totally evaded. Equally problematic, the first portrait presupposes that contemporary historians can feel what it was like to be in the minds of past actors. Yet, how could it be possible to imagine and ultimately feel what it was like to suffer from hunger, wounds, or even a simple headache? Obviously, there are limits to what the mind can imagine, feel, or accurately relive.

The second portrait (the necromancer) depicts the historical imagination as a sorcerer who, instead of adopting the identity and soul of the dead (as the psyche-snatcher), 'conjures a vision of the past action that a contemporary audience will find recognizable, intelligent, and plausible.'[24] The necromancer uses a literary genre and *trompe l'œil* to make the audience feel it experiences the past, whereas in reality the history given is merely an apparition of the past in the language of the present. The necromancer typifies, in many ways, contemporary historians' works as decried by postmodernists. In a critique of historicism, history, and imagination, for example, Hayden White claims that the historical imagination is a symptom of the 'linguistic determinism to which the conventional narrative historian remains enslaved.'[25]

The last portrait (the time-traveller) offers a more acceptable alternative to the first two. The time-traveller is projecting his or her own psyche into the minds of historical actors to relive the past. But, unlike the psyche-snatcher, the time-traveller does not lose his or her own sense of identity. The time-traveller remains a creature of the present who attempts to 'mentally relive events from the situation, though not necessarily from the standpoint, of the other.'[26]

The time-traveller may present the greatest promise for historians. Using the analogy of a black box (the input being an historical situation; the black box, the actor; and the output, the action or result), Shemilt demonstrates that for the psyche-snatcher, the goal is to become the black box and to act accordingly; and for the necromancer, to offer the audience a pair of spectacles to make the initially black box appears to be a glass one. However, the goal of the time-traveller, equipped with circuit diagrams, is to offer a detailed description of what the black box might look like and contain. Both the psyche-snatcher and necromancer are unlikely to support what Collingwood had in mind when he crafted his notion of historical imagination.

The psyche-snatcher may claim to explain the action 'from inside the black box' but does so by imposing his or her own sense of the action's significance, as it is simply impossible to relive a moment in the past (for every common-sense reason). The view of the historian as a necromancer is also dubious. Whereas the necromancer tries to explain the action from the inside, he or she does so entirely from the inside of current perspectives and not from those of historical actors.

The time-traveller, therefore, offers the best of the available options, although this personage presupposes a sort of transhistorical science of human nature, allowing forms of historical reasoning acceptable across time. Through thorough knowledge of historical actors and the use of 'the conceptual apparatus of the present,' the time-traveller attempts to construct a model of the past actor's mind (different from those of the present), 'into which known facts can be slotted and made good sense of.'[27] For Shemilt, this imaginative access to the past rests on principles of history, as outlined by Collingwood. It is based on the meticulous analysis of historical knowledge of the actors of the time, as available in re-enactable evidence.

7.2 The Nature of Historical Empathy

Collingwood's notions of historical thought and imagination and Shemilt's delineation of three types of historian, notably the time-traveller, offer valuable insight into people's power to feel and understand the perspectives of others. But the historical imagination does not adequately explain the concept of historical empathy and, more importantly for educators, the students' ability to engage in such imaginative, but not imaginary, re-creations. Part of the problem, as Lee observes, comes from the fact that the imagination 'covers a wide range of activities and achievements in history, and carries with it connotations deriving from the arts which in some cases appear to conflict with the fundamental tenets of history.'[28] The imagination can easily be confused with persuasive fantasy or mythology, and with the activities of the necromancer and psyche-snatcher. As a result, I propose to employ and focus on the related concept of historical empathy, which, thanks to psychologists, is now a subject of growing interest and recognition, both in historical research and in history education. Yet, the concept of historical empathy is far from unambiguous. Despite its presence in some national standards and teaching objectives, people typically misunderstand empathy as sympathy or a related kind of appreciative sentiment. Empathy, imagination, and understanding are related concepts but they are not the same and should not be used interchangeably.[29] Consequently, the objective of this section is to clarify what historical empathy is (and is not), relying on three interrelated concepts, largely employed in the discipline: historical imagination, historical contextualization, and moral judgment.

Historical Imagination

Because historians are not in direct contact with the people they study, and far less in a mutual relationship with them, it is impossible to know for sure what they believed, thought, or intended to do. The only possible way to understand more about past actors is to mentally recreate – to *imagine* – what it was like to be in their position, even if historians may (and often do) lack some of the keys to the past. As Collingwood put it, using the helpful analogy of a ship, 'If we look out over the sea and perceive a ship, and five minutes later look again and perceive it in a different place, we find ourselves obliged to *imagine* it as having occupied intermediate positions when we were not looking. That is already an example of historical thinking; and it is not otherwise that we find ourselves obliged to imagine Caesar as having travelled from Rome to Gaul when we are told that he was in these different places at these successive times.'[30] But critics of historical imagination have expressed their reservations. Indeed, some worry that the use of the imagination inevitably turns history into an unmethodological approach to the past because it would be an attempt to look into other people's minds, intuitively, and without any means or need to justify the outcome – a critique that I have already discussed. Part of the problem with the idea of the historical imagination comes from the difficulty of mentally controlling the creativity of the historian in trying to make sense of the 'intermediate positions of the ship,' so to speak, and the reality of historical actions.

Collingwood claimed that this worry could be dispelled. In an unpublished draft of his Waynflete lecture (1935), he made a useful comparison between what he called 'pure imagination' (as exercised by artists) and 'historical imagination.'[31] Whereas the former is not constrained by reality and self-reflection, the latter represents a complex act of mental perception, an inference to what historical actors did, valued, or believed. In the example of Caesar travelling from Rome to Gaul, it is possible (and in fact necessary) to imagine that Caesar was not at both places at the same time but travelled from one to the other and thus occupied intermediate positions, a mental representation both possible and historically real. Using another example from ordinary experience, Collingwood asserted, 'If I imagine the friend who lately left my house now entering his own, the fact that I imagine this event gives me no reason to believe it unreal.'[32]

Lee goes further by arguing that if historians may be right but also mistaken in their imagination (that is, inference) of an historical situation, they are nonetheless in a critical process of finding out, of understanding, what it was like. As he comments, 'In fact, empathy in history is much more like an *achievement*: it is knowing what someone (or some group) believed, valued, felt and sought to attain. It is being in a position to entertain (not necessarily to share) these beliefs, and being in a position to consider the impact of these emotions (not necessarily to feel them).'[33] In this sense, imagination would not be about entertaining fantasy feelings of people in the past (pure imagination), but a key disposition for making sense of historical actions, events, and evidence. Because historical thinking comes from knowing how people in the past felt, thought, and acted, historical knowledge would only be possible if contemporary actors rethink, recreate, or imagine how these people felt, thought, and acted. 'Whatever goes into it,' Collingwood concluded, 'goes into it not because [historians'] imagination passively accepts it, but because it actively demands it.'[34] Historians' understanding of the past is thus in every detail an imaginative picture because all the historical questions and selected evidence must be as imagined by historical and contemporary agents within their own respective forms of life.

But this imaginative achievement in understanding how people in the past felt, thought, and acted differently from people today demands thoughtful effort. As I argued in my discussion of progress, it necessitates the ability to view others from the past not as intellectually or morally inferior but as equal and different, with their own belief systems and forms of life. In this sense, it requires two somewhat complementary but incongruent elements: (1) an appreciation for different perspectives on human activities and beliefs; and (2) an acknowledgment of a shared humanity that transcends time, space, and culture. Indeed, historians cannot imagine predecessors' actions and behaviours unless they attempt to understand their fundamentally different positionalities. But historians can only imagine what it was like for predecessors if they can conceive of themselves as living inside that historical period or culture, even if it is fundamentally different from their own.

Clearly, successful use of the historical imagination can be extremely difficult and complex and still unlikely to offer a complete or perfect picture of the past, because, to be knowable, the past must have left traces capable of supporting a re-enactment. And, perhaps more importantly, contemporary actors must be able to imagine from re-enactable evidence how predecessors felt, thought, and acted. Historical inquiry, as Collingwood confessed, 'reveals to the historian the powers of his own mind ... Whenever he finds certain historical matters unintelligible, he has discovered a limitation of his own mind.'[35] Given this state of affairs, critics of Collingwood have come to the conclusion that the search for the historical imagination should be abandoned altogether. Because contemporary actors confront the past or relics of the past with their own mental frameworks, their own positionalities inescapably impinge on their relations to the past. Therefore, they cannot travel through time and rethink and recreate the situation as it actually was for those who lived then, because their inherent positionalities are fundamentally different. 'Imagination,' as VanSledright concludes, 'turns out to be the inquirer's best but perhaps least trustworthy ally.'[36]

So the best that historians can achieve, in these circumstances, would be to mentally *contextualize* the thoughts and relics of the past; that is, to situate them in the context of the time in question – the concept of historical empathy, which I address below. Yet, this critical position on the imagination fails to recognize the fact that while potentially different, the thoughts as expressed by predecessors and contemporary actors can legitimately exist in both contexts without losing their historical meaning and accuracy. They are thoughts both created and rendered possible by virtue of being forms of experience and mental activity grounded in evidence, and not purely imaginary feelings and sympathies. As Hughes-Warrington concludes in light of her analysis of Collingwood's works, 'historical imagination is not just one of a number of equal manifestations of imagination. It is located at the top of a hierarchical, cumulative scale of forms.'[37]

Historical Contextualization

If empathy is not simply a fellow feeling or an emotion for past actors but an imaginative construction (or 'picture') of the past, based on the evidence, then to be meaningful the thoughts of past actors must necessarily be contextualized, placed in the specific socio-spatial and -temporal location from which they emerged. Caesar, for example, could not have had breakfast in Rome and dinner in Gaul, as the means of transportation necessary to make such a day trip were simply not available at the time. Collingwood already argued that a relic becomes evidence 'only when some one contemplates it historically.' But what does it mean to contemplate the past historically? How can it be achieved?

I argued in chapter 6 that *contextualization* is an essential step in evaluating selected evidence. Only by placing a piece of evidence in its historical context can historians acquire a sense of its meaning. But the contextual framework, I have also noted, is not simply given by the evidence; it has to be constructed by historians through the mental act of empathetic reading.

To conceptualize this process, it might be useful to distinguish succinctly three contexts that historians take into account when empathizing with the past: the personal (inner), the sociocultural (outer), and contemporary (present-day). The personal context refers to the inner beliefs, perspectives, and environment of the author of the source. Relics and records, I argued in chapter 6, are traces left behind by predecessors. To grasp their particular meaning, it is necessary to attribute them to their authors in light of their own set of *mentalités* by asking questions such as Who created the source? For what purpose? What was the meaning of it for the author? What was the author's relation to the event?

Yet, the sources left behind do not so readily offer historians indications of the motivations, beliefs, intents, or values of their authors. These elements might be concealed in the sources or might, in fact, have been unknown to them. This is the reason why it is often astute to search for more pieces of information from the same author in order to get a better and potentially more accurate historical perspective, keeping in mind that other ways of configuring and analysing the sources may lead to different interpretations (and to different re-enactments).

But this consideration for personal contextualization should be complemented by the outer (sociocultural) context within which the author lived. Indeed, historical actors were not living and thinking in a vacuum; they had their positionalities 'deeply imbued with sociocultural, racial, ethnic, class, and gendered components.'[38] As for the inner context, key questions that might be useful to ask include What was the social, cultural, and economical context of the time? What was the author's role or participation in that context? What information do the sources reveal about the historical context? How is this context different from or similar to others and, ultimately, different from or similar to ours?

It is thus in this twofold light that historians should regard and empathize with predecessors. But contextualization could not be complete (or at least adequate) without thoughtful consideration of those who study the past – that is, ourselves. Indeed, the ever-changing *milieux* in which historians (or actors) find themselves shape the way they imagine and contextualize the past. Because history, as Carr observes, is an 'unending dialogue' between the past and the present, historical contextualization is only possible if contemporary actors can differentiate the past from the present and, thus, contextualize their own positionality in light of those of their predecessors. 'To understand what happened, as distinct from what people in the past thought or wanted others to think was happening,' Lowenthal contends, 'we must introduce our own thoughts. And just as present thoughts shape the known past, awareness of the past suffuses the present.'[39] Presentism is precisely the tendency of contemporary people not to differentiate the past from the present, to naively impose their present-day values and norms on predecessors, as if the two contexts could magically be merged into a single transhistorical entity, as projected by Shemilt's necromancer.

Consideration of the contemporary context represents one (perhaps the best) possible way of examining one's own positionality, as modelled by the community one inhabits. By virtue of being mentally aware of personal assumptions, values, and cultural contexts, historians can develop what VanSledright calls a 'strategic competence' in dealing with past actors in ways that reflect and recognize their historical positionalities (and thus limitations) by asking such questions as What type of thinking must I do to build an understanding of this context? How aware am I (or must I be) of the assumptions that I am making? What would it take to interpret the source differently? In an attempt to clarify his own sense of historical positionality, VanSledright concludes, '[If] the thought process involved in contextualizing – that is, "re-enacting" – the past ... can be wedded with "knowing ourselves to be doing so," then we learn much more about who we are, about our historical positionalities, and about the way we wield them.'[40] Given the predominant role of print and, to a growing extent, oral sources in history, language is a fundamental element to consider in historical contextualization. Because print materials were produced in another era, it is only through contextualized empathy that historians can rethink and re-enact what happened then or what the author had in mind. This is only possible if both the personal and larger societal contexts of the time are taken into consideration. Historical actors often used popular metaphors, concepts, words, or styles that may appear totally foreign to contemporary readers, even if produced in the same language. 'The language of history,' as Husbands argues, 'is not the language of the present. This is obviously true when we are attempting to describe societies linguistically different from our own ... but it is equally true of English-speakers of even the quite recent past.'[41] Indeed, historical words, such as 'gentlemen,' 'esquire,' 'class,' or even 'terror' (initially employed by Robespierre during the French Convention of 1793–4) may have very different meanings to contemporary people and, as such, lead to an ahistorical understanding of the past if the contemporary context is unnoticed and anachronistically imposed on predecessors. Contextualization viewed in these terms may thus push historians to self-examination of their own projections, beliefs, and frameworks of meaning.

Moral Judgment

If historical empathy aims to encourage us to appreciate past events within their historical context – but without losing our own sense of identity – how would we be supposed to judge past actors? How could Jews empathize with Adolf Hitler and Nazi Germany? How could African Americans appreciate President Abraham Lincoln? How would Aboriginal peoples be supposed to imagine Prime Minister John A. Macdonald? The central question here is whether moral judgment should play a role in historical empathy.

I argued earlier in this section that it is a major mistake to define empathy as a sort of blind feeling for past actors, even if their actions were later proven to be morally wrong or unacceptable. The confusion between sympathy and empathy is often brought up when revisionist histories challenge established assumptions or even conclusions about the past.[42] In education, the confusion is frequently generated by simplistic imaginative speculations framed in classroom exercises beginning with the typical 'Imagine you are ...' which make no historical sense unless accompanied with extensive re-enactable sources on, and from, the inner and outer contexts.

Yet, empathy is far more complex in that it is a way of making sense of the past by entertaining contextualized beliefs and values without accepting the past 'as it was.' The problem that historians face in this task is to give meaning to past actions and actors in hindsight, that is, appreciating the past while knowing the consequences of predecessors' actions. Because historians' interpretations are contextually situated in the present, these necessarily involve contemporary judgments on the meaning and significance of the selected past actions and actors. In this sense, historians would not, as Partington contends, 'simply investigate facts and leave the moral judgements to others, but must perforce often make moral judgements themselves.'[43]

Because historians live in a period that is the future – and, sometimes, the direct result – of the past they study, they cannot abstract themselves from their present-day perspectives and simply act as if they were psyche-snatchers. They know, for example, the consequences of the Nazis' Machiavellian program for the extermination of Jews. Therefore, trying to empathize with Adolf Hitler should not blind historians to the necessary judgments on the immediate and lasting consequences of his actions for millions of Jews, and ultimately for humanity. Thus, although *historical imagination* and *contextualization* help in understanding past realities potentially radically different from contemporary ones, these two elements are not sufficient to generate sophisticated empathy.[44] To explain the past to the present, it is necessary to consider the unfolding of the events, as well as the larger consequences for contemporary relevance and meaning. It might be argued, therefore, that historical empathy has a moral dimension because, as Partington contends, 'without some perspective as to *what ought to be valued* in human life and on what grounds there can be little meaning or significance in history for our pupils or for us.'[45] Otherwise, how would it be possible to reject brutal slave-holders, enthusiastic Nazis, or imperialist colonizers?

But imposing contemporary moral judgments on past actors is an extremely risky business.[46] As Oakeshott claimed, to draw moral lessons from the past is to make history into 'a field in which we exercise our moral and political opinions, like whippets in a meadow on a Sunday afternoon.'[47] Butterfield, a strong proponent of historicism, made a comparable remark when he claimed that 'he is the less a historian certainly if by any moral judgment he puts a stop to his imaginative endeavour, and if through moral indignation he cuts short the effort of historical understanding.'[48] Historians, from this view, are supposed to simply establish 'what actually happened.' Indeed, historicism demands that their role should not be to judge the past with present-day beliefs but to, more modestly, offer their contemporaries a better understanding and appreciation of what happened back then – as expressed in the old French saying *autres temps, autres mœurs.*

The critical problem outlined by Oakeshott and Butterfield is the absence in the history community of established standards for moral judgments to prevent historians making unacknowledged and unwarranted judgments or arbitrarily drawing moral lessons from the past. As Butterfield noted, 'it must be remembered that moral judgments are by their very nature absolute; in the sense that it is pointless to make them unless one can claim definitely to be right.'[49] As with the criteria of historical significance, establishing those of moral judgment invariably implies the imposition of an historically contextualized morality, which may well change from one generation of historians to another, and thus seems to imply turning history into an unpredictable, ever-changing minefield – a major problem for Oakeshott and Butterfield. There seems to be, as Robert Braun observes, 'a conflict between the moral authority of the narrator and the supposed moral authority of the past itself.'[50] Equally problematic is the fact that the conception of human reality (both past and present) cannot be scientifically conceived, independently of any given universe of cultural discourse. Individuals from the same temporal period but within different cultures may experience the same reality differently and, thus, establish their own set of standards. The study of the same past by different cultural actors can lead them to make contrasting judgments about the moral value of predecessors' actions.

But are all standards of moral judgment purely arbitrary? If this is the case, then historians should abandon all notions of progress, decline, advancement, or regression in their interpretations of past events. It is impossible to discuss the history of human rights, for example, unless historians have implicitly accepted non-arbitrary grounds for evaluating earlier and later forms of human agency. As with the notion of the imagination, historians' ability to make moral judgments requires that they entertain some criteria, or at least some assumptions about human nature (what ought to be valued) in history. Until the Enlightenment, questions of morality seemed to be more straightforward. Religion provided the necessary grounding for moral behaviour. Unfortunately, most historians, at least in the Western world, have resolutely abandoned religion as a reference point for morality. The result is, as philosopher Richard Vann contends, that 'there seems to be no foundation for moral action agreed upon by all or almost all philosophers that could be applicable at all times or places.'[51]

But saying this is not to say, however, that moral judgments should necessarily be put *à l'abandon*. Although most historians and even philosophers have paid little attention to the question in recent decades, a few have turned their minds to the issue. Partington and Oldfield are two examples pertinent to this discussion. Based on their respective but complementary works, it is fair to claim that at least two criteria seem to have emerged among Western historians in the late-twentieth century to judge the past: (1) criticism of rational action; and (2) appraisal of common humanity.[52] These two elements should not be viewed as definitive and comprehensive, as historians (now and later) could, with good reason, reject or amend them, on grounds of cultural imposition or omission.

Historians generally judge the past on the premise that although living in different times, historical actors behaved rationally. 'For both individuals and collectivities,' Shemilt contends, historians strive 'to posit modes of rational action and transitive meaning.'[53] Historians necessarily judge the actions of predecessors with the implicit reasoning that they had good or at least logical reasons to behave in the way they did, even if their thinking might appear on the surface to be unfounded, to diverge from the thinking even of their own past society, or to contradict these same predecessors' subsequent actions. The past, in this sense, is not presumed to be irrational but to be logical and understandable – a point with which postmodernists do not hesitate to quarrel. But, as Lee notes, '[Historians] are not content to give up when confronted with an action which resists the construction of any rationale. It is a kind of standing presupposition of history that (unless there is evidence to the contrary) people act for reasons which, from their own point of view at the moment of setting themselves to perform the action, are good reasons.'[54] It is still largely accepted in the history community that historians' empathetic explanations can only be accepted if they understand and judge rationally the thoughts (and potentially the feelings) of the people they study, that is, give convincing and coherent reasons, although historians may not (and often do not) agree with the conclusions drawn by their colleagues. Historians' judgments, Oldfield argues, are not made indiscriminately and without reflection. In his discussion of rational action, he further contends that if historians look at the past with the premise that predecessors acted logically, historical empathy requires that they establish the contextualized morality of predecessors' actions, even if their actions or decisions were later proven to be wrong or immoral. He refers to this as 'prudential judgment' because it involves the historian's ability to understand 'the codes of behavior which inform his subjects' actions.'[55] To support his point, he quotes historian William Gallie: 'To make a moral assessment of the character of an action certainly means to assess it in its own moral context, in relation to the moral inspiration, support, education and possibilities of action actually available to the agent.'[56] Although Oldfield recognizes that historians, or any contemporary actors, are not bound to accept the past and predecessors' judgments, he believes that understanding the morality of predecessors (i.e., what they thought, believed, or did) helps contextualize their own and historians' contemporary morality, and may encourage people to be more careful to judge predecessors' actions in light of the alternatives available at the time.

Through consideration of predecessors' actions in the proper historical context, with the alternatives available to them, it becomes possible for historians to say that predecessors acted properly or wrongly. Historians could thus judge past actors, pointing to instances of courage, justice, fairness, or their opposites and, by the same token, '[single] out examples of behavior which [they] thought praiseworthy or reprehensible, with the recommendation that we, as readers, should think likewise.'[57] Moral judgments would rely on contextualized, prudential reasoning and attitudes toward past actors' decisions, as supported by the evidence.

Perhaps the still-contested Dieppe raid of 1942 can serve as an example here. In trying to make sense of the Allies' first attempt to land on the beaches of Normandy and recapture the small French port during World War II, contemporary historians might be tempted to judge the raid of August 1942 a catastrophic failure of intelligence, planning, and execution by Canadian, British, and U.S. forces. In less than eight hours, over 3,000 soldiers were killed or captured by German troops on the beach. More than sixty years later, the infamous raid continues to divide historians: tactical failure or necessary lesson for D-Day? One key military historian who wrote about Dieppe is Colonel C.P. Stacey, a Canadian historical officer in England during World War II. In his book *Six Years of War*, he states, 'Tactically, [Dieppe] was an almost complete failure, for we suffered extremely heavy losses and attained few of our objectives. After the Normandy landings of 6 June 1944, however, it appeared in a new perspective. Historically, it is in the light of that later day that it must be judged.'[58] How can historians judge fairly what happened during this raid if, as Stacey suggests, it ought to be judged in the light of D-Day? Historical sources of the time do provide crucial details that can help historians make contextualized prudential judgments about Dieppe. One document in particular, Report No. 128, *The OPER-ATION at Dieppe, 19 Aug 42 – Some New Information*, is key to the case. Included in the military report is the official briefing that Canadian General H.D.G. Crerar delivered to officers on the D-Day landing of 6 June 1944. The now-declassified document reads,

> Until the evidence of Dieppe proved otherwise, it had been the opinion in highest command and staff circles in this country that an assault against a heavily defended coast could be carried out on the basis of securing tactical surprise, and without dependence on overwhelming fire support, in the cortical phases of closing the beaches and overrunning the beach defences ... Although at the time the heavy cost to Canada, and the non-success of the Dieppe operation seemed hard to bear, I believe that when this war is examined in proper perspective, it will be seen that the sobering influence of that operation on existing Allied strategical conceptions, with the enforced realization by the Allied Governments of the lengthy and tremendous preparations necessary before invasion could be attempted, was a Canadian contribution of the greatest significance to final victory.[59]

One can see how Stacey's prudential understanding of Dieppe in light of D-Day can be explained from the larger historical context of World War II, as well as from historical sources of the time. Key documents, such as General Crerar's briefing to Canadian officers, do yield crucial information on the operations at Dieppe and the strategic lessons learned for the landing of 6 June 1944. Overwhelming fire support, as Dieppe revealed, could not be replaced by tactical surprise in coastal assaults in Europe. Thus, rational thinking is rendered possible, and made legitimate, if historians' judgments are drawn from appropriate sources. These sources should be close to the event in question and offer details on how people felt, thought, or made decisions. This process is not necessarily straightforward or unanimously accepted, given historians' consideration for the historical context and the limited or conflicting sources available to them.

Yet, the use of historical agents' rationality by historians to make judgments requires also a sense of 'contingent relativism,' allowing temporally contextualized cultures certain forms of rational explanation that may seem alien to other groups. Even if historians can make prudential judgments based on re-enactable evidence, different sources and moral interpretations of the sources could lead to contrasting evaluations. Quoting twentieth-century anthropologist Edward Evans-Prit-chard, Partington writes,

> The fact that we attribute rain to meteorological causes alone while sav-ages believe that Gods or ghosts or magic can influence the rainfall is no evidence that our brains function differently from their brains. It does not show that we 'think more logically' than savages, at least not if this expression suggests some kind of hereditary psychic superiority. It is no sign of superior intelligence on my part that I attribute rain to physical causes ... This particular idea formed part of my culture long before I was born into it and little more was required of me than sufficient linguistic ability to learn it ... It would be absurd to say that the savage is thinking mystically and that we are thinking scientifically about rainfall. In either case, like mental processes are involved and, moreover, the content of our thought is similarly derived.[60]

One takes Evans-Pritchard's anthropological point at the risk of assum-ing our moral superiority in the study of history. Both Aboriginal and European explanations for the causes of rain can be construed as ratio-nal, depending on the perspective espoused. In either case, similar thinking processes are involved but in radically different cultural con-texts. Historians are correct to alert their contemporaries to the danger of anachronistically imposing their own morality on past historical actors. To go back to the Dieppe raid example, it is possible to offer dif-ferent judgments on the value and significance of the raid, based on dif-ferent perspectives on the issue.[61] One could argue, for instance, that military strategists had options available to them prior to the raid of August 1942. Heavy bombings and close support were initially contem-plated but later abandoned because of fears that such bombings would be inaccurate and thus potentially harmful to the landing and progress of Allied troops on the beach. Yet, if judgments in history are always relative and culturally situated, how could historians legitimately argue that Nazis, slave-holders, and colonizers were fundamentally *wrong* in their doing and thinking? How is it possible to harmonize his-torical relativism and morality? One way to address the issue is to con-sider the second criterion: appraisal of common humanity.

In the section on historical imagination, I argued that contemporary actors can only imagine what it was like for predecessors if they can conceive of themselves living in that historical period or culture. 'Our ability to make moral judgments in history,' Seixas argues, 'requires that we entertain the notion of a historically transcendent human commonality, a recognition of our humanity in the person of historical actors.'[62] The notion of common humanity supports the belief, found in the study of history, that despite the strangeness and contingency of past actions, there is continuity between the past and present and there are dimensions and forms of human life that, for historians, are potentially transhistorical. Writing a century before Germany's historicist tradition, Enlightenment thinker David Hume once argued that, 'It is universally acknowledged that there is a great uniformity among the actions of men, in all nations and ages, and that human nature remains still the same, in its principles and operations. The same motives always produce the same actions: The same events follow from the same causes. Ambition, avarice, self-love, vanity, friendship, generosity, public spirit: these passions, mixed in various degrees, and distributed through society, have been, from the beginning of the world, and still are, the source of all the actions and enterprises, which have ever been observed among mankind.'[63] Such generalization in history may appear unsustainable to a twenty-first-century reader. Like Newton and others in their explanations of the phenomena of nature, Hume assumes that humans and their actions typically follow set patterns so that understanding one instance in human affairs (with its principles and operations) results in understanding all instances across periods. Yet, I argued in chapter 2 that such positivist views about the past are not possible. Each individual and historical period is unique, with its own set of *mentalités*, and must be studied as such.

That being said, the earlier discussion on the unity of the past and present makes it difficult to reject *en bloc* Hume's arguments about human nature. If predecessors had their own contextualized forms of life, these are nonetheless genetically, and sometimes culturally, connected with historians' own forms of life.[64] 'The historian,' Shemilt maintains, 'is disciplined and guided by the fact that within any cultural tradition past "forms of life" are developmentally related to those of the present.'[65] It is precisely this transcendent commonality between now and then that renders anthropological studies possible. From the outlook of history, sharing a common humanity implies that certain aspects within forms of life, whether they are past or present, can be empathetically understood as transhistorical, that is, perceived as extending from one form of life to another. But the question of which aspects or concepts of humanity 'ought to be valued' over time is subject to lively debate in the history community and, *bien entendu*, varies over time and between cultures.

Of course, the struggle against the plagues of the human condition (scarcity of resources, natural disasters, existence of disease, aging, the inevitability of death, etc.) continues to be valued across cultures, and even more so in certain regions of the globe. But from a contemporary Western perspective, it is fair to claim that the more complex issues of equality, difference, and, ultimately, human rights are now seen as the driving force – what ought to be valued – in political, social, and even historical circles.[66] Increasingly, human differences (in gender, colour, ethnicity, language, sexual orientation, and so forth) appear to be morally irrelevant to inclusion or discrimination and historically relevant to study. The contemporary ideal of humanity, as initially advanced by the French *Révolutionnaires* and now embedded in the Universal Declaration of Human Rights, is more and more influenced by the notion that people ought to be treated equally (in politics, ethics, the workplace, history, etc.), regardless of their backgrounds or orientations.[67] As Ignatieff puts it, 'Whether someone is male or female, black or white, straight or gay may be central to their identity, but these differences should be strictly irrelevant to the way we treat them as persons. Our ideal should be that the way we treat people should depend not on who they are, but only on what they do and say. This is a new idea in history.'[68] So it is no surprise that many historians now ascribe value and significance to aspects of the past that they (consciously or not) believe deserve to be judged from the point of view of equality, rights, fairness, and justice. And even when historians are vigilant and critical of the implications of moral judgments in history, they frequently make unconcealed human rights judgments themselves.

Oldfield is thus right to contend that a major problem in the discipline is the failure of historians to make clear their moral positions, either because of literary genre or a desire to appear authoritative. But this is not to say that moral judgments have to be delivered 'thunderously' or lead to the formation of the minds of people whose moral convictions are *plus royalistes que le roi*. More modestly, moral judgments in the history classroom could serve as guides or examples of historical moral judgments, notably for the novice. From this point of view, moral judgments would not only be a requirement for sound historical interpretation but, perhaps more importantly for educators, a key part of a moral education. For novices, whose moral education is incomplete, as Oldfield concludes, 'the richly diverse resources of the historian can thus be harnessed to the task of moral education, without his having to crack his own whip.'[69] Employing the notion of appraisal of common humanity would not automatically lead historians (or historical actors) to agree, for example, with Stacey's evaluative judgment on Dieppe. More modestly, it could allow historians to appreciate more reflectively how and why another historian would make certain judgments about predecessors. It is conceivable that, facing the same situation and selected evidence, one would think of and re-enact the raid in the same way.

7.3 Students and Historical Empathy

Although historical imagination and empathy have been the subject of intense discussion in the discipline for over half a century, such attention to these concepts remained largely marginal in history education, despite some serious consideration in other school subjects, such as literature.[70] Until the 1960s, as Husbands observes, history education 'was generally characterized by approaches to history which encouraged the learning of "hard," "empirical" information about the past and hence was sceptical about the place of the imagination in history.'[71] Some researchers have, however, pointed to the limits and pitfalls of memory-history and suggested that children have the cognitive ability to engage in empathetic reconstruction and understanding of someone else's viewpoint.[72] The key problem, as Jacob Getzels and Philip Jackson argued in 1962, was that creative children were not encouraged by their teachers to develop their imaginations, as the focus was very much on the acquisition of factual knowledge.

The Schools' Council History Project (SHP) of the 1970s was influential and to a certain extent avant-garde, in its conceptualization and approach to British history education. Among other things, the SHP aimed to look at a 'student's understanding of the nature of enquiry by requiring him to empathize with the problems and motives of his predecessors, and to reconstruct frames of reference within which those problems and motives could seem both rationale and justifiable.'[73] Shemilt designed a conceptual framework for historical empathy, characterized by five levels (or 'stages') of progression, from very naive (sense of moral superiority) to sophisticated (empathetic contextualization and causal relations).[74] While finding no evidence of high-school students' ability to articulate historical empathy at the highest level, he nevertheless contended that they can learn this ability if empathy is taught as a cognitive (not affective) activity, empathy is introduced progressively, and empathy exercises and assessments emphasize historical dilemmas and contrasts between past and present.

Following the lead of Shemilt and the SHP, several more scholars in Europe and North America became interested in investigating issues of historical empathy, often characterized as 'historical imagination,' 'perspective-taking,' or 'perspective recognition.' Lee and Ashby, for example, conducted three specific research tasks (Claudius's decision to invade Britain, the murder of Pedanius by one of his slaves, and the Anglo-Saxon institution of trial by oath-helping and the ordeal) with British students (ages 7–14 years). They found that students with limited empathetic understanding, especially younger ones, generally explained these actions as due to some form of 'deficit.' Past actors, in the view of the students, did not possess scientific knowledge and institutions, or were morally deficient to deal with the problems they faced. To the question 'why do you think they used the ordeal?,' one student (Gemma), for example, replied bluntly, 'Because they didn't sort of have a court at that time ... And they didn't know what, sort of, to say in the court, so they just sort of tried, erm, these ordeals.'[75] Attempts to provide contextualized explanations were more frequent, but still limited, with older students. And even then, Lee and Ashby note, 'there was often still a stereotypical element in their suggestions.'[76] Related studies conducted in the United Kingdom, the United States, Canada, and elsewhere report similar findings, thus leading to the predictable conclusion that, for many students, notably younger ones, contemporary progressive views of humanity lead them to see predecessors naively as inherently inferior and ignorant.

Part of the problem, as Elizabeth Yeager and Stuart Foster contend, may well emanate from vague or divergent understandings of what is meant by historical empathy and how it can be achieved.[77] While the focus of this chapter has been on the cognitive role of empathy, psychological attention to emotional experiences (feelings) renders the application of the concept – in either research tasks or school activities – highly confusing to educators. School resources are of little assistance. If there are more and more imaginative scenarios for teachers to use to encourage students to empathize with past actors, these activities are largely unrealistic and ineffective as a result of the limited information they provide and the forms of students' writing they propose. The following 'digging deeper' exercise on gold seekers for a grade 8 Canadian history course is typical: 'Imagine you are a gold seeker or "overlander" in British Columbia in the 1860s. Write a postcard to a relative in Europe describing your experiences. Include an illustration on the front of the card.'[78] Unless students have already acquired some advanced abilities in the field of inquiry and are presented with a rich base of sources on the history of the BC gold rush, their postcard responses are likely to resemble what most gold seekers found in their venture – illusion. Supporting this view, Yeager and Doppen found in their recent study of Truman's decision to drop the atomic bombs in 1945 that high-school students' empathetic responses are largely influenced by the amount of information they can use and reference.[79] Those who had access only to a textbook generally answered by simply reciting the facts, without discussing or criticizing them. However, those given sources showing multiple perspectives on Truman's decision achieved better understanding of the historical context, 'viewed Truman's decision to use the bomb in relatively complex terms,' and made reference to multiple sources on the issue.[80] Equally interesting is the change of students' moral judgments with regard to the decision not to drop the bomb ('yes,' 'no,' 'yes and no,' 'don't know'). Among the latter group, the number of those who initially listed a mixed 'yes and no' response to the decision nearly doubled, whereas that of the 'don't know' decreased from ten to zero.[81] Yeager and Doppen concluded that students not only learn history better when they are provided with multiple sources of information but also significantly improve their ability to make more complex and empathetically contextualized answers.

A Model of Historical Empathy

Given this brief review of research on students and historical empathy, what can be done in history education? How can students successfully engage in meaningful experiences of historical empathy? How is it possible to imagine an irretrievable past without falling into the *Lord of the Rings* and *Harry Potter* type of historical fiction?

These questions urgently require some sophisticated and, to a certain extent, practical answers, given the influential role of popular media on students' historical thinking. 'The visual media,' as historian Robert Rosenstone argued, 'have become arguably the chief carrier of historical messages in our culture.'[82] Historically oriented movies, in particular, provide viewers with extremely powerful imagery and moral messages and may be unmatched in providing an 'empathic reconstruction to convey how historical people witnessed, understood, or lived their lives.'[83]

Drawing on the previous discussion on historical empathy, it is possible to stimulate students' ability to empathize with the past, without inevitably turning them into necromancers or psyche-snatchers. More importantly, empathy can be incorporated in meaningful learning activities building on other educational strengths and concepts, and not simply be an 'add-on' to the curriculum to make history more appealing to an immature audience. In this sense, empathizing with the past should not be viewed as a disconnected, merely emotional operation but as an imaginative way of thinking about past events, actions, and actors.

First, it is important to recognize the limits of and boundaries between 'history' and 'fiction' by clarifying the concept of the *imagination*. Second, students should engage in thoughtful historical *contextualization* of the sources. Finally, students should be given opportunities to evaluate and *judge* critically the past, with a self-awareness of all the implications of doing so. It is worth noting that the steps presented here are fluid and often deliberately merged in historical practice. But separating and sequencing them may serve useful educational purposes.

IMAGINING THE PAST

In chapter 2, I argued that framing courses and, more specifically, lessons in realistic historical inquiry leads students to acquire a more inquisitive and authentic appreciation of history. But, in this process, the *historical imagination* is necessary. One cannot immerse oneself in historical investigations without some mental re-creation, or imagination, of what it was like to be in the context of the time. Popular historically oriented movies, such as *Gladiator*, *Schindler's List*, *Braveheart*, or *Saving Private Ryan*, are powerful cinematographic tools precisely because they offer the audience authentic re-creations of events and people of the past, as conceived by the makers of these movies. Because they place the viewers in a realistic context, people often picture themselves as being part of the movie, with all the epistemological problems that creates. But the obstacle to the task of imagining the past is that it is per se inaccessible. Historians have access only to surviving relics and records.

One way of addressing the issue is to provide students with a rich base of historical sources to not only help contextualize the period but also offer students a wide range of 'multimodal' (multiple-sense) sources capable of facilitating re-enactment. It is well established in special education that students with learning disabilities learn more successfully if content is presented in concrete and stimulating ways, building on their various sensory abilities (e.g., visual learners learn better if the information is presented non-verbally, such as in pictures, videos, and animations).[84] Psychologist Richard Mayer argues from empirical research in cognitive theory that students acquire and retain more knowledge when information is presented to them in multiple processing channels, that is, using dual or multiple channels of delivery simultaneously (e.g., auditory, visual, and tactile). An animation with on-screen text, for example, would be better than text only because it uses two modes of delivery (print and visual media). But animation with vocal narration (e.g., a movie) would be preferred, as it uses two distinct delivery paths (visual and auditory) to convey the same information. Multimodal sources of information would thus create a 'modality effect,' increasing retention, imagination, and understanding.

Equally interesting is the emotional reaction of students to the sources. Research findings suggest that emotions based on the senses can enhance students' experiences and retention of historical information.[85] But as people in general do not necessarily react the same way to the same source, it might be important to include sources to arouse the students' capacity to feel some of the messages conveyed by other sources. In the context of the Dieppe raid, for example, a personal account from a Canadian or German officer on the front line (print source) could be supplemented with graphically explicit photographs and maps of the raid (visual sense) and an authentic uniform or weapon from the Canadian or German army (visual, tactile, and even olfactory senses). One can see here the potential power of experiential learning through such activities as dramatic re-enactment, role-playing, a field trip, or even virtual history, which would be meant to enhance people's ability to experience the past from evidence.[86]

While the historical imagination can be used to arouse students' interest in history, students' ability to imagine the past and predecessors should ultimately be employed in the analysis of sources and the creation of historical interpretations.

CONTEXTUALIZING THE PAST

A major difference between poetry and history is the focus of historians on events that really happened, as understood and corroborated in the available sources. Historians' interpretations must not only be internally coherent and effective in conveying specific messages but also be contextualized in space and time and in relation to the evidence. But contextualizing the past is complex and intellectually rigorous.

This task demands, first, that students acquire a synoptic comprehension of the historical period. Too often, school activities are designed and presented to students as if empathizing with particular past actors could be magically achieved without the students' understanding the differences of time, space, and *mentalités* of those who lived then. Making sense of the concentration camp account provided by Levi in the introduction to this chapter, for example, is possible only if students have acquired some chronological and conceptual understanding of total war, Nazism, anti-Semitism, and final solution. Any attempt to study the past without such historical comprehension is likely to lead to presentist impositions, as evidenced by the 'smart' student's solution to the Jews' escape problem. Because students' prior knowledge could differ considerably, it is important for educators to present sufficient background information.

Second, the success of historical inquiry largely depends on the nature, quantity, and examination of sources. As I noted in chapter 6, primary sources used by students must be selected carefully so as to offer multiple viewpoints and increase their understanding of the situation. For that matter, it is important to engage students in the critical evaluation of evidence, based on four interrelated steps (or stages): (1) identification; (2) attribution; (3) contextualization; and (4) corroboration.

Finally, it is important to pay attention to the students' contemporary context. Because history is an 'unending dialogue' between the past and the present, historical contextualization requires an appreciation of one's own positionality in light of those of past actors. Only by virtue of being mentally aware of personal assumptions, values, and cultural contexts can contemporary actors appreciate the 'pastness' of the past and potentially avoid imposing their own framework of meaning on others in their interpretations.

JUDGING THE PAST

The last step involved in empathizing with the past is probably the most difficult and contentious for educators. It is not easy to give meaning and significance to the past without infusing some moral judgments on the consequences of the decisions and actions of historical actors. Students may imagine, for example, how Hitler, Lincoln, or Macdonald felt, thought, and acted as leaders of their countries, but the students' empathetic understanding ultimately involves a moral assessment of past actors in light of 'what ought to be valued,' according to certain moralities. 'Judgements and moral attitudes,' as history educator John Slater clearly puts it, 'lie at the heart of historical language.'[87] Yet, moral judgments in history may (and often do) lead to anachronistic impositions of present-day standards. So how can students judge the past critically without exercising their moral opinions, like 'whippets in a meadow on a Sunday afternoon,' to use Oakeshott's *façon de parler*?

This question is extremely pertinent to history education, given the moral dimension of schooling in contemporary society. As Husbands puts it, 'We teach and learn history in schools in a moral and social context.'[88] To resolve the issue, the works of Oldfield and Partington might be useful on two different but complementary levels.

First, it might be useful for teachers to clarify with students their own set of contextualized moralities, when introducing students to historical inquiry. This means that before or while confronting the past, students ought to consider and examine carefully their own belief systems, including all the implicit and explicit assumptions that they make about human life, technology, progress, and so forth. Barton and Levstik refer to this process as the 'contextualization of the present,' noting also that 'history educators have not devoted much attention, either theoretical or empirical, to this element of perspective recognition.'[89] Two reasons would account for this neglect. The progressive and teleological perspective of national history presented to U.S. students leads educators to instinctively consider the past as an illumination of the present. From this point of view, historical events happened because they had to (logical necessity). Furthermore, contextualizing the present would imply reassessing – and potentially confronting – the multiple beliefs and values that make up U.S. society, a highly controversial exercise in multiethnic schools where some dominant views about the collective past are still legitimated and inculcated. My own and others' work with students in Canada suggests that Canadian students also lack opportunity and experience in contextualizing their own belief systems.[90] The result is the absence in history education of established criteria of moral judgment, such as criticism of rational actions and appraisal of common humanity, to judge the past critically.

Second, the works of Oldfield and Partington also suggest that the students should be encouraged to judge past actors in their own historically situated context and on its terms. Oldfield indicates that if historians look at the past with the premise that predecessors acted logically, historical empathy requires that they establish the contextualized morality of predecessors' actions, even if their actions or decisions were later proven to be wrong or immoral. As with the concept of historical contextualization, the educational challenges of teaching students different historical moralities are many. Typically, as Shemilt has found, students' ability to empathize with past actors goes as far as the level of 'everyday empathy,' at which stage they think of themselves as historical actors but do not enter into the minds of predecessors.[91] Although these students seriously employed the concept, they failed to see the potential difference of moralities between now and then and, as a result, unconsciously imposed their own contemporary morality on the past. The following student's explanation of Germans' mass acceptance of Nazism, using a 'supermarket' analogy, is telling: 'It's the psychological force of numbers on your free will – it makes you willing to surrender it and want what you think others want. More people buy things they don't want in supermarket than they do in a corner shop, and it was the same in Germany.'[92]

In brief, moral judgments can hardly be avoided in history education, since judgments are employed at every step of an evidence-based inquiry. Whether they are contemporary personal judgments in the development of research questions or moral judgments on the past in the form of 'prudential judgments' in the analysis of sources, students should be aware of both their own belief systems and the impacts of these beliefs on their historical thinking.

7.4 Conclusion

People in the past not only had different forms of life but also experienced, interpreted, and acted according to different norms, values, and belief systems. In trying to make sense of the ways these people felt, thought, and acted, historians must recreate and imagine the situation through empathetic understanding. More importantly, they must contextualize the past according to their own contemporary assumptions and moral judgments, while remaining conscious of all the problems empathy generates in historical-knowledge production.

With the recent focus of school history on issues of imagination, empathy, and moral education, it becomes imperative for students to be introduced to this procedural concept in the study of history. If they are to imagine what it was like to be a 'gold seeker' or to understand the motivations for key past actors' decisions that now appear morally wrong (whether it is the Holocaust or the dropping of the atomic bomb), they must do so in ways that enhance their historical thinking. Instead of simply telling students that Hitler was evil, educators should lead them to discover why he is considered evil, on what grounds, and from what re-enactable evidence. Only with such a sophisticated approach to the past would it become possible to teach students how to empathize with predecessors and use moral judgments appropriately in history. Unfortunately, popular culture in general, and school resources in particular, typically fail to engage students in realistic and authentic performances set to meet the target of sophisticated thinking. The result is that students often empathize with predecessors in naive and presentist ways, entertaining decontextualized views and unconsciously projecting their own morality, from which deviance is infamy.

Because school history is not intended, as I have argued in previous chapters, to turn children into professional historians, it would be unrealistic (and unworkable) to require them to engage empathetically at the highest level established by Shemilt. Yet, the present school situation, as evidenced by various studies around the world, is clearly not acceptable. Students cannot understand history if, in every attempt to make sense of predecessors, they see their actions as reflective of deficit and moral inferiority. What might be required, then, is to conceptualize historical empathy as an achievement: striving to imagine what it was like, knowing that humans may lack the necessary tools or abilities to accomplish this task at the highest level of empathy. For this reason, scholars should be more tolerant of students' performances in research tasks and recognize the necessity of engaging them in more activities designed to foster their historical thinking. Historical empathy, as Primo Levi makes clear, is essential to a citizenry because it allows one to consider one's own and others' perspectives on a contested past and collectively envisioned future.

8 Conclusion

The recent transformations in history have taken a variety of forms and led to unprecedented consequences for human societies in spheres of activity as diverse as international relations, environmental affairs, global economy, the military, immigration, and education. More than ever, progress, welcomed *à bras ouverts* by optimistic voices, benefits those who can take advantage of the new means of generating knowledge, goods, and wealth, just as it devastates all those not prepared to respond adequately and positively to change.

In the field of history, the magnitude, profundity, and rapidity of global change have generated passionate debate about the role, nature, and ultimately the pertinence of historical knowledge. In a world where collective memories, heritage practices, and other *lieux de mémoire* furiously compete with disciplinary-history, it is no surprise that historians have lost the traditional control they once exercised over the interpretation of the past. More than half a century ago, visionary historian Carl Becker alerted his colleagues to the danger of producing 'dry' historical knowledge that would be of little importance to 'Mr Everyman.' Nowadays, historians are far from alone in manufacturing the past. It is a role they share with judges, legislators, bureaucrats, curators, publishers, media, movie producers, and amateurs.[1]

The recent global changes and historical disputes have significantly affected history education. Although there is growing social and political interest in 'resurrecting' history in school, there is far less consensus on the direction and approach to take. The contending purposes of public schooling, coupled with sensitive issues of collective memory, heritage, commemoration, and identity politics, now render the manufacturing, teaching, and assessment of history highly explosive.

Yet, from the discussion and review presented in this book, it is fair to claim that it is futile in this day and age, characterized by competing claims and appropriations of the past, to teach students an uncontested memory-history of the collective past. Traditions and practices long taken for granted are no longer adequate to provide direction, meaning, and understanding in the twenty-first century. In 1920, H.G. Wells proclaimed that human history was engaged in a race between education and catastrophe.[2] In light of the previous discussion on progress and decline, it seems that his statement is still relevant today. Rapid and profound transformations bearing down on the whole world population require from students historical knowledge and thinking not to be acquired from simple teleological stories of 'what actually happened,' no matter how intense and emotionally powerful they might be.

In these circumstances, I hope to have made it clear that teaching students to *think historically* can be a valuable contribution to the short- and long-term challenges awaiting them. Acquiring historical knowledge in the form of 'stories' and 'facts' is certainly vital to students' interests, understanding, and place in the world. But this substantive knowledge is clearly not sufficient to move beyond intuitive and manipulative forms of thinking about the past. To think historically, students must engage in analytic practices allowing them to study and question the competing historical accounts they encounter and ultimately to construct their own historical arguments and interpretations, using the agreed-on procedures, concepts, and standards of the discipline. It is true that most students will never grow into professional historians or even contemplate the profession. But it is equally fair to maintain that students cannot understand or ultimately use *any* history if they have no exposure to, or experience of, the discipline. Going back to my introductory analogy, students cannot make sense of the history 'game' if they never get to practise and play it themselves. As Bruner makes clear with reference to learning, intellectual activity is the same anywhere, whether at the frontier of knowledge or in a history classroom. The difference, he notes, is in *degree* not in kind.

Students are already exposed to masses of conflicting stories and, to various degrees, engaged in some forms of historical practice. The family stories they hear and share at home and in their community, the historically oriented movies they take pleasure in watching, the visits they make to memorials, museums, or cemeteries, the headlines they read in the newspapers or magazines, the personal information they record in diaries and journals, the virtual discussions they have on Bin

Laden or George W. Bush, and the lessons they learn (and too quickly forget) in school are to varying degrees forms of historical knowledge and practice.

Yet, without the intervention of a formal sense of how historical knowledge is developed, manipulated, or conveyed, students are left naively apprehending what is presented to them by authorities, whether they are political leaders, movie producers, parents, or teachers. Since the nineteenth century the history profession has developed useful concepts, procedures, and ways of thinking about the past that are quite pertinent to the concerns of contemporary students. Outlining disciplinary-history as a set of procedural concepts employed by historians can help students make sense of the analytic process of producing and disseminating historical knowledge. From their initial areas of interest and significance, through their underlying ideas of change, progress, and decline, to the selection of evidence, and, finally, empathetic writing about predecessors, historians (or historical writers in general) are, consciously or not, engaged in a complex evaluative process of judging and interpreting the past from their own contemporary, situated frames of reference. Procedural concepts are essential constructs, or 'tools,' that shape historians' work and help them arrive at more sophisticated thinking and claims about the past they investigate.

Perhaps more important and stimulating for educators, introducing students to the contested but nonetheless legitimate work of historical investigation and interpretation puts the students in charge of their own learning and encourages them to take pride in and responsibility for their own education and ultimately their future. To paraphrase Wiggins and McTighe, by *uncovering* (as opposed to covering) the past, educators put students in a position to learn far more on their own than they ever could learn from history textbooks, educators, or any authority. Far from reducing the power of history, such an approach to the past opens up the knowledge doors of historical meaning-making and practice.

Clearly, engaging students in historical thinking is a long and arduous process that is likely to put educators at odds with memory-history practices, rigid curriculum expectations and content standards, and sometimes the students themselves. It is much easier and perhaps reassuring to have students intuitively accept the 'correct' story of the past than to initiate them into the contentious field of historical scholarship, particularly in jurisdictions where standardized testing is the rule.

For that reason, and many others, the recent studies conducted with student teachers or beginning history teachers often present an unrealistic, or at least incomplete, portrayal of the educational world.[3] As with other liberal professions, it would be totally unfair to expect junior teachers, who are teaching in adverse conditions and school environments, to carry out their responsibilities in an exemplary manner – or in the way scholars see fit. As educators are well aware, thorough background knowledge (through in-service training and lifelong learning), teaching experience and self-confidence, and professional autonomy are fundamentals to unconventional teaching approaches.[4] It may be discouraging, as Barton and Levstik seem to suggest, that despite greater efforts to promote historical thinking in teacher education, there is little evidence of improvement in classroom practice. It is well known that in every aspect of life, culture is the main impediment to change precisely because change threatens existing values, behaviours, habits, norms, identities, and ultimately the sense of security. Resistance to change is likely to occur in any society and in any educational system. Yet, some groups and some teachers are better positioned and equipped for the challenges of the twenty-first century than others. It is obvious that those with experience of the discipline, confidence and effectiveness in their teaching role and autonomy, and who are well disposed toward the profession, are in a better position to teach students to think historically than those who lack these strengths.

History suggests that it is unlikely that highly politicized and bureaucratic educational systems will somehow magically change their mission statements and objectives, alter their culture, and retool their organizations overnight. All of these imply long-term transformations. In some jurisdictions these transformations started many decades ago, and we only see today some of the positive impacts on students' historical learning. The purpose of this book is not to provide a blueprint for such transformations. Its goal is the more modest one of shedding light on what historical thinking entails in procedural knowledge and in how educators facing impeding changes might more effectively prepare their students to think historically. I leave it to them to examine whether the arguments presented in this book are of some pertinence.

Notes

1. Introduction

1 Nora, 'Reasons for the Current Upsurge' (online), 1.
2 Nora, 'General Introduction,' 1.
3 Keegan, 'Diary' (online).
4 Husbands et al., *Understanding History Teaching*, 4.
5 See, for instance, Talbott and Chanda, *Age of Terror*, esp. chs. 1, 3, and 6.
6 Booth and Dunne, Preface, ix.
7 Nora, 'Reasons for the Current Upsurge,' 5.
8 Fukuyama, *End of History*.
9 James Wertsch, 'Is It Possible?' 38–50; van der Leeuw-Roord, *History Changes*. See also examples of newly developed resources for history education in post-Soviet Europe, such as *Understanding a Shared Past, Learning for the Future: Everyday Life in Albania, Bulgaria and Macedonia 1945–2000* and *Ukraine and Europe from 1900–1939: The History of an Epoch through the Eyes of an Individual*. For more details on these resources, see the EuroClio website: http://www.eurocliohistory.org/.
10 Seixas, 'Purposes of Teaching Canadian History' (online).
11 See Ignatieff, *Blood and Belonging*; Boyko, *Last Steps to Freedom*; and Stanley, 'Whose Public? Whose Memory?' 32–49.
12 Nora, 'General Introduction,' 3.
13 Anderson, *Imagined Communities*.
14 The term 'heritage fashioner' was coined by David Lowenthal; see Lowenthal, *Heritage Crusade*, xi.
15 Nora, 'General Introduction,' 1.
16 On the powerful role and influence of historically oriented movies in recent cinematographic productions, see Lind, 'Screening out the Awkward Facts,' R3.

17 Gardner and Boix-Mansilla, 'Teaching for Understanding in the Disciplines – and Beyond,' 198–218.
18 Gardner and Boix-Mansilla, 'Teaching for Understanding – Within and across the Disciplines,' 17.
19 Gardner and Boix-Mansilla, 'Teaching for Understanding in the Disciplines – and Beyond.'
20 Ibid., 145.
21 Wineburg, *Historical Thinking*, 5.
22 Nora, 'General Introduction,' 3.
23 Lowenthal's acclaimed book *The Heritage Crusade and the Spoils of History* is typical. Although he does not hesitate to engage in a hyperbolic condemnation of school history for instilling historical faith (p. 116), and not without some supporting evidence, his book surprisingly offers few theoretical insights or practical procedures for 'the purpose and practice of history' (ch. 5) to guide history educators in their battle against the 'heritage crusade.'
24 George Ross, quoted in Jain, 'Nationalism and Educational Politics,' 41.
25 See, for example, Beard, 'Use of Sources in Instruction,' 40–50; Keatinge, *Studies*; Fling, 'One Use of Sources,' 206–10; and Jeffreys, *History in Schools*. For a review of advocates of disciplinary-history during the first half of the twentieth century, see Aldrich, 'New History,' 210–24; Whelan, 'Social Studies for Social Reform,' 288–315; and Osborne, 'Fred Morrow Fling,' 466–501.
26 Fred Morrow Fling, in Ibid., 471.
27 Hodgetts, *What Culture? What Heritage?*; Trudel and Jain, *Canadian History Textbooks*; Sylvester, 'Change and Continuity'; and Robert Phillips, *History Teaching*.
28 Stearns et al., 'Introduction,' 3–7.
29 See Higham, *History*; and the many related articles on this topic in the *Journal of Social History* (available from http://muse.jhu.edu/journals/jsh/). For more specific reference to school history, see Woyshner, 'Political History as Women's History,' 354–80.
30 See Appleby et al., *Telling the Truth about History*, ch. 3. On the impact of social, postmodern, feminist, postcolonial, and post-structural history on history education, see Segall, 'Critical History,' 358–74.
31 Osborne, *Education*, 87.
32 Gardner, *Mind's New Science*.
33 Boix-Mansilla, 'Beyond the Lessons,' 49.
34 OECD, *Développement de l'enseignement supérieur*.
35 For more details on the history of teacher education programs in international jurisdictions, see Wilson, et al., *Canadian Education*; Lomax, *Education of Teachers in Britain*; *European Perspectives in Teacher Education*; Lucas, *Teacher*

Education in America; Long and Riegle, *Teacher Education*; and Gidney, *From Hope to Harris.*

36 Bruner, *Process of Education*, 33.

37 Ibid., 14.

38 Ibid., 11.

39 Ibid., 60.

40 Stearns et al., 'Introduction,' 13.

41 Appleby et al., *Telling the Truth about History,* 9.

42 Sellers, 'Is History on the Way Out?' 510. A more recent argument on historians' lack of public engagement has been made by Jonathan Zimmerman in light of the Florida debate on relativism in history; see his post on the History News Network (online).

43 Wineburg, *Historical Thinking*, 50.

44 See, for example, a selection of works from Booth, 'Longitudinal Study of Cognitive Skills'; Shemilt, *History 13–16*; Wineburg, 'On the Reading of Historical Texts,' 495–519; Carretero and Voss, *Cognitive and Instruction Processes*; Seixas, 'Students' Understanding of Historical Significance,' 281–304; Audigier, 'Histoire et géographie,' 61–89; Barton and Levstik, '"It Wasn't,"' 478–513; Martineau, *L'histoire à l'école*; and VanSledright, *In Search of America's Past*. The great majority of these works focus exclusively on specific age levels and jurisdictions, with limited comparison with or reference to others. In Canada, most studies have been conducted in a few provinces (predominantly in British Columbia, Ontario, and Québec), with limited student samples, not necessarily representative of Canada's highly diverse and regional student populations.

45 Jeffreys, *History in Schools*, 4–5.

46 Jerome Bruner, in Krug, *History and the Social Sciences*, 118.

47 Stevens et al., 'Comparative Understanding of School Subjects,' 125–57.

48 Barton and Levstik, 'Why Don't More History Teachers?' 358–61. See also Hartzler-Miller, 'Making Sense of "Best Practice,"' 672–95; and Husbands et al., *Understanding History Teaching*, esp. chs. 4–6.

49 VanSledright, 'What Does It Mean?' 230.

50 This conception of disciplinary thinking has been informed by Gardner, *Unschooled Mind*; 'Discipline, Understanding, and Community,' 233–6; Bruner, *Process of Education*, ch. 4; and Wertsch, 'Is It Possible?' 38–50.

51 American Historical Association, *Study of History in Schools*, 18. Instead of using the term 'historical thinking,' the Committee preferred the related concept of 'historical-mindedness.'

52 Here, I have in mind the arguments presented notably by Schlesinger, *Disuniting of America*; and Granatstein, *Who Killed Canadian History?* For a

review of these and related arguments and their implications for history
education, see Zimmerman, *Whose America?*; Osborne, 'Teaching History in
Schools,' 585–626; Husbands et al., *Understanding History Teaching*, ch. 1; and
Barton and Levstik, *Teaching History*, ch. 1.

53 VanSledright, *In Search of America's Past*, 9.

54 Fernand Braudel, in Evans, *In Defence of History*, 11.

55 Evans, *In Defence of History*, 3.

56 See, for instance, John Slater, *Teaching History*; Seixas, 'Schweigen!' 19–37;
and Stevens et al., 'Comparative Understanding of School Subjects,' 125–57.

57 Nova Scotia history teacher, in Shields and Ramsay, *Teaching and Learning*,
63.

58 This theoretical framework relies extensively on Dickinson and Lee, 'Making Sense of History,' 117–53; Lee and Ashby, 'Progression in Historical
Understanding,' 199–222; and VanSledright and Franks, 'Concept- and Strategic-Knowledge Development,' 239–83.

59 Gaffield, 'Toward the Coach,' 12.

2. The Nature of History and Historical Thinking

1 *Report of the Royal Commission*, 138.

2 Ibid., 142.

3 Ibid., 137.

4 See Lévesque, 'History and Social Studies,' ch. 3.

5 Barton and Levstik, *Teaching History*, 1.

6 On oral history, Thucydides notes at the beginning of his *History of the
Peloponnesian War*, that 'Either I was present myself at the events I have
described or else I heard them from eye-witnesses whose reports I have
checked with as much thoroughness as possible. Not that even so the truth
was easy to discover: different eye-witnesses give different accounts of the
same events' (p. 10).

7 Thucydides, in Breisach, *Historiography*, 17. See also R.G. Collingwood's critical comments on Herodotus and Thucydides in *The Idea of History*, 25–31.

8 Stanford, *Companion*, 251.

9 Tosh, *Pursuit of History*, 10.

10 Evans, *In Defence of History*, 16.

11 Appleby et al., *Telling the Truth about History*, 73–4.

12 von Laue, *Leopold Ranke*, 19–20.

13 Tosh, *Pursuit of History*, 11. Philology, as defined in the *Oxford English Dictionary*, refers to 'the study of the development of specific languages or language families, especially research into phonological and morphological

history based on written documents.' See the definition of *philology* in the *Oxford English Dictionary Online*.

14 Tosh, *Pursuit of History*, 18.

15 von Ranke, Preface, 57.

16 Ibid., 57 (editor's translation).

17 Von Laue is careful to mention, however, that Ranke was clearly not the first historian to apply the philological techniques in the study of history. 'The philological method of analyzing and evaluating authors and their works,' he comments, 'had long been practiced by men like Friedrich August and Ranke's own teacher Gottfired Hermann' (von Laue, *Leopold Ranke*, 19).

18 Breisach, *Historiography*, 263.

19 de Coulanges, 'Inaugural Lecture,' 179.

20 Bury, 'Inaugural Lecture,' 211.

21 Edward Gaylord Bourne, in American Historical Association, *Annual Report for 1897*, 67.

22 Trevelyan, 'Clio, Rediscovered,' 229.

23 Thomas Macaulay, in Stanford, *Companion*, 93 (my emphasis).

24 Croce, *History as the Story of Liberty*, 19.

25 Collingwood, *Idea of History*, 317.

26 Ibid., 317.

27 See, for instance, Gallie, *Philosophy and the Historical Knowledge*; Danto, *Analytical Philosophy of History*; White, *Foundations of Historical Knowledge*; Scholes and Kellogg, *Nature of Narrative*; and Ricoeur, *Temps et récit*.

28 David Carr, *Time, Narrative, and History*, 59.

29 G.M. Trevelyan, in Evans, *In Defence of History*, 250.

30 Thomson, *Aims of History*, 57.

31 Tosh, *Pursuit of History*, 12.

32 See Osborne, 'Fred Morrow Fling,' 480.

33 Elton, 'What Sort of History?' 225. A similar argument was presented by the American Committee of Seven in their report of 1899. See American Historical Association, *Study of History in Schools*, 101–6.

34 The term 'appropriation' is borrowed from socio-cognitive psychology (neo-Vygotsky). As one of the leading scholars in the domain, James Wertsch contends that it refers to a particular relationship between the learner and cultural tools (texts, language, etc.). The process of appropriation involves the ability not only to use (or employ) such cultural tools but also to make them one's own. This sense of appropriating cultural tools, for Wertsch, goes beyond the dimension of cognitive mastery (or use) because it involves an emotional dimension that favours its internalization. In simple terms, Wertsch refers to appropriation as the process of 'knowing and

believing,' whereas mastery typically means for the learner 'knowing but not believing.' In education, mastery would be used in reference to students' processes of learning an historical narrative for the sake of an exam, whereas appropriation would imply learning this narrative to acquire and internalize it in personal attributes, values, and identity. See Wertsch, 'Is It Possible?' 38–50. See also his *Mind as Action*, ch. 5.

35 Lee, 'History Teaching and Philosophy,' 26.
36 Dewey, *Democracy and Education*, 151.
37 Gardner, *Unschooled Mind*, 9.
38 Ibid., 9.
39 Bruner, *Process of Education*, 25.
40 Stearns, *Why Study History?*
41 Arthur et al., *Citizenship through Secondary History*, 53.
42 VanSledright, 'What Does It Mean?' 230.
43 Lee, 'History Teaching and Philosophy of History,' 21–8. A related but more complex model has also been presented by VanSledright and Franks, 'Concept- and Strategic-Knowledge Development,' 239–83.
44 Lee and Ashby, 'Progression in Historical Understanding,' 199.
45 Lee, 'History Teaching and Philosophy of History,' 25.
46 Lee and Ashby, 'Progression in Historical Understanding,' 199.
47 Ibid., 200.
48 Bruner, *Process of Education*, 28.
49 Haydn et al., *Learning to Teach History*, 84.
50 See Hertzberg, 'History and Progressivism,' 80–9. Barton and Levstik's most recent book, *Teaching History for the Common Good*, also typifies this interdisciplinary emphasis.
51 VanSledright, *In Search of America's Past*, 141.
52 Osborne, 'To the Past,' 117–18. See also his 'History and Social Studies,' 74.
53 Seixas, 'Conceptualizing,' 32.
54 Levstik and Barton, *Doing History*, 13.
55 See Haydn et al., *Learning to Teach History*, ch. 6. An online version of the National Curriculum for England, with details on the programs of study for history (key stage 1 to key stage 3), is available online from http://www.nc.uk.net/.
56 National Standards for History in the Schools, *National Standards* (online).The electronic version presents all the elements of the printed one, except for charts, illustrations, and appendices.
57 Barton and Levstik, *Teaching History*, 7.
58 For Australia, see Taylor, *Future of the Past*; for France, see France, Ministère de l'Éducation Nationale, *Histoire-géographie et éducation civique*; and for

Germany and other European countries, see von Borries, 'Exploring,' 25–49; and Macdonald, *Approaches to European Historical Consciousness*, esp. secs. 4 and 5.

59 Ahonen, 'Past, History, and Education,' 739.
60 Rogers, 'Why Teach History?' 23.
61 Grant Wiggins and Jay McTighe, *Understanding by Design*, 105.
62 Ibid., 109.
63 Ibid., 228.
64 E.H. Carr, *What Is History?* 28.
65 Bruner, *Process of Education*, 58.
66 VanSledright and Franks, 'Concept- and Strategic-Knowledge Development,' 246.

3. What Is Important in the Past? – Historical Significance

 1 E.H. Carr, *What Is History?* 49.
 2 Dallaire, *Shake Hands with the Devil*, xvii.
 3 Roméo Dallaire, in Allen, 'The General and the Genocide.'
 4 E.H. Carr, *What Is History?* 44.
 5 Ibid., 44.
 6 Ignatieff, *Human Rights*, 39.
 7 Ibid., 39
 8 E.H. Carr, *What Is History?* 5–6.
 9 Lomas, *Teaching and Assessing*, 41.
10 von Ranke, 'The Ideal of Universal History,' 55.
11 Ibid., 59.
12 Elton, *Practice of History*, 13.
13 Partington, *Idea of an Historical Education*, 110.
14 See Braudel, *On History*. Original work published in French in 1969 as a collection of Braudel's occasional papers from his work with the *Annales*.
15 Rogers, 'The Past,' 6. See also Thomson, *Aims of History*, 55.
16 Thomas Carlyle, in Carr, *What Is History?* 49.
17 E. Pauline Johnson, cited in McMaster University, *Pauline Johnson Archives*. See also a copy of her last work in E. Johnson, *E. Pauline Johnson*.
18 See Lyon, 'Pauline Johnson,' 136–59; Gray, *Flint & Feather*; and Strong-Boag and Gerson, *Paddling Her Own Canoe*.
19 Strong-Boag, 'No Longer Dull,' 55.
20 Ibid., 56.
21 Seixas, 'Mapping the Terrain,' 22.
22 E.H. Carr, *What Is History?* 29.

23 Ibid., 30.
24 On the 'relevance' of history, see Butterfield, *Whig Interpretation of History*; Oakeshott, *Experience and Its Modes*; Tosh, *Pursuit of History*, ch. 1; Lowenthal, *The Past Is a Foreign Country*, ch. 5; and David Carr, *Time, Narrative, and History*, ch. 7.
25 A good example of this implicit understanding of scientific history is the recent case of U.S. historian Michael Bellesiles. Following the scandal over the unwarranted conclusion of his book *Arming America: The Origins of a National Gun Culture*, which was awarded Columbia University's Bancroft Prize, Professor Bellesiles was forced to resigned from his academic position in 2002. An investigating committee, headed by professor Stanley Katz, in *The Emory Wheel* (http://www.emorywheel.com/vnews/display.v/ART/2002/10/25/3db9bc0a08df2 [accessed 22 October 2004]), concluded that 'Bellesiles was guilty of both substandard research methodology and of willfully misrepresenting specific evidence in Arming America.'
26 Phillips, 'Historical Significance,' 14–19.
27 Lee, 'Historical Imagination,' 87.
28 Partington, *Idea of an Historical Education*, 112.
29 Ibid., 112.
30 On history by numbers, see Tosh, *Pursuit of History*, ch. 9.
31 Ibid., 169.
32 Keegan, *Iraq War*, 1.
33 Butterfield, *Whig Interpretation of History*, 31.
34 Ibid., 13–14.
35 Oakeshott, *Experience and Its Modes*, 103.
36 E.H. Carr, *What Is History?* 38.
37 Appleby et al., *Telling the Truth about History*, 295.
38 Becker, 'Everyman His Own Historian,' 235.
39 *The New York Times* book review, in MacMillan, *Paris 1919*, back cover.
40 Lowenthal, *The Past Is a Foreign Country*, 216.
41 Barton and Levstik, '"It Wasn't,"' 479.
42 Symcox, *Whose History?* 2–3.
43 For a review of these 'history crises' in French and English Canada, see Osborne, '"Our History Syllabus,"' 404–35.
44 Granatstein, *Who Killed Canadian History?*, 43.
45 On this last point, see VanSledright, *In Search of America's Past*, ch. 3.
46 Seixas, 'Students' Understanding of Historical Significance,' 285.
47 Barton, 'Cultural Context,' 5.
48 Seixas, 'Students' Understanding of Historical Significance,' 285.
49 Wertsch, 'Is It Possible?' 42.

50 Barton, "'You'd Be Wanting to Know,'" 102.
51 Ibid., 89–106; Epstein, 'Deconstructing Differences,' 397–423; Létourneau and Moisan, 'Mémoire et récit,' 325–56; Seixas, 'Mapping the Terrain,' 22–7; and Yeager et al., 'How Eighth Graders,' 199–219.
52 Epstein, 'Deconstructing Differences,' 418.
53 Lis Cercadillo has also elaborated a set of five similar criteria (contemporary, causal, pattern, symbolic, and present or future) in 'Significance in History,' 116–45. See also the related criteria developed by Denos and Case, *Teaching about Historical Thinking*, 9–14.
54 Rosenzweig, 'How Americans Use and Think,' 264.
55 Lévesque, 'Teaching Second-Order Concepts' (online).
56 Wertsch, 'Is It Possible?' 38–9.
57 Ibid., 39.
58 Barton and Levstik, "'It Wasn't,'" 484.
59 Lévesque, 'Teaching Second-Order Concepts.' Original quote was removed from the online edition of the text.
60 Levstik, 'Articulating the Silences,' 290.
61 The limited reference to and consideration of World War I, and particularly Vimy Ridge, by French Canadian students was also observed in the study of young Québec francophones by Létourneau and Moisan, 'Mémoire et récit,' 332–3. It should be noted, however, that World War I represents a pivotal change in French-Canadians' attitudes toward the military. The establishment of the Fusiliers de Sherbrooke in 1910 and the Royal 22e Régiment in 1914, for instance, led to increased enrolments in French Québec, notably in the infantry. See Morton, *Military History of Canada*.
62 Simon Schama, in Seaton, 'Blast from the Past' (online), 1.
63 Henry Buckle, in Stanford, *Companion*, 260.
64 Lee, 'Why Learn History?' 6.
65 Ibid., 7.
66 Ibid., 10.
67 Yeager et al., 'How Eighth Graders,' 210, 215.
68 Seixas, 'Students' Understanding of Historical Significance,' 294.
69 Student, in ibid., 294.
70 VanSledright, *In Search of America's Past*, 140.

4. What Changed and What Remained the Same? – Continuity and Change

1 Donovan, *Historical Thought in America*, 92.
2 Lester B. Pearson, in Matheson, *Canada's Flag*, 73.
3 John Diefenbaker, in House of Commons, *Debates*, 11,004.

4 Diefenbaker, *One Canada*, 243.
5 Pearson, in Matheson, *Canada's Flag*, 161.
6 Pearson, in ibid., 75.
7 In 1957, Prime Minister Diefenbaker authorized a change of the colour of the maple leafs embedded in the Canadian coat of arms (from green to red), which were incorporated in the Red Ensign.
8 Mink, 'Autonomy of Historical Understanding,' 32.
9 Ibid., 40.
10 Ibid., 40.
11 Ibid., 42.
12 Ibid., 30
13 Ibid., 33.
14 Shemilt, 'Caliph's Coin,' 91. For a similar argument, with students, see Stanford, *Companion*, 176.
15 Collingwood, *Idea of History*, 215.
16 Lowenthal, *The Past Is a Foreign Country*, 219–20.
17 Pollard, *Idea of Progress*, 201.
18 Burston, *Principles of History Teaching*, 23.
19 Tosh, *Pursuit of History*, 96.
20 Thomson, *Aims of History*, 58. Karl Marx did offer a more nuanced and perhaps prudent statement of human agency, where he claimed that 'Man makes his own history, but he does not make it out of the whole cloth; he does not make it out of conditions chosen by himself, but out of such as he finds close at hand. The tradition of all past generations weighs like an alp upon the brain of the living.' See Marx, *Eighteenth Brumaire of Louis Bonaparte*, 5.
21 Richard Tawney, *History and Society*, 54.
22 See Meinecke, 'Historicism and its Problems,' 267–88.
23 Burston, *Principles of History Teaching*, 63 (emphasis in the original).
24 Ibid., 63–4.
25 On 'subjectivity' in historical explanation, see the critical discussion of Martin, 'Causes, Conditions, and Causal Importance,' 53–74.
26 E.H. Carr, *What Is History?* 85.
27 Shemilt, 'Caliph's Coin,' 91.
28 Stanford, *Companion*, 203 (my emphasis).
29 Mink, 'Autonomy of Historical Understanding,' 30.
30 Rüsen, 'Historical Narration,' 89. A similar statement was also made a century earlier, where Frederick Jackson Turner argued in his essay 'The Significance of History' that 'in history there is a unity and continuity. Strictly speaking, there is no gap between ancient, medieval, and modern history.' See Turner, 'American Definition of History,' 202.

31 Hayden White, in Partner, 'Hayden White,' 165
32 Walsh, *Introduction to Philosophy of History,* 59.
33 Ibid., 59.
34 McCullagh, 'Colligation and Classification in History,' 267.
35 Walsh, 'Colligatory Concepts in History,' 75.
36 Seixas, 'Conceptualizing,' 771.
37 Shemilt makes a similar claim where he writes that 'the historian must not be false to the chronicle of events but must also construct meaningful accounts that impute narrative significance to events by means of quantitative and colligatory generalizations, analysis of trends and turning points, and intentional and causal explanations.' See Shemilt, 'Caliph's Coin,' 95.
38 Walsh, 'Colligatory Concepts in History,' 77.
39 Ibid., 79 (emphasis in the original).
40 Ibid., 79–80.
41 Ibid., 83.
42 McCullagh, 'Colligation and Classification in History,' 284.
43 Ibid., 278.
44 Haydn, et al., *Learning to Teach History,* 105.
45 See Ontario Ministry of Education, *Canadian and World Studies, Grades 11 and 12,* 114.
46 National Standards for History in the Schools, *National Standards* (online).
47 Bogle et al., *Canada: Continuity and Change.*
48 Haydn et al., *Learning to Teach History,* 106. On the limited reference to and usage of continuity and change in history education, see also Barton, 'Sociocultural Perspective on Children's Understanding,' 881–913.
49 Shemilt, *History 13–16,* 35.
50 Ibid., 35.
51 Ibid., 36.
52 For example, Husbands et al.'s study of English history teachers concludes that concepts, such as 'causation,' are often poorly defined and employed in class by teachers. The result is a sense of confusion in their application and usage by students and teachers themselves. See Husbands et al., *Understanding History Teaching,* 141–2.
53 VanSledright and Brophy, 'Storytelling, Imagination, and Fanciful Elaboration,' 837–59.
54 VanSledright, *In Search of America's Past,* 89.
55 U.S. student, in Barton, 'Narrative Simplifications,' 67.
56 Shemilt, 'Caliph's Coin,' 90.
57 Ibid., 90.
58 Seixas, 'Conceptualizing,' 771.
59 Ibid., 772.

60 Lévesque, '"Bin Laden Is Responsible,"' 186–7.
61 Seixas, 'Conceptualizing,' 772.
62 Stanford, *Companion*, 175.
63 National Standards for History in the Schools, *National Standards*, standard 1.
64 For more evidence on students' chronological thinking, see Levstik and Barton, '"They Still Use,"' 531–76.
65 Shemilt, 'Caliph's Coin,' 94.
66 National Standards for History in the Schools, *National Standards*, standard 1.
67 Drake and Nelson, *Engagement in Teaching History*, 81.
68 Levstik and Barton, *Doing History*, 136–7.
69 E.H. Carr makes a similar argument where he claims that significance is necessary for the selection of both the 'facts' and the 'causes' pertinent to historians' explanations and interpretations. See Carr, *What Is History?* 99–100.
70 Thompson, 'Colligation and History Teaching,' 96–7.
71 Tosh, *Pursuit of History*, 97.
72 Shemilt, 'Caliph's Coin,' 99.
73 Ibid., 100.

5. Did Things Change for Better or Worse? – Progress and Decline

1 Koselleck, *Practice of Conceptual History*, 221.
2 Voltaire, *Age of Lewis XIV*, 4.
3 Ibid., 4.
4 Condorcet, *Esquisse d'un tableau historique*, 77.
5 Condorcet, in Breisach, *Historiography*, 207.
6 Ibid., 208. On Enlightenment and progress, see Dumas, *Histoire de la pensée*.
7 Malthus, *Essay*, 1.
8 Ibid., 13–14.
9 Paul Kennedy, *Preparing*, 4.
10 Ibid., 13.
11 Ibid., 6. See also data from Migration Watch, United Kingdom, http://www.migrationwatchuk.org/frameset.asp?menu=researchpapers&page=briefingpapers/history/nationemigrants.asp [21 March 2005].
12 Ignatieff, *Rights Revolution*, 140.
13 Wright, *Short History of Progress*, 3.
14 Ibid., 31.
15 Ibid., 129.

16 A closely related argument is also put forth by Diamond, *Collapse*.
17 Paul Kennedy, *Preparing*, 11.
18 Ibid., 12.
19 Ibid., 11.
20 Koselleck, *Practice of Conceptual History*, 219.
21 Graham, *Shape of the Past*, 45.
22 Pollard, *Idea of Progress*, 180.
23 Bury, *Idea of Progress*, 21.
24 Breisach, *Historiography*, 206.
25 See Comte, *Cours de philosophie positive*.
26 Koselleck, *Practice of Conceptual History*, 219.
27 E.H. Carr, *What Is History?* 111.
28 Koselleck, *Practice of Conceptual History*, 221 (emphasis in the original).
29 Cronon, 'A Place for Stories,' 1347–76.
30 Ibid., 1348.
31 Ibid.
32 Ibid., 1364.
33 Ibid., 1373.
34 Koselleck, *Practice of Conceptual History*, 227.
35 Ibid., 230.
36 Ibid.
37 Ibid., 227.
38 Ibid., 229.
39 Ibid., 232.
40 Mercier, *Memoirs of the Year Two Thousand Five Hundred*. Because the year 2440 was set arbitrarily by Mercier in his original publication, the editor of the English version noted in the preface that it was rounded up for practical purposes.
41 Mercier, *Memoirs*, 72–3.
42 Bury, *Idea of Progress*, 193.
43 R.G. Collingwood, in van der Dussen, 'Collingwood,' 33.
44 Ibid., 31.
45 Collingwood, *Idea of History*, 329.
46 Collingwood, in van der Dussen, 'Collingwood,' 31.
47 Collingwood, *Idea of History*, 330.
48 van der Dussen, 'Collingwood,' 34.
49 Collingwood, *Idea of History*, 330.
50 Butterfield, *Whig Interpretation of History*, 11.
51 Graham, *Shape of the Past*, 51–2.
52 Ibid., 57 (emphasis in the original).

53 A related problem has to do with historians' perception of what counts as valid standards. Some may talk about progress in aspects of life (e.g., the development of 'smart' weapons) that would be considered to be either a decline or even an inappropriate standard to judge human development for others (e.g., in terms of universal peace or human agency). Technological advances in weaponry are not necessarily a guarantee of international security or even of a decrease in casualties if one takes 'security' or 'casualties' as a measure of progress.

54 Graham, *Shape of the Past*, 56.

55 Cronon, 'A Place for Stories,' 1373.

56 Graham, *Shape of the Past*, 52–3.

57 Jeffreys, *History in Schools*, 21.

58 Trevelyan, 'Clio, Rediscovered,' 236.

59 See, for instance, Igartua, 'What Nation, Which People?'; Johnson, *Teaching of History*, chs. 2–3; Osborne, '"Our History Syllabus,"' 404–35; Stanley, 'White Supremacy,' 39–56; and Yeandle, 'Empire.'

60 Yeandle, 'Empire,' 2.

61 Shemilt, 'Caliph's Coin,' 87–8.

62 Ibid., 88 (emphasis in the original).

63 Husbands et al., *Understanding History Teaching*, 125.

64 Secondary school teacher, in ibid., 125.

65 Wertsch and O'Connor, 'Multivoicedness in Historical Representations,' 295–309.

66 Barton and Levstik, '"It Wasn't,"' 484–5.

67 Barton and Levstik, *Teaching History*, 169.

68 Létourneau, 'Remembering Our Past,' 74. Original research findings have been published in Létourneau and Moisan, 'Mémoire et récit,' 325–56.

69 Seixas and Clark, 'Murals as Monuments,' 146–71.

70 Ibid., 156. As noted by the authors, the total number of 57 test responses does not match the numbers presented (18, 29, and 8), as some responses spanned two categories and two students' responses were not categorized because of the lack of information provided.

71 Ibid., 157.

72 Ibid., 158.

73 Ibid. 158.

74 Ibid., 168.

75 Ontario Ministry of Education, *Canadian and World Studies, Grades 9–10*, 37. These grade 9–10 curriculum guidelines were revised in 2005. The reference to Wilfrid Laurier has disappeared.

76 Granatstein, *Who Killed the Canadian Military?* 33.

77 Barton and Levstik, *Teaching History*, 180.
78 Appleby et al., *Telling the Truth about History*, 103.

6. How Do We Make Sense of the Raw Materials of the Past? – Evidence

1   Lowenthal, *The Past Is a Foreign Country*, 212–13.
2   Bush, 'President's Remarks.'
3   Powell, 'U.S. Secretary of State.'
4   Hans Blix, in PBS, *Interviews*.
5   Secretary of State Collin Powell, in BBC, 'Powell Admits Iraq Evidence Mistake.' See also his more recent declaration on ABC, 'Colin Powell on Iraq.'
6   Deputy Secretary of Defense Paul Wolfowitz, in *USA Today*, 'Wolfowitz Comments Revive Doubts.'
7   Stanford, *Companion*, 135.
8   John Adams, in Edward Kennedy, 'Speech to the Council.'
9   Barton and Levstik, *Teaching History*, 83.
10 Husbands, *What Is History Teaching?* 16.
11 C.R. Cheney, in Tosh, *Pursuit of History*, 50.
12 Ranke, in von Laue, *Leopold Ranke*, 116.
13 Arnaldo Momigliano, in Evans, *In Defence of History*, 93.
14 For a similar argument, see Stanford, *Companion*, 155–8.
15 Husbands, *What Is History Teaching?* 13.
16 Tosh, *Pursuit of History*, 49.
17 John Dewey, in Levstik and Barton, *Doing History*, 23.
18 Collingwood, *Idea of History*, 248.
19 Fling, 'One Use of Sources,' 206–10. See also Osborne's review of Fling's method in Osborne, 'Fred Morrow Fling,' 484.
20 Hammond, 'Framework of Plausibility,' 47–58.
21 Bloch, *Historian's Craft*, 61.
22 Felix Branhan, in Ambrose, *D-Day*, 420.
23 Ibid., 403.
24 Spears, 'Dear Diary,' A2.
25 See Heller, 'Netanyahu Calls for Referendum,' A14 (my emphasis).
26 McParland, 'Call Them the Terrorists,' A11.
27 Ringrose, 'Beyond Amusement,' 209–28.
28 Trask, 'Did the Sans-Coulottes Wear Nikes?'
29 Dynneson et al., *Designing Effective Instruction*, 160.
30 For more details on teaching with digital sources and hypermedia, see Brush and Saye, 'Scaffolding Critical Reasoning'; Craver, *Using Internet Primary*; Cantu and Warren, *Teaching History*; and Friedman, 'World History,'

124–41. On the role of digital sources and the Internet for historical-knowledge production and publication, see Cohen and Rosenzweig, *Digital History*.

31 See, for example, American Psychological Association, *Publication Manual*, 268–81.

32 Tosh, *Pursuit of History*, 53.

33 For an insightful, theoretical discussion on the reading and meaning of text in light of the recent postmodernist debate, see McCullagh, *Truth of History*, ch. 5.

34 Stanford, *Companion*, 32.

35 On the *mentalités* and their French cultural origins and adaptation in English, see Le Goff, 'Mentalities,' 166–80.

36 See Cantor and Schneider, *How to Study History*, 42.

37 House of Commons, *Debates*, 3118–19 (my emphasis).

38 VanSledright, *In Search of America's Past*, 111.

39 Daniel Gordon, in Lowenthal, 'Dilemmas and Delights,' 66 (my emphasis).

40 Ibid., 78.

41 VanSledright, *In Search of America's Past*, 112.

42 Collingwood, in Pattiz, 'Idea of History Teaching,' 3.

43 On the usefulness and limits of the courtroom analogy in history, see Clark, *Critical Historian*, 13–18.

44 Collingwood, *Idea of History*, 257.

45 Hallam, 'Piaget and Thinking in History,' 162–78.

46 See Stones, 'An Analysis'; and de Silva, 'Formation of Historical Concepts,' 174–82.

47 Elton, 'What Sort of History?' 221 (my emphasis).

48 On the recent use of evidence in the English curriculum, see Sylvester, 'Change and Continuity,' 18–19.

49 Booth, 'Longitudinal Study of the Cognitive Skills,' 61–9.

50 Cooper, *Teaching of History*. See also her 'Historical Thinking and Cognitive Development,' 101–21.

51 Shemilt, *History 13–16*, 36.

52 More recent materials and ideas on the progression of British students with evidence can be found in Shemilt, 'Adolescent Ideas about Evidence,' 39–61.

53 Lee and Ashby, 'Progression in Historical Understanding,' 213.

54 VanSledright, *In Search of America's Past*, 29.

55 For the United States, see Barton, '"I Just Kind of Know,"' 407–30; 'Primary Children's Understanding,' 21–30; Foster and Yeager, '"You've Got to Put Together,"' 286–317; Grant, *History Lessons*; Mayer, 'Learning to Teach Young People'; Levstik and Smith, '"I've Never Done This Before,"' 105–9;

and Wineburg, 'On the Reading of Historical Texts,' 495–519. For Canada, see Seixas, 'Community of Inquiry,' 305–24; 'Student Teachers Thinking Historically,' 310–41; Martineau, 'Les conceptions des futurs enseignants'; *L'Histoire à l'école*; and Lévesque, 'Learning about the October Crisis.'

56 VanSledright, *In Search of America's Past*, 141.
57 Barton, 'Primary Children's Understanding,' 28–9.
58 See Osborne, 'Teaching History in Schools,' 585–626; and Lévesque, 'Teaching History and Social Studies,' 55–70.
59 Wilson and Sykes, 'Toward Better Teacher Preparation,' 273.
60 Ibid., 274.
61 See, for instance, Kirman, *Elementary Social Studies*, chapters 18–19.
62 VanSledright, *In Search of America's Past*, 51.
63 Partington, *Idea of an Historical Education*, 74.
64 On the use of the historical method with students, see the critical review of Seixas, 'When Psychologists Discuss Historical Thinking,' 107. On the ways of introducing students to evidence in the classroom, see Dickinson et al., 'Evidence in History and the Classroom,' 1–20; and Lee, 'Historical Knowledge,' 41–8.
65 Wiggins and McTighe, *Understanding by Design*, 121.
66 Ibid., 119.
67 Ibid., 119 (my emphasis).
68 Roland Tharp and Ronald Gallimore, in Bain, 'Into the Breach,' 336.
69 See Haydn et al., *Learning to Teach History*, 115; and VanSledright, *In Search of America's Past*, 84.
70 Husbands, *What Is History Teaching?*, 109.
71 Dickinson et al., 'Evidence in History,' 16.
72 See, for instance, the discussion in Lee, 'Explanation and Understanding in History,' 72–93.
73 VanSledright, *In Search of America's Past*, 50.
74 Bruner, *Acts of Meaning*, 97.
75 Voss and Wiley, 'Case Study,' 383–4.
76 Barton and Levstik, *Teaching History*, ch. 7; and VanSledright and Brophy, 'Storytelling, Imagination, and Fanciful Elaboration,' 837–59. On children and stories in general, see the psychological work of Miller and Sperry, 'Early Talk about the Past,' 293–325; and Dunn, *Beginnings of Social Understanding*.
77 Voss and Wiley, 'Case Study,' 384.
78 Ibid., 385.
79 Ibid., 384.
80 Boscolo and Mason, 'Writing to Learn,' 83–104.

81 Ibid., 101.
82 Barton, '"I Just Kind of Know,"' 420.
83 Bain, 'Into the Breach,' 335
84 Husbands, *What Is History Teaching?* 26 (my emphasis).
85 Lee, 'Historical Knowledge,' 45.

7. How Can We Understand Predecessors Who Had Different Moral Frameworks? – Historical Empathy

1 Partington, *Idea of an Historical Education*, 51.
2 Levi, *Drowned and the Saved*, 38.
3 Ibid., 158–9.
4 Ibid., 161.
5 Ibid., 152.
6 Student, in ibid., 157. I am in debt to Sam Wineburg for pointing out this book to me.
7 Ibid., 157.
8 Ibid., 158.
9 Ibid., 158.
10 Seixas, 'Conceptualizing,' 773–4.
11 Leopold von Ranke, in Partington, *Idea of an Historical Education*, 194.
12 Collingwood, *Idea of History*, 215.
13 Ibid., 218.
14 Ibid., 218.
15 Ibid., 231.
16 Ibid., 247.
17 See, for instance, Walsh, 'R.G. Collingwood's Philosophy of History,' 154–8; Gardiner, 'Objects of Historical Knowledge,' 211–20; and Toynbee, *Study of History*, esp. 730–4. For a review of the criticism of Collingwood, see Goldstein, 'Collingwood's Theory of Historical Knowing,' 3–36; and Nielsen, 'Re-enactment and Reconstruction,' 1–31.
18 Patrick Gardiner, in Nielsen, 'Re-enactment and Reconstruction,' 6 (emphasis in the original).
19 Part of the controversy, as Nielson observes, comes from the posthumous edition of *The Idea of History* by Malcolm Knox. This version includes a collection of lectures and essays but ignores some earlier unpublished manuscripts of Collingwood on re-enactment and imagination. See Nielsen, 'Re-enactment and Reconstruction,' 2–3. See also the work of Marnie Hughes-Warrington, '*How Good an Historian?*'
20 A clear statement showing that Collingwood was not an intuitionist but an

evidence-based methodologist can be found in a lecture entitled 'II C.T.T. 1929,' originally inserted in 'Outlines of a Philosophy of History' written at Le Martouret, Die, 1928. These documents, stored in the Bodleian Library at the University of Oxford, are included in Nielsen, 'Re-enactment and Reconstruction,' 9–10, as well as in Hughes-Warrington, *'How Good an Historian?'* 60.

21 Collingwood, in ibid., 246 (my emphasis).
22 Shemilt, 'Beauty and the Philosopher,' 41–3.
23 Ibid., 41
24 Ibid., 43.
25 Hayden White, in Hughes-Warrington, *'How Good an Historian?'* 124.
26 Ibid., 41.
27 Ibid., 44.
28 Peter Lee, 'Historical Imagination,' 85.
29 For an in-depth discussion of empathy, sympathy, and imagination in history education, notably in the British context, see Hughes-Warrington, *'How Good an Historian?'* ch. 1–2.
30 Collingwood, *Idea of History,* 241 (my emphasis).
31 Collingwood, 'Inaugural: Rough Notes,' 135.
32 Ibid., 241.
33 Lee, 'Historical Imagination,' 89.
34 Ibid., 245.
35 Ibid., 218.
36 VanSledright, 'From Empathic Regard to Self-Understanding,' 59.
37 Hughes-Warrington, *'How Good an Historian?'* 153.
38 VanSledright, 'From Empathic Regard to Self-Understanding,' 57.
39 Lowenthal, *The Past Is a Foreign Country,* 234–5.
40 VanSledright, 'From Empathic Regard to Self-Understanding,' 66.
41 Husbands, *What Is History Teaching?* 31.
42 The recent German movie *Der Untergang* (The Downfall), about the Nazi dictator's final days in his Berlin bunker, is a good public example. Based on the work of historian Joachim Fest and the memoirs of Traudl Junge, the movie presents Hitler with an intimate and more humanizing realism than portrayed so far, thus leading some critics to argue that humanizing Hitler necessarily legitimizes him and his evil actions. See Hundley, 'New Film Re-examines Hitler.'
43 Partington, *Idea of an Historical Education,* 74.
44 Ashby and Lee, 'Children's Concepts,' 63.
45 Partington, *Idea of an Historical Education,* 239 (my emphasis).
46 See Sheehan, 'Problems of Moral Judgments,' 37–50.

47 Oakeshott, *Rationalism in Politics*, 165.

48 Butterfield, *Whig Interpretation of History*, 119.

49 Ibid., 118. Butterfield likely had Lord Acton in mind here. See Acton's inaugural lecture at Cambridge in 1895 in Acton, *Lectures on Modern History*, 27.

50 Braun, 'The Holocaust,' 182.

51 Vann, 'Historians and Moral Evaluation,' 24.

52 Partington, *Idea of an Historical Education*, 278–86; and Oldfield, 'Moral Judgments in History,' 260–77.

53 Shemilt, 'Beauty and the Philosopher,' 48.

54 Peter Lee, in ibid., 48.

55 Oldfield, 'Moral Judgments in History,' 269

56 Gallie, in ibid., 270.

57 Ibid., 273.

58 Stacey, *Six Years of War*, 397.

59 Lieutenant-General H.D.G. Crerar, in Canadian Military Headquarters, *OPERATION at Dieppe*, 40.

60 Partington, *Idea of an Historical Education*, 79–80.

61 For a different interpretative judgment on Dieppe, see Villa, *Unauthorized Action*.

62 Seixas, 'Conceptualizing,' 776.

63 Hume, *Enquiry concerning Human Understanding*.

64 Shemilt, 'Beauty and the Philosopher,' 47.

65 Ibid., 47–8.

66 See, for instance, Cmiel, 'Recent History of Human Rights'; Ishay, *History of Human Rights*, esp. chs. 5–6; and Ignatieff, *Rights Revolution*. Recent evidence of the growing interest of historians in issues of human rights and civil liberties: In 2003 members of the American Historical Association created the network Historians against War to promote world peace through non-military interventions in Iraq and elsewhere (information available from http://www.historiansagainstwar.org). A related international organization, called the Network of Concerned Historians, was created in 1995 to study and disseminate information on human rights abuses around the world (http://www.concernedhistorians.org).

67 Saying that human equality (in the forms of rights) is now seen as a precondition for a shared humanity does not, however, solve the problem of deciding what doctrine or institution best protects or enhances these rights. Such moral claims, as Nathan Rotenstreich observes, must necessarily be measured empirically or conceptually analysed to expose their fallacies (or connectnesses). See Rotenstreich, 'Idea of Historical Progress,' 211.

68 Ignatieff, *Right Revolution*, 14.
69 Oldfield, 'Moral Judgments in History,' 275.
70 See, for instance, Charles Dickens, *Hard Times*, esp. ch. 1.
71 Husbands, *What Is History Teaching?* 54.
72 See Flavell, *Cognitive Development*; Jones, *Fantasy and Feeling in Education*; and Watts, *Learning of History*. For an historical discussion of empathy and cognitive development, see Cooper, 'Historical Thinking and Cognitive Development,' 107–111.
73 School Council History Project, in Stockley, 'Empathetic Reconstruction of History,' 53.
74 Shemilt, 'Beauty and the Philosopher,' 50.
75 Lee and Ashby, 'Empathy, Perspective,' 40.
76 Ibid., 33.
77 Yeager and Foster, 'Role of Empathy,' 13–19.
78 Cruxton and Wilson, *Flashback Canada*, 88.
79 Yeager and Doppen, 'Teaching and Learning Multiple Perspectives,' 97–114.
80 Ibid., 110.
81 Ibid., 108. Yet, the authors also found that despite the inclusion of British and Russian sources, students in the second group adopted essentially two perspectives on the issue (U.S. and Japanese). It is no surprise, the researchers observe, the U.S. viewpoint figured prominently in students' answers.
82 Robert Rosenstone, in Weinstein, 'Movies as Gateway to History,' 27. On the influence of popular media, notably films and books, on U.S. citizens, see Rosenzweig, 'How Americans Use and Think,' 273–5.
83 Richard Raack, in Weinstein, 'Movies as Gateway to History,' 27.
84 See Haydn, et al., *Learning to Teach History*, ch. 7.
85 Husbands, *What Is History Teaching?* 66.
86 On the growing importance of experiential learning and virtual history, see my 'Learning by Playing,' 68–71.
87 John Slater, in Husbands et al., *Understanding History Teaching*, 123.
88 Husbands, *What Is History Teaching?* 65. On the important role of moral beliefs for English history teachers, see Husbands et al., *Understanding History Teaching*, ch. 8.
89 Barton and Levstik, *Teaching History*, 219.
90 See my '"Bin Laden Is Responsible,"' 174–202; Létourneau and Moisan, 'Mémoire et récit,' 325–56; and Seixas, 'Confronting the Moral Frames,' 261–85.
91 Shemilt, 'Beauty and the Philosopher,' 54.
92 Ibid., 53.

8. Conclusion

1 Nora, 'Reasons for the Current Upsurge,' 5.
2 Wells, *Outline of History.*
3 See, for instance, van Hover, '"Making" Students Better People?' 219–32; Barton and Levstik, 'Why Don't More History Teachers?' 358–61; Hartzler-Miller, 'Making Sense of "Best Practice,"' 672–95; Gillaspie and Davis, 'Historical Constructions,' 35–45; and Seixas, 'Student Teachers Thinking Historically,' 310–41.
4 For a more extensive discussion of some of these elements, see Shulman, 'Knowledge and Teaching,' 1–22.

Bibliography

ABC (American Broadcasting Corporation). 'Colin Powell on Iraq, Race, and Hurricane Relief.' *ABC News*, 8 September 2005. http://abcnews.go.com/2020/Politics/story?id=1105979&page=1 (accessed 9 September 2005).

Acton, John. *Lectures on Modern History*. London: Macmillan, 1906. http://oll.libertyfund.org/ToC/0028.php (27 January 2005).

Ahonen, Sirkka. 'The Past, History, and Education.' *Journal of Curriculum Studies* 33, no. 6 (2001): 737–51.

Aldrich, R. 'New History: An Historical Perspective.' In Dickinson et al., *Learning History*, 210–24.

Allen, Terry. 'The General and the Genocide.' *Amnesty International Now* (Winter 2002). http://www.thirdworldtraveler.com/Heroes/Gen_Romeo_Dallaire.html (accessed 20 October 2004).

Ambrose, Stephen. *D-Day: The Climactic Battle of World War II*. New York: Simon & Schuster, 1994.

American Historical Association. *Annual Report for 1897*. Washington, DC: Government Printing Office, 1897.

– *The Study of History in Schools: Report to the American Historical Association by the Committee of Seven*. 1899. New York: Macmillan, 1906.

American Psychological Association. *Publication Manual of the American Psychological Association*. 5th ed. Washington, DC: American Psychological Association, 2001.

Anderson, Benedict. *Imagined Communities: Reflections on the Origin and Spread of Nationalism*. New York: Verso, 1991.

Appleby, Joyce, Lynn Hunt, and Margaret Jacob. *Telling the Truth about History*. New York: W.W. Norton & Company, 1994.

Arthur, James, Ian Davies, Andrew Wrenn, Terry Haydn, and David Kerr. *Citizenship through Secondary History*. New York: Routledge-Falmer, 2001.

Ashby, Rosalyn, and Peter Lee. 'Children's Concepts of Empathy and Understanding in History.' In Portal, *History Curriculum*, 62–88.

Audigier, François. 'Histoire et géographie: Des savoirs scolaires en question entre les définitions officielles et les constructions des élèves.' *Spirale* 15 (1995): 61–89.

Bain, Robert. 'Into the Breach: Using Research and Theory to Shape History Instruction.' In Stearns et al., *Knowing, Teaching, and Learning History*, 331–52.

Ballard, Martin, ed. *New Movements in the Study and Teaching of History*. London: Temple Smith, 1970.

Barton, Keith. 'The Cultural Context of Historical Understanding among Children in Northern Ireland.' Paper presented at the annual meeting of the American Educational Research Association, San Diego, CA, 13–17 April 1998.

– '"I Just Kind of Know": Elementary Students' Ideas about Historical Evidence.' *Theory and Research in Social Education* 25, no. 4 (1997): 407–30.

– 'Narrative Simplifications in Elementary Students' Historical Thinking.' In Brophy, *Advances in Research on Teaching*, 51–84.

– 'Primary Children's Understanding of the Role of Historical Evidence: Comparisons between the United States and Northern Ireland.' *International Journal of Historical Learning, Teaching and Research* 1, no. 2 (2001): 21–30.

– 'A Sociocultural Perspective on Children's Understanding of Historical Change: Comparative Findings from Northern Ireland and the United States.' *American Educational Research Journal* 38, no. 4 (2001): 881–913.

– '"You'd Be Wanting to Know about the Past": Social Contexts of Children's Historical Understanding in Northern Ireland and the USA.' *Comparative Education* 37, no. 1 (2001): 89–106.

Barton, Keith, and Linda Levstik. '"It Wasn't a Good Part of History": National Identity and Students' Explanations of Historical Significance.' *Teachers College Record* 99, no. 3 (1998): 478–513.

– *Teaching History for the Common Good*. Mahwah, NJ: Lawrence Erlbaum Associates, 2004.

– 'Why Don't More History Teachers Engage Students in Interpretations?' *Social Education* 67, no. 6 (2003): 358–61.

BBC (British Broadcasting Corporation). 'Powell Admits Iraq Evidence Mistake.' London, British Broadcasting Corporation, 3 April 2004. http://news.bbc.co.uk/2/hi/middle_east/3596033.stm (accessed 9 September 2004).

Beard, Charles A. 'The Use of Sources in Instruction in Government and Politics.' *History Teachers Magazine* 1 (1919): 40–50.

Becker, Carl. 'Everyman His Own Historian.' *American Historical Review* 37, no. 2 (1932): 221–36.

Bellesiles, Michael. *Arming America: The Origins of a National Gun Culture*. New York: Alfred A. Knopf, 2000.

Bloch, Marc, *The Historian's Craft*. Trans. Peter Putnam. Manchester: Manchester University Press, 1954.

Bogle, Don, Eugene D'Orezio, and Don Quinlan. *Canada: Continuity and Change – A History of Our Country from 1900 to the Present*. Markham, ON: Fitzhenry & Whiteside, 2000.

Bohan, Chara, and O.L. Davis. 'Historical Constructions: How Social Studies Student Teachers' Historical Thinking Is Reflected in Their Writing of History.' *Theory and Research in Social Education* 26, no. 2 (2004): 173–97.

Boix-Mansilla, Veronica. 'Beyond the Lessons from the Cognitive Revolution.' *Canadian Social Studies* 32, no. 2 (1998): 49–51.

Booth, Ken, and Tim Dunne. Preface to *Worlds in Collision: Terror and the Future of Global Order*, ed. Ken Booth and Tim Dunne, i–x. New York: Palgrave Macmillan, 2002.

Booth, Martin. 'Cognition in History: A British Perspective.' *Educational Psychologist* 29, no. 2 (1994): 61–9.

– 'A Longitudinal Study of Cognitive Skills, Concepts and Attitudes of Adolescents Studying Modern World History Syllabus and an Analysis of Their Adductive Historical Thinking.' PhD thesis. Reading: Reading University, 1979.

Boscolo, Pietro, and Lucia Mason. 'Writing to Learn, Writing to Transfer.' In *Writing as a Learning Tool: Integrating Theory and Practice*, ed. Paivi Tynjala, Lucia Mason, and Kirsti Lonka, 83–104. Studies in Writing 7. Dordrecht: Kluwer Academic Publishers, 2001.

Bourdillon, Hilary, ed. *Teaching History*. London: Open University Press, 1994.

Boyko, John. *Last Steps to Freedom: The Evolution of Canadian Racism*. Winnipeg: Watson & Dwyer, 1995.

Braun, Robert. 'The Holocaust and the Problem of Historical Representation.' *History and Theory* 33, no. 2 (1994): 172–97.

Breisach, Ernst. *Historiography: Ancient, Medieval, and Modern*. 2nd ed. Chicago: University of Chicago Press, 1994.

Braudel, Fernand. *On History*. 1960. Trans. Sarah Matthews. Chicago: University of Chicago Press, 1980.

Brophy, Jere, ed. *Advances in Research on Teaching*. Greenwich, CO: JAI Press, 1996.

Bruner, Jerome. *Acts of Meaning*. Cambridge, MA: Harvard University Press, 1990.

– *The Process of Education.* 2nd ed. Cambridge: Harvard University Press, 1977.

Brush, Thomas, and John Saye. 'Scaffolding Critical Reasoning in History and Social Studies: Tools to Support Problem-Based History Inquiry.' Paper presented at the annual meeting of the American Educational Research Association, San Francisco, CA, 7–11 April 2006.

Burston, William. *Principles of History Teaching.* Norfolk: Methuen, 1964.

Burston, William, and David Thompson, eds. *Studies in the Nature and Teaching of History.* London: Routledge and Kegan Paul, 1967.

Bury, John Bagnell. *The Idea of Progress: An Inquiry into Its Origin and Growth.* New York: Dover, 1932.

– 'Inaugural Lecture: The Science of History.' 1902. In Stern, *Varieties of History,* 209–26.

Bush, George W. 'President's Remarks at the United Nations General Assembly.' Washington, DC: The White House, 12 September 2002. http://www.whitehouse.gov/news/releases/2002/09/20020912–1.html (accessed 9 September 2004).

Butterfield, Herbert. *The Whig Interpretation of History.* London: G. Bell & Sons, 1931. Republished in Eliohs Electronic Library of Historiography, http://www.eliohs.unifi.it/testi/900/butterfield (accessed 21 October 2004).

Canadian Military Headquarters. *The OPERATION at Dieppe, 19 Aug 42 – Some New Information.* Report no. 128. Ottawa: Department of National Defence, 1944.

Cantor, Norman, and Richard Schneider. *How to Study History.* New York: Thomas Y. Crowell, 1967.

Cantu, Antonio, and Wilson Warren. *Teaching History in the Digital Classroom.* New York: M.E. Sharpe, 2003.

Carr, David. *Time, Narrative, and History.* Bloomington: Indiana University Press, 1986.

Carr, E.H. *What Is History?* London: Macmillan, 1962.

Carretero, Mario, and James Voss, eds. *Cognitive and Instruction Processes in History and Social Sciences.* Hillsdale, NJ: Erlbaum, 1994.

Cercadillo, Lis. 'Significance in History: Students' ideas in England and Spain.' In *Raising Standards in History Education: International Review of History Education,* ed. Alaric Dickinson, Peter Gordon, and Peter Lee, 116–45. London: Woburn Press, 2001.

Clark, Kitson. *The Critical Historian.* London: Heinemann, 1967.

Cmiel, Kenneth. 'The Recent History of Human Rights.' *The American Historical Review* 109, no. 1 (2004). http://www.historycooperative.org (accessed 19 September 2005).

Cohen, Daniel J., and Roy Rosenzweig. *Digital History: A Guide to Gathering,*

Preserving, and Presenting the Past on the Web. Philadelphia: University of Pennsylvania Press, 2006.

Collingwood, R.G. *The Idea of History*. 1946. New York: Oxford University Press, 1956.

– 'Inaugural: Rough Notes.' In Hughes-Warrington, *'How Good an Historian?'* 5.

Comte, Auguste. *Cours de Philosophie Positive*. 6 vols. 1830–42. Paris: J.B. Baillière et Fils, 1864.

Condorcet, Jean-Antoine-Nicolas de Caritat de. *Esquisse d'un tableau historique des progrès de l'esprit humain*. Paris: Agasse, 1795.

Cooper, Hilary. 'Historical Thinking and Cognitive Development in the Teaching of History.' In Bourdillon, *Teaching History*, 101–21.

– *The Teaching of History*. London: David Fulton, 1992.

Craver, Kathleen. *Using Internet Primary Sources to Teach Critical Thinking Skills in History*. Westport, CT: Greenwood Press, 1999.

Croce, Benedetto. *History as the Story of Liberty*. Trans. Sylvia Sprigge. London: Allen and Unwin Ltd, 1941.

Cronon, William. 'A Place for Stories: Nature, History, and Narrative.' *Journal of American History* 78, no. 4 (1992): 1347–76.

Cruxton, Bradley, and Douglas Wilson. *Flashback Canada*. 4th ed. Don Mills, ON: Oxford University Press, 2000.

Dallaire, Roméo. *Shake Hands with the Devil: The Failure of Humanity in Rwanda*. Toronto: Random House, 2003.

Danto, Arthur. *Analytical Philosophy of History*. Cambridge: Cambridge University Press, 1965.

Davis, O.L. 'In Pursuit of Historical Empathy.' In Davis et al., *Historical Empathy and Perspective Taking*, 1–12.

Davis, O.L., Elizabeth Yeager, and Stuart Foster, eds. *Historical Empathy and Perspective Taking in the Social Studies*. Lanham, MD: Rowman & Littlefield, 2001.

de Coulanges, N.D. Fustel. 'Inaugural Lecture.' 1862. Trans. Fritz Stern. In Stern, *Varieties of History*, 179–90.

Denos, Mike, and Roland Case. *Teaching about Historical Thinking*. Vancouver: Pacific Educational Press, 2006.

de Silva, W.A. 'The Formation of Historical Concepts through Conceptual Clues.' *Educational Research* 24, no. 3 (1972): 174–82.

Dewey, John. *Democracy and Education: An Introduction to the Philosophy of Education*. 1916. New York: Free Press, 1997.

Diamond, Jared. *Collapse: How Societies Choose to Fail or Succeed*. New York: Viking, 2005.

Dickens, Charles. *Hard Times*. 1854. Toronto: Bantam Books, 1981.

Dickinson, Alaric, and Peter Lee, ed. *History Teaching and Historical Understanding*. London: Heinemann, 1978.

‒ 'Making Sense of History.' In Dickinson et al., *Learning History*, 117–53.

Dickinson, Alaric, A. Gard, and Peter Lee. 'Evidence in History and the Classroom.' In Dickinson and Lee, *History Teaching and Historical Understanding*, 1–20.

Dickinson, Alaric, Peter Lee, and Peter Rogers, eds. *Learning History*. London: Heinemann, 1984.

Diefenbaker, John. *One Canada: Memoirs of the Right Honorable John G. Diefenbaker, 1962–1967*. Toronto: Macmillan, 1977.

Donovan, Timothy. *Historical Thought in America: Postwar Patterns*. Norman, OK: University of Oklahoma Press, 1973.

Drake, Frederick, and Lynn Nelson. *Engagement in Teaching History: Theory and Practice for Middle and Secondary Teachers*. Upper Saddle River, NJ: Pearson Education, 2005.

Dray, William. *Philosophy of History*. Englewood Cliffs, NJ: Prentice Hall, 1964.

Dumas, Jean-Louis. *Histoire de la pensée: Renaissance et siècle des Lumières*. Paris: Tallandier, 1990.

Dunn, Judy. *The Beginnings of Social Understanding*. Cambridge, MA: Harvard University Press, 1988.

Dynneson, Thomas, Richard Gross, and Michael Berson. *Designing Effective Instruction for Secondary Social Studies*. 3rd ed. Englewood Cliffs, NJ: Merrill-Prentice Hall, 2003.

Elton, G.R. *The Practice of History*. London: Methuen & Co., 1967.

‒ 'What Sort of History Should We Teach?' In Ballard, *New Movements*, 221–32.

Epstein, Terrie. 'Deconstructing Differences in African-American and European-American Adolescents' Perspectives on U.S. History.' *Curriculum Inquiry* 28, no. 4 (1998): 397–423.

Evans, Richard. *In Defence of History*. London: Granta Books, 1997.

Flavell, John. *Cognitive Development*. Englewood Cliffs, NJ: Prentice Hall, 1977.

Fling, Fred Morrow. 'One Use of Sources in the Teaching of History.' *The Social Studies* 85, no. 5 (1994): 206–10. (Originally published in *The Social Studies* vol. 1.)

Foster, Stuart. 'Historical Empathy in Theory and Practice: Some Final Thoughts.' In Davis et al., *Historical Empathy and Perspective Taking*, 167–82.

Foster, Stuart, and Elizabeth Yeager. '"You've Got to Put Together the Pieces": English 12-Year-Olds Encounter and Learn from Historical Evidence.' *Journal of Curriculum and Supervision* 14, no. 4 (1999): 286–317.

France, Ministère de l'Éducation Nationale. *Histoire-géographie et éducation civique, programmes et accompagnement*. Paris: Centre National de Documentation Pédogogique, 2002.

Friedman, Adam. 'World History Teachers' Use of Digital Primary Sources: The Effect of Training.' *Theory and Research in Social Education* 34, no. 1 (2006): 124–41.

Fukuyama, Francis. *The End of History and the Last Man*. New York: Free Press, 1992.

Gaffield, Chad. 'Toward the Coach in the History Classroom.' *Canadian Issues/ Thèmes canadiens* (October–November 2001): 12–14.

Gagnon, Paul, ed. *Historical Literacy: The Case for History in American Education*. New York: Macmillan Publishing, 1989.

Gallie, W.B. *Philosophy and the Historical Knowledge*. New York: Schocken, 1964.

Gardiner, Patrick. 'The Objects of Historical Knowledge.' *Philosophy* 27 (1952): 211–20.

Gardner, Howard. 'Discipline, Understanding, and Community.' *Journal of Curriculum Studies* 36, no. 2 (2004): 233–6.

– *The Mind's New Science: A History of the Cognitive Revolution*. New York: Basic Book, 1987.

– *The Unschooled Mind: How Children Think and How Schools Should Teach*. New York: Basic Books, 1991.

Gardner, Howard, and Veronica Boix-Mansilla. 'Teaching for Understanding in the Disciplines – and Beyond.' In *The Development and Education of the Mind: The Select Works of Howard Gardner*, ed. Howard Gardner, 145–58. New York: Routledge, 2006. Originally published in *Teachers College Record* 96, no. 2 (1994): 198–218.

– 'Teaching for Understanding – Within and across the Disciplines.' *Educational Leadership* 51, no. 5 (2004): 14–18.

Gidney, Robert. *From Hope to Harris: The Reshaping of Ontario Schools*. Toronto: University of Toronto Press, 1999.

Gillaspie, Melanie, and O.L. Davis. 'Historical Constructions: How Elementary Student Teachers' Historical Thinking Is Reflected in Their Writing of History.' *International Journal of Social Education* 12, no. 2 (1997–8): 35–45.

Goldstein, Leon. 'Collingwood's Theory of Historical Knowing.' *History and Theory* 9, no. 1 (1970): 3–36.

Graham, Gordon. *The Shape of the Past: A Philosophical Approach to History*. New York: Oxford University Press, 1997.

Granatstein, Jack. *Who Killed Canadian History?* Toronto: HarperCollins, 1998.

– *Who Killed the Canadian Military?* Toronto: HarperCollins, 2004.

Grant, S.G. *History Lessons: Teaching, Learning, and Testing in U.S. High School Classrooms*. Mahwah, NJ: Lawrence Erlbaum, 2003.

Gray, Charlotte. *Flint & Feather: The Life and Times of E. Pauline Johnson, Tekahion-wake*. Toronto: HarperCollins, 2002.

Hallam, Roy. 'Piaget and Thinking in History.' In Ballard, *New Movements*, 162–78.

Hammond, Michael. 'A Framework of Plausibility for an Anthropological Forgery: The Piltdown Case.' *Anthropology* 3, nos. 1–2 (1997): 47–58.

Harris, Paul. *The Work of the Imagination*. Malden, MA: Blackwell, 2000.

Hartzler-Miller, Cynthia. 'Making Sense of "Best Practice" in Teaching History.' *Theory and Research in Social Education* 29, no. 4 (2001): 672–95.

Haydn, Terry, James Arthur, and Martin Hunt. *Learning to Teach History in the Secondary School: A Companion to School Experience*. New York: Routledge, 1997.

Heller, Jeffrey. 'Netanyahu Calls for Referendum on Gaza Plan.' *National Post*, 14 September 2004, A14.

Hertzberg, Hazel. 'History and Progressivism: A Century of Reform Proposals.' In Gagnon, *Historical Literacy*, 80–9.

– Preface to Gagnon, *Historical Literacy*, xii–xiii.

Hexter, John. *The History Primer*. New York: Basic Books, 1971.

Higham, John. *History: Professional Scholarship in America*. Baltimore: Johns Hopkins University Press, 1989.

Hodgetts, A.B. *What Culture? What Heritage?* Toronto: Ontario Institute for Studies in Education, 1968.

Holt, Tom. *Thinking Historically: Narrative, Imagination, and Understanding*. New York: The College Board, 1990.

House of Commons. *Debates*. 5th Parliament, 3rd Session. Ottawa: Maclean, Roger & Co., June 6, 1885 to July 20, 1885.

– *Debates*. Vol. 10. Ottawa: E. Cloutier, Queen's Printer, 1964.

Hughes-Warrington, Marnie. *'How Good an Historian Shall I Be?'*: R.G. Collingwood, The Historical Imagination and Education. Charlottesville, VA: Imprint Academic, 2003.

Hume, David. *An Enquiry concerning Human Understanding*. Raleigh, NC: Alex Catalogue, 2005. http://www.netlibrary.com/Details.aspx.

Hundley, Tom. 'New Film Re-examines Hitler.' *Chicago Tribune*, 19 September 2004. http://www.chicagotribune.com/news/nationworld/ch0409190263sep19,1,4800189.story (accessed 14 December 2004).

Husbands, Chris. *What Is History Teaching? Language, Ideas, and Meaning in Learning about the Past*. Buckingham: Open University Press, 1993.

Husbands, Chris, Alison Kitson, and Anna Pendry. *Understanding History Teaching: Teaching and Learning about the Past in Secondary Schools*. Maidenhead: Open University Press, 2003.

Igartua, José. 'What Nation, Which People? Representations of National Identity in English-Canadian History Textbooks from 1945–1970.' Paper presented at the International Congress of Historical Sciences, Sydney, Australia, 3–9 July 2005.

Ignatieff, Michael. *Blood and Belonging: Journeys into the New Nationalism.* Toronto: Penguin Books, 1993.

– *Human Rights as Politics and Idolatry.* Princeton: Princeton University Press, 2001.

– *The Rights Revolution.* Toronto: Anansi Press, 2000.

Ishay, Micheline. *The History of Human Rights: From Ancient Times to the Globalization Era.* Berkeley, CA: University of California Press, 2004.

Jain, Geneviève. 'Nationalism and Educational Politics in Ontario and Québec, 1867–1914.' In *Canadian Schools and Canadian Identity,* ed. Alf Chaiton and Neil McDonald, 38–56. Toronto: Gage Educational Press, 1977.

Jeffreys, M.V.C. *History in Schools: The Study of Development.* London: Pitman House, 1939.

Jenkins, Keith. *Re-thinking History.* New York: Routledge, 1991.

Johnson, E. Pauline. *E. Pauline Johnson (Tekahionwake): Poetess.* Toronto : Musson Book Co., 1913.

Johnson, Henry. *Teaching of History in Elementary and Secondary Schools with Applications to Allied Studies.* New York: Macmillan, 1940.

Jones, Richard. *Fantasy and Feeling in Education.* New York: New York University Press, 1968.

Keatinge, M.W. *Studies in the Teaching of History.* London: A&C Black, 1910.

Keegan, John. 'Diary.' *The Spectator,* 6 October 2001. www.spectator.co.uk/article.php?table=old&section=current&issue=-04–17&id=1166&search Text= (accessed 27 October 2003).

– *The Face of Battle.* New York: Penguin Books, 1978.

– *The Iraq War.* Toronto: Key Porter Books, 2004.

Kennedy, Edward. 'Speech to the Council on Foreign Relations.' Washington, DC: 5 March 2004. http://kennedy.senate.gov/newsroom/speech.cfm?id =88ff759f-aeba-4208-b8c2–80d3a5f14c61 (accessed 13 September 2004).

Kennedy, Paul. *Preparing for the Twenty-First Century.* New York: Random House, 1993.

Kirman, Joseph. *Elementary Social Studies: Creative Classroom Ideas.* 3rd ed. Toronto: Prentice Hall, 2002.

Koselleck, Reinhart. *The Practice of Conceptual History: Timing History, Spacing Concepts.* Stanford: Stanford University Press, 2002.

Krug, Mark. *History and the Social Sciences: New Approaches to the Teaching of Social Studies.* Waltham, MA: Blaisdell, 1967.

Lee, Peter. 'Explanation and Understanding in History.' In Dickinson and Lee, *History Teaching and Historical Understanding*, 72–93.

– 'Historical Imagination.' In Dickinson et al., *Learning History*, 87–112.

– 'Historical Knowledge and the National Curriculum.' In *History in the National Curriculum*, ed. R. Aldrich, 39–65. London: Kogan Page, 1991.

– 'History Teaching and Philosophy of History.' *History and Theory* 22, no. 4 (1983): 19–49.

– 'Why Learn History?' In Dickinson et al., *Learning History*, 1–19.

Lee, Peter, and Rosalyn Ashby. 'Empathy, Perspective Taking, and Rational Understanding.' In Davis et al., *Historical Empathy and Perspective Taking*, 21–50.

– 'Progression in Historical Understanding among Students Ages 7–14.' In Stearns et al., *Knowing, Teaching, and Learning History*, 199–222.

Le Goff, Jacques. 'Mentalities: A History of Ambiguities.' In *Constructing the Past: Essays in Historical Methodology*, ed. Jacques Le Goff and Pierre Nora, 166–80. New York: Cambridge University Press, 1985.

Létourneau, Jocelyn. 'Remembering Our Past: An Examination of the Historical Memory of Young Québécois.' In Sandwell, *To the Past*, 70–87.

Létourneau, Jocelyn, and Sabrina Moisan. 'Mémoire et récit de l'aventure historique du Québec chez les jeunes Québécois d'héritage canadien-français: coup de sonde, amorce d'analyse des résultats, questionnements.' *The Canadian Historical Review* 84, no. 2 (2004): 325–56.

Lévesque, Stéphane. '"Bin Laden Is Responsible, It Was Shown on Tape": Canadian High School Students' Historical Understanding of Terrorism.' *Theory and Research in Social Education* 31, no. 2 (2003): 174–202.

– 'Discovering the Past: Engaging Canadian Students in Digital History.' *Canadian Social Studies* 40(1) (2006). http:// www.quasar.ualberta.ca/css (accessed 27 January 2007).

– 'Learning about the October Crisis in Ontario History Classrooms: An Experimental Study Using the Virtual Historian.' Research report. London, ON: University of Western Ontario, 2007. http:// www.virtualhistorian.ca (accessed 25 June 2007).

– 'Learning by Playing: Engaging Students in Digital History.' *Canadian Issues/Thèmes canadiens* (Fall 2006): 68–71.

– 'Teaching History and Social Studies in Québec: An Historical Perspective.' In Sears and Wright, *Challenges and Prospects*, 55–72.

– 'Teaching Second-Order Concepts in Canadian History: The Importance of Historical Significance.' *Canadian Social Studies* 39, no. 2 (2005). http:// www.quasar.ualberta.ca/css (accessed 23 November 2004).

Levi, Primo. *The Drowned and the Saved*. Trans. Raymond Rosenthal. New York: Vintage Books, 1989.

Levstik, Linda. 'Articulating the Silences: Teachers' and Adolescents' Conceptions of Historical Significance.' In Stearns et al., *Knowing, Teaching, and Learning History,* 284–305.

Levstik, Linda, and Keith Barton. *Doing History: Investigating with Children in Elementary and Middle Schools.* Mahwah, NJ: Laurence Erlbaum Associates, 2001.

– '"They Still Use Some of Their Past": Historical Salience in Elementary Children's Chronological Thinking.' *Journal of Curriculum Studies* 28, no. 5 (1996): 531–76.

Levstik, Linda, and Dehea Smith. '"I've Never Done This Before": Building a Community of Inquiry in a Third-Grade Classroom.' In Brophy, *Advances in Research on Teaching,* 85–114.

Lind, Laura. 'Screening Out the Awkward Facts.' *Globe and Mail,* 15 November 2002, R3.

Lomas, Tim. *Teaching and Assessing Historical Understanding.* London: The Historical Association, 1990.

Lomax, Donald, ed. *The Education of Teachers in Britain.* New York: John Wiley, 1973.

– ed. *European Perspectives in Teacher Education.* New York: John Wiley, 1976.

Long, Delbert, and Rodney Riegle. *Teacher Education: The Key to Effective School Reform.* Westport, CT: Bergin and Garvey, 2002.

Lowenthal, David. 'Dilemmas and Delights of Learning History.' In Stearns et al., *Knowing, Teaching, and Learning History,* 63–82.

– *The Heritage Crusade and the Spoils of History.* Cambridge: Cambridge University Press, 1998.

– *The Past Is a Foreign Country.* New York: Cambridge University Press, 1985.

Lucas, Christopher. *Teacher Education in America: Reform Agendas for the Twenty-First Century.* New York: St Martin's Press, 1997.

Lyon, George. 'Pauline Johnson: A Reconsideration.' *Studies in Canadian Literature* 66, no. 2 (1992): 136–59.

Macdonald, Sharon, ed., *Approaches to European Historical Consciousness – Reflections and Provocations: Shaping European History.* Vol. 1. Hamburg: Körber-Stiftung, 2000.

MacMillan, Margaret. *Paris 1919: Six Months That Changed the World.* New York: Random House, 2002.

Malthus, Robert Thomas. *An Essay on the Principle of Population; Or a View of Its Past and Present Effects on Human Happiness.* 3rd ed. Vol. 1. London: J. Johnson, 1806.

Martin, Raymond. 'Causes, Conditions, and Causal Importance.' *History and Theory* 21, no. 1 (1982): 53–74.

Martineau, Robert. 'Les conceptions des futurs enseignants d'histoire inscrits

dans les universités québécoises: un enjeu majeur de formation.' Research
report. Trois-Rivières, QC: Université du Québec à Trois-Rivières, 1999.
– L'histoire à l'école, matière à penser ... Paris: L'Harmattan, 1999.
Marx, Karl. The Eighteenth Brumaire of Louis Bonaparte. Champaign, IL: NetLi-
brary, n.d. http://www.netlibrary.com/Details.aspx (accessed 25 January
2005).
Matheson, John. Canada's Flag: A Search for a Country. Belleville, ON: Mika
Publishing, 1986.
Mayer, Robert. 'Learning to Teach Young People How to Think Historically: A
Case Study of One Student Teacher's Experience.' Paper presented at the
annual meeting of the American Education Research Association, San Diego,
CA, 12–16 April 2004.
McCullagh, Behan. 'Colligation and Classification in History.' History and The-
ory 17, no. 3 (1978): 267–84.
– The Truth of History. New York: Routledge, 1998.
McMaster University. Pauline Johnson Archives. Hamilton: McMaster Univer-
sity, n.d. http://www.humanities.mcmaster.ca/~pjohnson/mock.html
(accessed 21 October 2004).
McParland, Kelly. 'Call Them the Terrorists They Are.' National Post, 25 Sep-
tember 2004, A11.
Meinecke, Friedrich. 'Historicism and its Problems.' 1928. Trans. Julian Frank-
lin. In Stern, Varieties of History, 267–88.
Mercier, Louis-Sébastien. Memoirs of the Year Two Thousand Five Hundred. 2 vols.
1771. Trans. W. Hooper. London: G. Robinson, 1772.
Migration Watch, United Kingdom. A Nation of Emigrants – Emigration from the
UK. Briefing paper. Guilford: Migration Watch. http://www.migration-
watchuk.org/frameset.asp?menu=researchpapers&page=briefingpapers/
history/nationemigrants.asp (accessed 21 March 2005).
Miller, Peggy, and Linda Sperry. 'Early Talk about the Past: The Origins of
Conversational Stories of Personal Experience.' Journal of Child Language 15
(1988): 293–325.
Mink, Louis. 'The Autonomy of Historical Understanding.' History and Theory
5, no. 1 (1996): 24–7.
Morton, Desmond. A Military History of Canada: From Champlain to Kosovo. 4th
ed. Toronto: McClelland and Stewart, 1999.
National Standards for History in the Schools. National Standards in United
States and World History. Los Angeles: University of California at Los Angeles, 1996. http://nchs.ucla.edu/standards/thinking5–12–1.html (accessed
27 January 2005).
Nielsen, Margit. 'Re-enactment and Reconstruction in Collingwood's Philosophy of History.' History and Theory 20, no. 1 (1981): 1–31.

Nora, Pierre. 'General Introduction: Between Memory and History.' In *Realms of Memory: The Construction of the French Past*, ed. Lawrence Kritzman, 1–20. New York: Columbia University Press, 1996.

– 'The Reasons for the Current Upsurge in Memory.' *Eurozine*, 19 April 2002. www.eurozine.com (accessed 25 March 2005).

Novick, Peter. *That Noble Dream: The 'Objectivity Question' and the American Historical Profession*. Cambridge: Cambridge University Press, 1988.

Oakeshott, Michael. *Experience and Its Modes*. Cambridge: Cambridge University Press, 1933.

– *Rationalism in Politics, and Other Essays*. London: Methuen, 1962.

OECD (Organization for Economic Co-operation and Development). *Développement de l'enseignement supérieur, 1950–1967: Rapport analytique*. Paris: Organization for Economic Co-operation and Development Publications, 1971.

Oldfield, Adrian. 'Moral Judgments in History.' *History and Theory* 20, no. 3 (1981): 260–77.

Ontario Ministry of Education. *Canadian and World Studies, Grades 9–10*. Toronto: Queen's Printer, 1999.

– *Canadian and World Studies, Grades 11 and 12*. Toronto: Queen's Printer, 2000.

Osborne, Ken. *Education: A Guide to the Canadian School Debate – Or, Who Wants What and Why?* Toronto: Penguin Books, 1999.

– 'Fred Morrow Fling and the Source-Method of Teaching History.' *Theory and Research in Social Education* 31, no. 4 (2003): 466–501.

– 'History and Social Studies: Partners or Rivals?' In Sears and Wright, *Challenges and Prospects*, 73–89.

– '"Our History Syllabus Has Us Gasping:" History in Canadian Schools – Past, Present, and Future.' *The Canadian Historical Review* 81, no. 3 (2000): 404–35.

– 'Teaching History in Schools: A Canadian Debate.' *Journal of Curriculum Studies* 35, no. 5 (2003): 585–626.

– 'To the Past: Why We Need to Teach and Study History.' In Sandwell, *To the Past*, 103–31.

Oxford English Dictionary Online. Oxford: Oxford University Press, 2007. http://dictionary.oed.com (accessed 20 August 2004).

Partington, Geoffrey. *The Idea of an Historical Education*. Windsor, UK: NFER Publishing, 1980.

Partner, Nancy. 'Hayden White: The Form of the Content.' *History and Theory* 37, no. 2 (1998): 162–72.

Pattiz, Anthony. 'The Idea of History Teaching: Using Collingwood's Idea of History to Promote Critical Thinking in the High School History Classroom.' *The History Teacher* 37, no. 2 (2004). http://www.historycooperative.org/journals/ht/37.2/pattiz.html (accessed 10 September 2004).

PBS (Public Broadcasting Service). *Interviews: Hans Blix*. Alexandria, VA: Public Broadcasting Service, November 2003. http://www.pbs.org/wgbh/pages/frontline/shows/wmd/interviews/blix.html (cited 9 September 2004).

Phillips, Robert. 'Historical Significance – The Forgotten "Key Concept"?' *Teaching History* 106 (2002): 14–19.

– *History Teaching, Nationhood and the State: Study in Educational Politics*. London: Cassell, 1998.

Pollard, Sidney. *The Idea of Progress: History and Society*. London: C.A. Watts, 1968.

Portal, Christopher, ed. *The History Curriculum for Teachers*. London: Falmer Press, 1987.

Powell, Colin. 'U.S. Secretary of State Colin Powell Addresses the U.N. Security Council.' Washington, DC: The White House, 5 February 2003. http://www.whitehouse.gov/news/releases/2003/02/20030205-1.html (accessed 9 September 2004).

Ravitch, Diane. 'The Educational Background of History Teachers.' In Stearns et al., *Knowing, Teaching, and Learning History*, 143–55.

Report of the Royal Commission of Inquiry on Education in the Province of Québec. Vol. 3. Québec City: Government of Québec, 1965.

Ricoeur, Paul. *Temps et récit*. Vol. 1. Paris: Seuil, 1983.

Ringrose, Daniel. 'Beyond Amusement: Reflections on Multimedia, Pedagogy, and Digital Literacy in the History Seminar.' *The History Teacher* 34, no. 2 (2001): 209–28. http://www.historycooperative.org (accessed 9 September 2004).

Rogers, Peter. 'The Past as a Frame of Reference.' In Portal, *History Curriculum*, 3–21.

– 'Why Teach History?' In Dickinson et al., *Learning History*, 20–38.

Rosenstone, Robert. *Visions from the Past: The Challenges of Film to Our Idea of History*. Cambridge, MA: Harvard University Press, 1995.

Rosenzweig, Roy. 'How Americans Use and Think about the Past: Implications from a National Survey for the Teaching of History.' In Stearns et al., *Knowing, Teaching, and Learning History*, 162–283.

Rotenstreich, Nathan. 'The Idea of Historical Progress and Its Assumptions.' *History and Theory* 10, no. 2 (1971): 197–221.

Rüsen, Jörn. 'Historical Narration: Foundation, Types, Reason.' *History and Theory* 26, no. 4 (1987): 87–97.

Sandwell, Ruth, ed. *To the Past: History Education, Public Memory, and Citizenship in Canada*. Toronto: University of Toronto Press, 2006.

Schlesinger, Arthur, Jr. *The Disuniting of America*. New York: Norton, 1992.

Scholes, Robert, and Robert Kellogg. *The Nature of Narrative*. New York: Oxford University Press, 1966.

Sears, Alan, and Ian Wright, eds. *Challenges and Prospects for Canadian Social Studies.* Vancouver: Pacific Educational Press, 2004.

Seaton, Matt. 'Blast from the Past.' *The Guardian,* 19 February 2003. http://www.guardian.co.uk/g2/story/0,,898341,00.html (accessed 23 November 2004).

Segall, Avner. 'Critical History: Implications for History/Social Studies Education.' *Theory and Research in Social Education* 27, no. 3 (1999): 358–74.

Seixas, Peter. 'The Community of Inquiry as a Basis for Knowledge and Learning: The Case of History.' *American Educational Research Journal* 30, no. 2 (1993): 305–24.

– 'Conceptualizing the Growth of Historical Understanding.' In *The Handbook of Education and Human Development,* ed. David Olson and Nancy Torrance, 765–83. Oxford: Blackwell, 1996.

– 'Confronting the Moral Frames of Popular Film: Young People Respond to Historical Revisionism.' *American Journal of Education* 102 (May 1994): 261–85.

– 'Mapping the Terrain of Historical Significance.' *Social Education* 61, no. 1 (1997): 22–7.

– 'The Purposes of Teaching Canadian History.' *Canadian Social Studies* 36, no. 2 (2002). http://www.quasar.ualberta.ca/css (accessed 31 January 2006).

– 'Schweigen! die Kinder: or, Does Postmodern History Have a Place in the Schools?' In Stearns et al., *Knowing, Teaching, and Learning History,* 19–37.

– 'Students' Understanding of Historical Significance.' *Theory and Research in Social Education* 22, no. 3 (1994): 281–304.

– 'Student Teachers Thinking Historically.' *Theory and Research in Social Education* 26, no. 3 (1998): 310–41.

– 'When Psychologists Discuss Historical Thinking: A Historian's Perspective.' *Educational Psychologist* 29, no. 2 (1994): 107–9.

Seixas, Peter, and Penney Clark. 'Murals as Monuments: Students' Ideas about Depictions of Civilization in British Columbia.' *American Journal of Education* 110, no. 2 (2004): 146–71.

Sellers, Charles. 'Is History on the Way Out of the Schools and Do Historians Care?' *Social Education* 33, no. 5 (1969): 509–16.

Sheehan, Bernard. 'The Problems of Moral Judgments in History.' *South Atlantic Quarterly* 84, no. 1 (1985): 37–50.

Shemilt, Denis. 'Adolescent Ideas about Evidence and Methodology in History.' In Portal, *History Curriculum,* 39–61.

– 'Beauty and the Philosopher: Empathy in History and Classroom.' In Dickinson et al., *Learning History,* 39–83.

– 'The Caliph's Coin.' In Stearns et al., *Knowing, Teaching, and Learning History,* 83–101.

– *History 13–16: Evaluation Study*. Edinburgh: Holmes McDougall, 1980.

Shields, Patricia, and Douglas Ramsay. *Teaching and Learning about Canadian History across Canada*. Toronto, ON: Historica Foundation, Canada, 2002.

Shulman, Lee. 'Knowledge and Teaching: Foundations of a New Reform.' *Harvard Educational Review* 57, no. 1 (1987): 1–22.

Slater, John. *Teaching History in the New Europe*. London: Cassell, 1995.

Spears, Tom. 'Dear Diary: I'm Totally Depressed.' *National Post*, 21 September 2004, A2.

Stacey, C.P. *Six Years of War: The Army in Canada, Britain and the Pacific*. Vol. 1. Ottawa: Queen's Printer, 1955.

Stanford, Michael. *A Companion to the Study of History*. Cambridge: Blackwell, 1994.

Stanley, Timothy. 'White Supremacy and the Rhetoric of Educational Indoctrination: A Canadian Case Study.' In *Children, Teachers, and Schools in the History of British Columbia*, ed. Jean Barman, Neil Sutherland, and J. Donald Wilson, 39–56. Calgary: Detselig, 1995.

– 'Whose Public? Whose Memory? Racisms, Grand Narratives and Canadian History.' In Sandwell, *To the Past*, 32–49.

Stearns, Peter. *Why Study History?* Washington, DC: American Historical Association Publications, n.d. http://www.historians.org/pubs/Free/Why-StudyHistory.htm (accessed 24 August 2004).

Stearns, Peter, Peter Seixas, and Sam Wineburg. Introduction to Stearns et al., *Knowing, Teaching, and Learning History*, 1–17.

– eds. *Knowing, Teaching, and Learning History: National and International Perspectives*. New York: New York University Press, 2000.

Stern, Fritz, ed. *The Varieties of History: From Voltaire to the Present*. London: Macmillan, 1956.

Stevens, Reed, Sam Wineburg, Leslie Ruper Herrenkohl, and Philip Bell. 'Comparative Understanding of School Subjects: Past, Present, and Future.' *Review of Educational Research* 75, no. 2 (2005): 125–57.

Stockley, David. 'Empathetic Reconstruction of History and History Teaching.' *History and Theory* 22, no. 4 (1983): 50–65.

Stones, S.K. 'An Analysis of the Growth of Adolescent Thinking in Relation to their Comprehension of School History Material.' MEd thesis. Birmingham: University of Birmingham.

Strong-Boag, Veronica. 'No Longer Dull: The Feminist Renewal of Canadian History.' *Canadian Social Studies* 32, no. 2 (1998): 55–7.

Strong-Boag, Veronica, and Carole Gerson. *Paddling Her Own Canoe: The Times and Texts of E. Pauline Johnson (Tekahionwake)*. Toronto: University of Toronto Press, 2002.

Sylvester, David. 'Change and Continuity in History Teaching, 1900–93.' In Bourdillon, *Teaching History*, 9–23.

Symcox, Linda. *Whose History? The Struggle for National Standards in American Classrooms*. New York: Teachers College Press, 2002.

Talbott, Strobe and Nathan Chanda, eds. *The Age of Terror: America and the World after September 11*. New York: Basic Books, 2001.

Tawney, Richard. *History and Society: Essays*. Boston: Routledge and Paul, 1978.

Taylor, Tony. *The Future of the Past: Final Report of the National Inquiry into School History*. Victoria, Australia: Faculty of Education, Monash University, 2000. http://www.dest.gov.au/sectors/school_education/publications_resources/national_inquiry_into_school_history/the_future_of_the_past_final_report.htm (accessed 30 January 2006).

Thompson, David. 'Colligation and History Teaching.' In Burston and Thompson, *Studies*, 85–106.

Thomson, David. *The Aims of History: Values of the Historical Attitude*. London: Thames & Hudson, 1969.

Thucydides. *History of the Peloponnesian War*. Trans. Rex Warner. Harmondsworth: Penguin Book, 1965.

Tosh, John. *The Pursuit of History: Aims, Methods, and New Directions in the Study of History*. New York: Longman, 1986.

Toynbee, Arnold. *A Study of History*. New York: Oxford University Press, 1957.

Trask, David. 'Did the Sans-Coulottes Wear Nikes? The Impact of Electronic Media on the Understanding and Teaching of History.' *The History Teacher* 35, no. 4 (2002). http:www.historycooperative.org (accessed 20 September 2004).

Trevelyan, George Macaulay. 'Clio, Rediscovered.' 1913. In Stern, *Varieties of History*, 227–46.

Trudel, Marcel, and Genvième Jain. *Canadian History Textbooks: A Comparative Study*. Ottawa: Queen's Printer, 1970.

Turner, Frederick Jackson. 'An American Definition of History.' 1891. In Stern, *Varieties of History*, 197–208.

UNESCO (United Nations Educational, Scientific, and Cultural Organization). *The UNESCO Courier*, July–August, 1999. http://unesdoc.unesco.org/images/0011/001165/116578e.pdf#116585 (accessed 5 February 2007).

United Kingdom, Department for Education and Skills, and Qualifications and Curriculum Authority. *The National Curriculum for England*. London: Qualifications and Curriculum Authority, 2002. http://www.nc.uk.net/ (accessed 29 March 2005).

USA Today. 'Wolfowitz Comments Revive Doubts over Iraq's WMD.' *USA*

214   Bibliography

Today, 30 May 2003. http://www.usatoday.com/news/world/iraq/2003–05–30-wolfowitz-iraq_x.htm (accessed 9 September 2004).

van der Dussen, Jan. 'Collingwood and the Idea of Progress.' *History and Theory* 29, no. 4 (1990): 21–41.

van der Leeuw-Roord, Joke, ed. *History Changes: Facts and Figures about History Education in Europe since 1989.* The Hague: EuroClio, 2004.

van Hover, Stephanie. '"Making" Students Better People? A Case Study of a Beginning History Teacher.' *International Social Studies Forum* 3, no. 1 (2003): 219–32.

Vann, Richard. 'Historians and Moral Evaluation.' *History and Theory* 43, no. 4 (2004): 3–30.

VanSledright, Bruce. 'From Empathic Regard to Self-Understanding: Im/Positionality, Empathy, and Historical Contextualization.' In Davis et al., *Historical Empathy and Perspective Taking,* 51–68.

– *In Search of America's Past: Learning to Read History in Elementary Schools.* New York: Teachers College Press, 2002.

– 'What Does It Mean to Think Historically ... and How Do You Teach It?' *Social Education* 68, no. 3 (2004): 230–3.

VanSledright, Bruce, and Jere Brophy. 'Storytelling, Imagination, and Fanciful Elaboration in Children's Historical Reconstructions.' *American Educational Research Journal* 29, no. 4 (1992): 837–59.

VanSledright, Bruce, and Lisa Franks. 'Concept- and Strategic-Knowledge Development in Historical Study: A Comparative Exploration of Two Fourth-Grade Classrooms.' *Cognition and Instruction* 18, no. 2 (2000): 239–83.

Villa, Brian Loring. *Unauthorized Action: Mountbatten and the Dieppe Raid.* Don Mills, ON: Oxford University Press, 1989.

Voltaire (François-Marie Arouet). *The Age of Lewis XIV.* 2nd ed. Vol. 1. 1751. Trans. M. Chambaud. London: R. Dodsley, 1752.

von Borries, Bodo. 'Exploring the Construction of Historical Meaning: Cross-Cultural Studies of Historical Consciousness among Adolescents.' In *Reflections on Educational Achievement: Papers in Honour of T. Neville Postlethwaite,* ed. Wilfried Bos and Rainer Lehmann, 25–49. New York: Waxmann, 1995.

von Laue, Theodore. *Leopold Ranke: The Formative Years.* Princeton: Princeton University Press, 1950.

von Ranke, Leopold. 'The Ideal of Universal History.' In Stern, *Varieties of History,* 55.

– Preface to *Histories of the Latin and Germanic Nations from 1494 to 1514.* Trans. Fritz Stern. In Stern, *Varieties of History,* 55–8.

Voss, James, and Jennifer Wiley. 'A Case Study of Developing Historical Understanding via Instruction: The Importance of Integrating Text Components and Constructing Arguments.' In Stearns et al., *Knowing, Teaching, and Learning History*, 375–89.

Wagar, Warren, ed. *The Idea of Progress since the Renaissance*. New York: John Wiley, 1969.

Walsh, William. 'Colligatory Concepts in History.' In Burston and Thompson, *Studies*, 65–84.

– *An Introduction to Philosophy of History*. London: Hutchinson's University Library, 1961

– 'R.G. Collingwood's Philosophy of History.' *Philosophy* 22 (1947): 154–8.

Watts, David. *The Learning of History*. Boston: Routledge and Kegan Paul, 1972.

Weinstein, Paul. 'Movies as Gateway to History: The History and Film Project.' *The History Teacher* 35, no. 1 (2001). http://www.historycooperative.org (accessed 14 December 2005).

Wells, H.G. *The Outline of History, Being a Plain History of Life and Mankind*. 1920. New York: Macmillan, 1921.

Wertsch, James. 'Is It Possible to Teach Beliefs, as Well as Knowledge about History?' In Stearns et al., *Knowing, Teaching, and Learning History*, 38–50.

– *Mind as Action*. New York: Oxford University Press, 1998.

Wertsch, James, and Kevin O'Connor. 'Multivoicedness in Historical Representations: American College Students' Accounts of the Origins of the United States.' *Journal of Narrative and Life History* 4, no. 4 (1994): 295–309.

Whelan, Michael. 'Social Studies for Social Reform: Beard's Vision of History and Social Studies Education.' *Theory and Research in Social Education* 25, no. 3 (1997): 288–315.

White, Hayden. 'Historical Text as Literary Artifact.' In *The Writing of History: Literary Form and Historical Understanding*, ed. Robert Canary and Henry Kozicki, 81–100. Madison: University of Wisconsin Press, 1978.

White, Morton. *Foundations of Historical Knowledge*. New York: Harper and Row, 1965.

Wiggins, Grant, and Jay McTighe. *Understanding by Design*. 2nd ed. Alexandria, VA: Association for Supervision and Curriculum Development, 2005.

Wilson, J. Donald, Robert Stamp, and Louis-Philippe Audet, eds. *Canadian Education: A History*. Scarborough, ON: Prentice Hall, 1970.

Wilson, Suzanne, and Gary Sykes. 'Toward Better Teacher Preparation and Certification.' In Gagnon, *Historical Literacy*, 268–86.

Wineburg, Sam. *Historical Thinking and Other Unnatural Acts: Charting the Future of Teaching the Past*. Philadelphia: Temple University Press, 2001.

– 'On the Reading of Historical Texts: Notes on the Breach Between School and Academy.' *American Educational Research Journal* 28, no. 3 (1991): 495–519.

Woyshner, Christine. 'Political History as Women's History: Toward a More Inclusive Curriculum.' *Theory and Research in Social Education* 30, no. 3 (2002): 354–80.

Wright, Ronald. *A Short History of Progress.* Toronto: Anansi Press, 2004.

Yeager, Elizabeth, and O.L. Davis. 'Between Campus and Classroom: Secondary Students-teachers' Thinking about Historical Texts.' *Journal of Research and Development in Education* 29 (1995): 1–8.

Yeager, Elizabeth, and Frans Doppen. 'Teaching and Learning Multiple Perspectives on the Use of the Atomic Bomb: Historical Empathy in the Secondary Classroom.' In Davis et al., *Historical Empathy and Perspective Taking*, 97–114.

Yeager, Elizabeth, and Stuart Foster. 'The Role of Empathy in the Development of Historical Understanding.' In Davis et al., *Historical Empathy and Perspective Taking*, 13–19.

Yeager, Elizabeth, Stuart Foster, and Jennifer Greer. 'How Eighth Graders in England and the United States View Historical Significance.' *The Elementary School Journal* 103, no. 2 (2002): 199–219.

Yeandle, Peter. 'Empire, Englishness and Elementary School History Education, c.1880–1914.' *International Journal of Historical Learning, Teaching and Research* 3, no. 1 (2003). http://www.centres.ex.ac.uk/historyresource/journalstart.htm (cited 1 March 2005).

Zimmerman, Jonathan. *Whose America? Culture Wars in the Public Schools.* Cambridge, MA: Harvard University Press, 2002.

– Post on the *History News Network*, 7 June 2006. Fairfax, VA: George Mason University. http://hnn.us/roundup/entries/26426.html (accessed 20 June 2006).

Index